Environmental Geography

Jack Gillett

Longman

Longman Group UK Limited,
Longman House, Burnt Mill Harlow,
Essex CM20 2JE, England
and Associated Companies throughout the world.

First published 1990

Set in 10/12 point Palatino

Produced by Longman Group (FE) Ltd
Printed in Hong Kong

ISBN 0 582 23178 7

British Library Cataloguing in Publication Data

Gillett, Jack
   Environmental geography. – (Key themes in geography).
   1. Environment – for schools
   I. Title   II. Series
   333.7

For Cliff Humphreys
We are grateful to the following for permission to
reproduce copyright material;

British Pharmaceutical Industry for the advertisement 'The
British Diet'; British Waste Paper Association for the article
'We keep Supply and Demand in balance say Waste Paper
People' in *EYE News* (October 1987); Central Electricity
Generating Board for a slightly adapted extract from *The
Need for Nuclear Energy*; The Daily Telegraph PLC for the
following articles in *The Daily Telegraph*, 'Plans laid for
'healthier' egg' by Agriculture Correspondent (26.7.86),
'Campaign's coffin-shaped pie angers meat traders' by
Peter Pallot (4.5.87), 'Britain 'killing all life in North Sea' by
Charles Clover (22.4.87), 'Greenpeace claims of 'dead'
North Sea challenged' by Godfrey Brown (24.4.87), 'Call for
early tax cut on unleaded petrol' by John Langley (26.6.87),
'Most polluted river 'now 75pc cleaner'' (21.6.86), 'Bird
haven bought for £70,000' by Robert Bedlow (23.3.87),
'Food firms cause salt problems' (23.3.87), 'Fat-free diets
can break your bones' by Dr K C Hutchin (14.7.86), 'Call for
'wave power'' by Parliamentary Staff (20.10.85), extracts
from the article 'BNFL fined £10,000 over radiation leak' by
John Williams (24.7.85) and an adapted article 'A wave of
anger rises, along a poisoned river' by Maurice Weaver
(19.12.86); Department of Energy (UK) for adapted extracts
from *Review* Issue 1 (September 1987); Diet Center, Inc for
an adapted extract from '100 Diet Tips That Can Change
Your Life' by Sybil Ferguson, Founder, President Diet
Center, Inc. Copyright © 1987 by Diet Center, Inc; HMSO
for an extract from Ordnance Survey 1:50,000 Landranger,
sheet 129, Nottingham & Loughborough, © Crown
Copyright; Northern Examining Association for question 2
(c) in *NEA Joint Examination in Geography, Paper 2* (1987);
North West Evening Mail Ltd for an extract from an article
in *North West Evening Mail* (5.5.87); Overseas Development
Administration for an extract from *The Environment and the
British Aid Programme*, Crown Copyright.

We are grateful to the following for permission to
reproduce photographs: A-Z Collection, page 48; Aaron
Photographic, page 125 *right*; Airviews Scott Ltd, page 143;
Associated Press, pages 58, 115, 128; Australian High
Commission, page 38 *below*; Australian News &
Information Bureau, page 39 *below* (photo: John Crowther);
Barnabys Picture Library, page 107 *above*; Dr Alan
Beaumont, page 30; S. Bennetts, page 118 *above left*; Anne
Bolt, page 56 *right*; Bristol Press & Picture Agency, page 50
right; British Antarctic Survey, page 120 (photo: C.J.
Gilbert); British Coal, page 28; Camera Press, page 138 *right*
(photo: Les Wilson); Bruce Coleman, pages 87 *above left*
(photo: Hans Reinhard); 118 *above right*; Colorific, page 139
(photo: A.B. Joyce); Consolidated Gold Fields, page 5 *left*;
Daily Telegraph, page 60 *right*; *Farmer's Weekly*, page 43
below (photo: Philip Felkin); *The Guardian*, page 84; Brendan
Hearne, pages 26, 35, 45, 47, 59, 64 *above*, 80, 135, 146;
Highlands & Islands Development Board, pages 87 *above
right*, 87 *centre*, 87 *below*; Eric & David Hosking, page 83
(photo: D.P. Wilson); Hulton Deutsch Collection, pages 43
above left, 43 *above right*, 117 *above*, 124 *left*; Alan Hutchison
Library, pages 20, 68 *right*, 99; Institute of Agricultural
History of Museum of English Rural Life, University of
Reading, pages 42, 44 *left*; Dr Peter Jordan, page 103; Frank
Lane Picture Agency, page 5 *right* (photo: Braun
Waldsterben); the Mansell Collection, page 44 *right*; Tony
Marsh, page 62 *left*; Ministry of Agriculture, Fisheries &
Food, page 50 *left*; Marion & Tony Morrison, South
American Pictures, page 15 *right*; Dr S. Nakagawa, page
114; National Portrait Gallery, London, pages 43 *centre*, 107
centre; National Power, page 72; Netherlands Embassy,
page 126; North of Scotland Hydro-Electric Board, page 96
(photo: John Dewar); Axel Poignant Archive, page 38 *above*;
Popperfoto, pages 62–63, 64 *below*, 100, 117 *below*, 118 *below*;
The Royal Collection, page 107 *below*; *Selby Times*, page 27;
The Scotsman Publications Ltd, page 95; Ronald Sheridan
Photo Library, page 101 (photo: John P. Stevens); Robert
Stephenson, Brighton Polytechnic, page 60 *left*; Swedish
Institute, page 69; Thames Water, page 90; Tropix, page 138
left (photo: V.J. Birley); Dr C Tydeman, page 23; Viewfinder
Colour Photo Library, pages 92 (photo: Nick Meers), 123;
Water Research Centre, page 108 *below*; Yorkshire Dales
National Park, page 29; Zefa Picture Library, pages 15 *left*
(photo: D. Frobisch), 37 (photo: Smith Robin), 39 *above*, 56
left, 65.

Cover: Thames Barrier; International Stock Exchange Photo
Library

Contents

Preface

The Longman *Key Themes in Geography* Series meets the requirements of many of the GCSE syllabi introduced in 1986. Teachers involved in Schools Council (Avery Hill/GYSL) based courses should find this series particularly helpful as its topics have been grouped together under economic, environmental and urban/rural headings.

The books in the series have been designed to enable students to achieve the high academic aims specified in the GCSE National Criteria. Emphasis has been placed on practical work and enquiry-based techniques, as these inevitably bring students into the closest possible contact with the subject material. Ample opportunities for individual research and group role-play have been built into the teaching programmes, and each book contains a selection of both aim and hypothesis-based fieldwork topics to meet course study requirements. Additional guidance and recommended activities for this vital component are provided by *Fieldwork Studies in Geography* (Longman; ISBN 0 582 22442 X).

The teaching units are designed to convey basic concepts, knowledge and skills; all units include a set of questions which are graded in difficulty. Some of these questions invite class discussion and are deliberately 'open-ended'; this allows the teacher to dictate how much information the students are expected to put into their answers. The three books in the series each end with a test/revision section – also carefully graded.

Topics are examined at local, regional/national, and international/global scales, as required by the National Criteria. An appendix to each book carries a world map on which studies at the last scale are located. A further appendix in each book provides a glossary of key terms; these are highlighted in the text by bold type.

The authors welcome constructive comments on the books in this series, and ask that these be directed through the publishers.

Jack Gillett
Series Editor

Companion Volumes
Economic Geography (ISBN 0 582 23177 9)
Urban and Rural Geography (ISBN 0 582 23176 0)

1

The Natural Environment

1.1 Introduction: population pressures

This book is about the natural world in which we live, and how we use it to meet our needs. Unfortunately, the story it has to tell is not always a happy one for people often act in a careless and selfish way and give too little thought to the long-term effects of what they are doing. Here are some examples:

☐ In the lowlands of the Amazon Basin, large areas of forest are being felled much faster than they can be replaced.

☐ In the Mediterranean Sea, many coastal waters have been over-fished and now produce much less food.

☐ In the North American states of Kansas, Nebraska and Oklahoma, huge quantities of fertile soil were 'lost' in the 1930s due to harmful farming methods.

1 On an outline map of the world, locate the examples of mis-use given in the text and shown in the photographs on this page. Each location must bear its name and a brief description of what happened there.

2 Locate any local examples of mis-use on a map of your own area, possibly having discussed them openly in class first.

We will need to examine many of these problems later in the book, and suggest ways in which they might be tackled. But first it is necessary to introduce two important concepts (ideas): over-population and the natural environment.

▼ **Figure 1.1** Open cast mining for gold in South Africa

▲ **Figure 1.2** Trees in a West German forest affected by acid rain

Over-population

Study the population distribution map in Figure 1.3. It highlights those places where large numbers of people live (the **densely populated** areas) as well as others having fewer people (the **sparsely populated** ones). Either of these types of area may be said to be **over-populated**. This means that they do not meet the basic needs of all the people living in them. It may be that there is insufficient food and water, or perhaps a lack of essential materials needed to make clothes and build homes. Hot, dry areas for example may be inhabited by very few people, but are still over-populated if there isn't enough pasture or water for their animals. On the other hand, certain densely populated areas such as south-east England are not really over-populated. Can you suggest reasons why this is so? The two main reasons why many densely populated areas are under increasing pressure are shown in Figures 1.4 and 1.5.

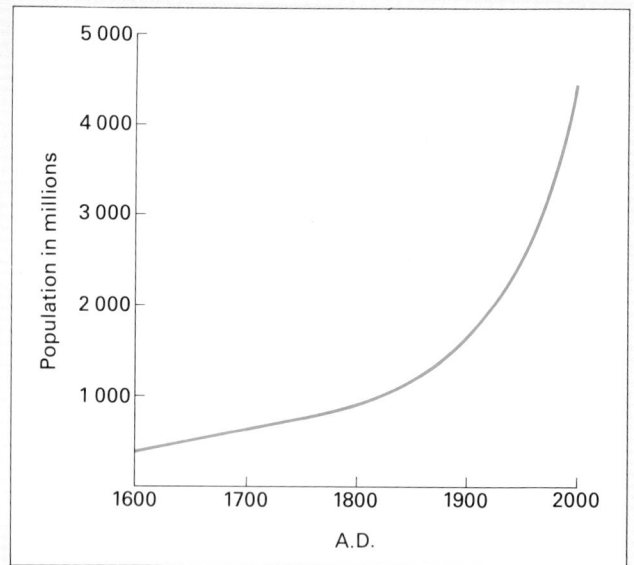

▲ **Figure 1.4** World population increase from AD 1600

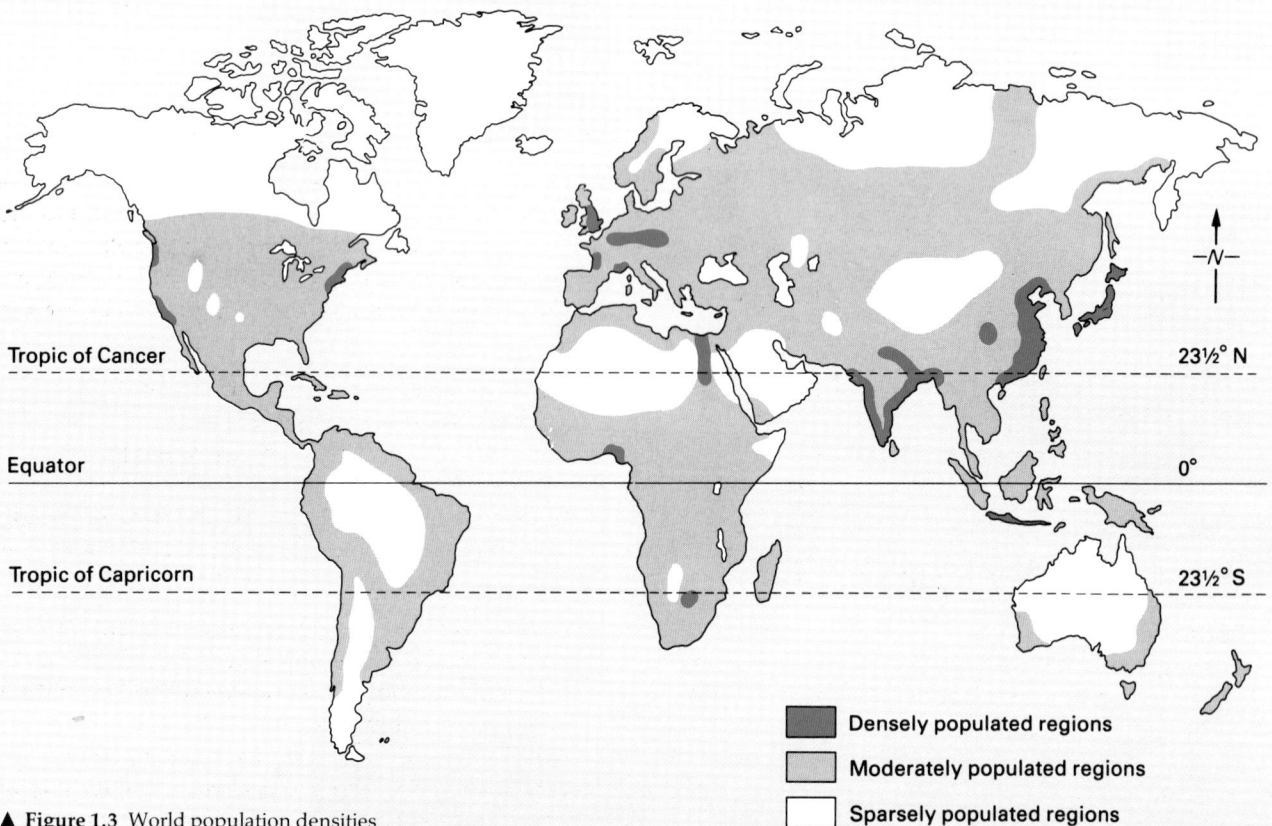

▲ **Figure 1.3** World population densities

Densely populated regions

Moderately populated regions

Sparsely populated regions

Description of suitability for farming	% of world's total land area
Climate too dry	30
Climate too cold	16
Land too steep/high	10
Soil too shallow/infertile	10
Land which could be made productive	24
Land which is already very productive	10

▲ and ▶ **Figure 1.5** How suitable is the world's land area for farming?

3 Pair up these five important terms with their correct meanings:
Densely populated . . .
Over-populated . . .
Population distribution . . .
Sparsely populated . . .
Uninhabited . . .
. . . describes an area in which few people live.
. . . describes an area in which many people live.
. . . describes an area in which no people live.
. . . describes an area which cannot meet the basic needs of all its people.
. . . describes how people are 'spaced out' over a part of the world's land surface.

4 Copy out each of these statements based on Figure 1.3, choosing the correct words to fill the blanks.
a The world's population is distributed very . . . (evenly *or* unevenly) over its land surface.
b Most of the densely populated areas arc to the . . . (north *or* south) of the Equator.
c Most of the densely populated areas are . . . (on or near a coast *or* well inland).
d Most of the densely populated areas are . . . (between *or* outside) Latitudes 60°N and 60°S.

5 Plot the information in Figure 1.5 in the form of a divided bar graph. The skeleton graph will help you to do this.

6 **a** Write down the world's population (to the nearest 100 million) in 1600, 1800, 1900 and 1980.
b Describe the changes in the world's population since 1600. You will need to say much more than 'It has increased'!
c Suggest what problems might result from a continuing rise in world population.

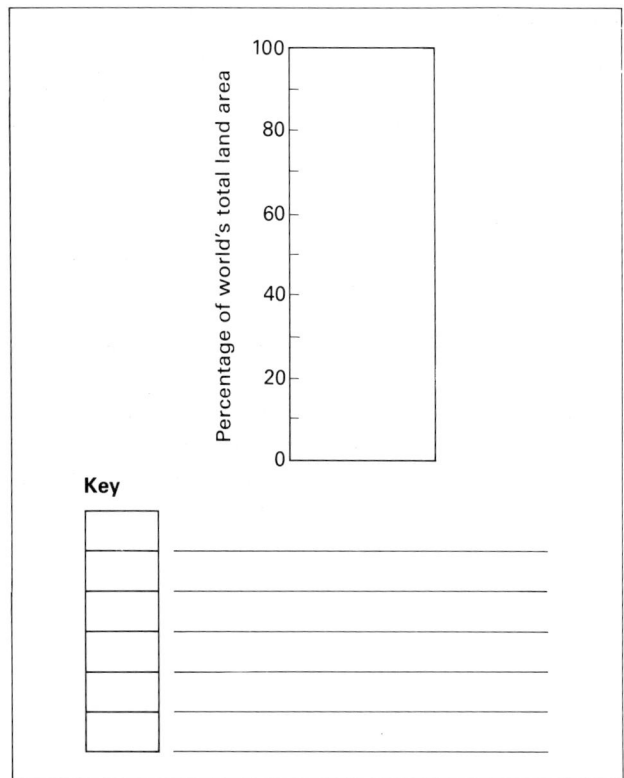

Percentage of world's total land area

Key

The natural environment

Much of this book studies the effects of population increase on what is called the **natural environment**. These are the surroundings in which people live, but which are not of their own making. Any natural environment may be fully described under certain key topic headings:

☐ relief (the height and shape of the land)
☐ climate (temperature, rainfall, wind)
☐ water features (seas, rivers, lakes, etc.)
☐ soils
☐ natural vegetation (the trees and smaller plants which are so well suited to a particular area that they grow there without any 'help' from people).

7 **a** What aspects of natural environment are *not* covered by the five topics listed above?
b Describe the *differences* between the two natural environments shown in Figures 1.6 and 1.7. Do this with the help of your amended topic list. (Hint: you will have to base your assessment of soil fertility on other information given in the two scenes.)

▲ Figure 1.6

▼ Figure 1.7

1.2 Local climate study

Unit 1.1 stressed the importance of climate to natural environments. This practical study investigates selected climate patterns within the local area. It can be undertaken without expensive equipment and adapted to suit individual needs. There are no restrictions as to site and duration, but the same place(s) and time(s) must be used each day. The following notes should prove helpful when choosing the topics to study:

Wind direction The 'wet-finger' technique may be used or the movement of trees, chimney smoke, flags or weather vanes observed. Only *general* wind directions are needed (e.g. 'from the south-west').

Air temperature An ordinary thermometer can be used, preferably in a shaded and sheltered position.

Cloud cover Can only be judged by eye. It is done by estimating how many oktas (eighths) of the sky are obscured by cloud (e.g. a half-covered sky would be recorded as 4 oktas).

Rainfall Requires the use of a rain guage (Figure 1.8). The amount which has collected in the previous 24 hours is measured and recorded in mm.

It is important to keep a careful record of all your observations; these could be displayed in the classroom and up-dated as necessary.

The completed study consists of a series of stages, and these should be tackled in the following order.

Title The precise wording is up to you to decide, but it could be as short as the title of this study.

Aim or **hypothesis** These begin with the words 'To ...' and 'That ...' respectively. They should state very clearly what your study is designed to investigate. The examples on page 154 should help you to get the wording right.

Location Draw a labelled sketch map to show the general location of the chosen site, then explain why that particular site was chosen.

Duration State the first and last dates on which recordings were taken. You should also note down the set time(s) of the daily observation(s).

Method Summarise how you obtained the required information (e.g. What equipment was available? How did you use it?)

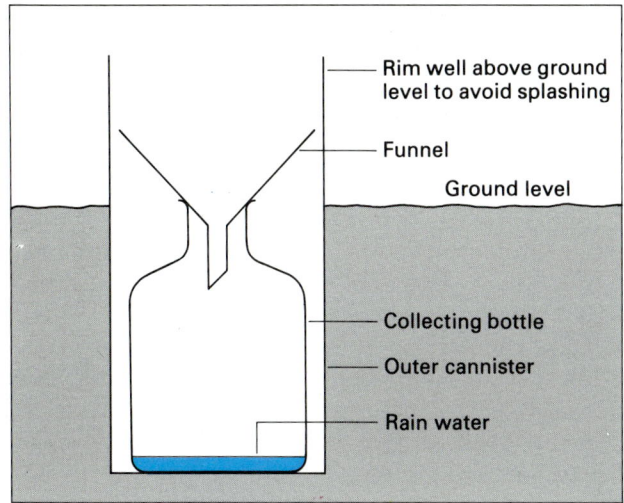

▲ **Figure 1.8** A rain gauge. The contents of the bottle are emptied into a special graduated cylinder to be measured

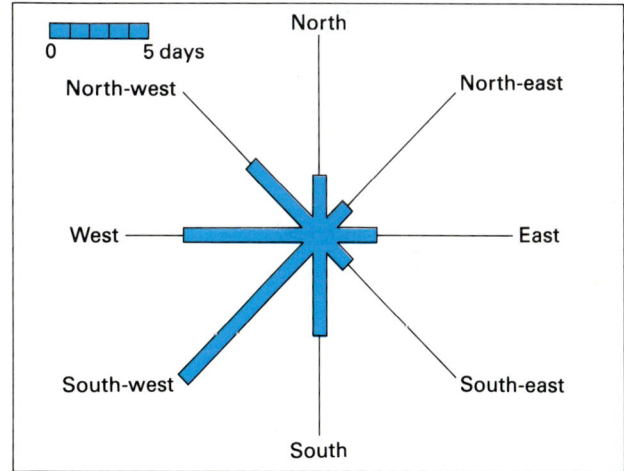

▲ **Figure 1.9** A wind rose – to show the frequency of wind directions

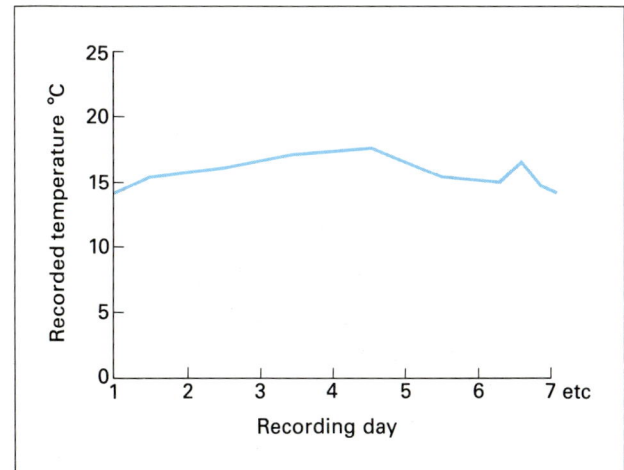

▶ **Figure 1.10** Sample air temperature line graph

Results and interpretation This stage is the 'heart' of the study and will take the most time to complete. It could be sub-divided into two sections:

☐ **Data recording** Show the data for each climate topic in table or graph form. Try to use a variety of graphing techniques (see Figures 1.9–1.12). *It is most important* that you write about each of these illustrations. This stage of 'talking on paper' need not be very long, but examiners often look especially carefully at how well you do this.

☐ **Data comparison** A series of scatter graphs like the one in Figure 1.13 will help you to see how closely each pair of topic data sets is linked. As before, full written descriptions and attempted explanations are required in every case.

General conclusions These can be quite brief as you should have been drawing 'mini' conclusions throughout the previous stage. As the general conclusions must answer the question posed at the beginning of the study, it is wise to re-read the Aim or Hypothesis before summarising your most important findings.

Appendix Having completed your study, think back to what you have done and achieved. Any important weaknesses/recommendations highlighted by doing this should be added as an appendix to the study.

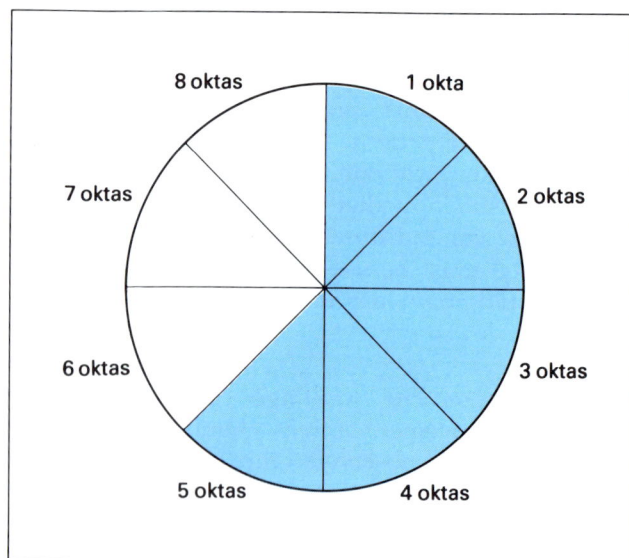

▲ **Figure 1.11** Sample cloud cover pie graph. This shows a sky five-eighths covered by cloud. A cloudless sky would need an unshaded graph

▼ **Figure 1.12** Sample rainfall bar graph

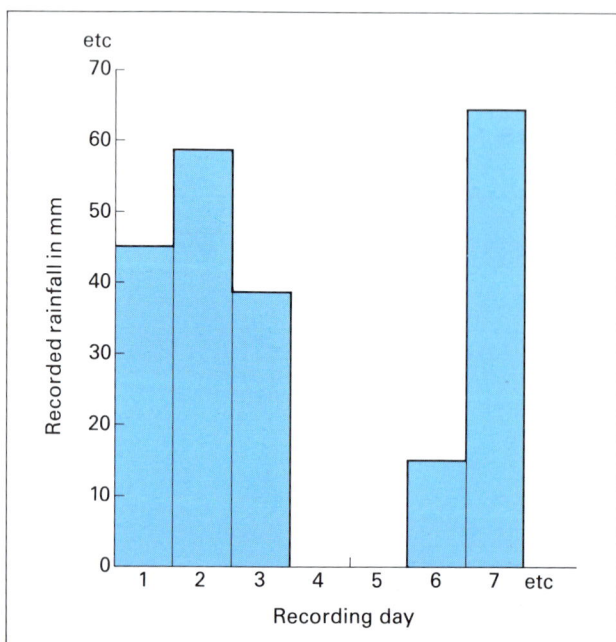

▼ **Figure 1.13**

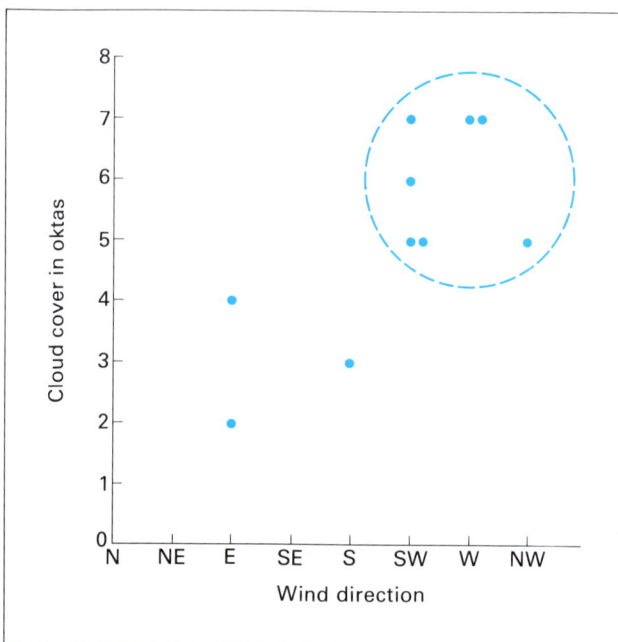

1.3 Africa's natural regions

Climate is greatly influenced by the heating effect of the sun and the direction of the wind. On the world scale, the basic temperature pattern is fairly simple – it gets steadily cooler with increasing latitude (distance from the Equator). However, most places have one season which is much warmer than the others. This is because the overhead position of the sun moves northwards and then southwards again between the Tropics of Cancer and Capricorn in the course of a full year. This movement of the sun's overhead position also affects the main wind belts around the Earth.

The effects of this link between sun and wind on Africa's climates are shown in Figure 1.14. Similar patterns also occur over the other parts of the world between latitudes 40°N and 40°S. The places which have the same wind direction throughout the year are usually wet or dry, depending on whether this wind has already passed over sea or land. It follows that a seasonal change in wind direction usually brings much wetter or drier weather. The effects of wind belt movements over Africa are shown in Figure 1.15. Both maps have been drawn to the same scale, to make it easier for you to answer the questions. Figure 1.15 also includes a typical climate graph for each of the four main **natural regions** shown on this second map.

1 Copy the map in Figure 1.15, then add onto it the information shown in Figure 1.14. You will need to 'combine' the keys in both illustrations.

2 Follow these instructions to complete a copy of the table at the bottom of this page.
2nd and 3rd columns – look at the climate graphs to get the highest and lowest temperatures. The spaces in brackets are for descriptions of these temperatures; the words to use are shown in the table below.

Temperature range	Temperature description
Below – 10°C	Very cold
– 10°C to 0°C	Cold
0°C to 10°C	Cool
11°C to 20°C	Warm
21°C to 30°C	Hot
Over 30°C	Very hot

4th and 5th columns – shade each box either blue (for months with more than 40mm of rain) or red (for those with fewer than 40mm). This monthly figure has been chosen because areas constantly receiving less rainfall are classified as desert or semi-desert.

Summary of Africa's four major climate regions; this information is for places north of the Equator.

▼ Figure 1.14 The effects of the sun's overhead position on the seasonal movements of wind belts over Africa

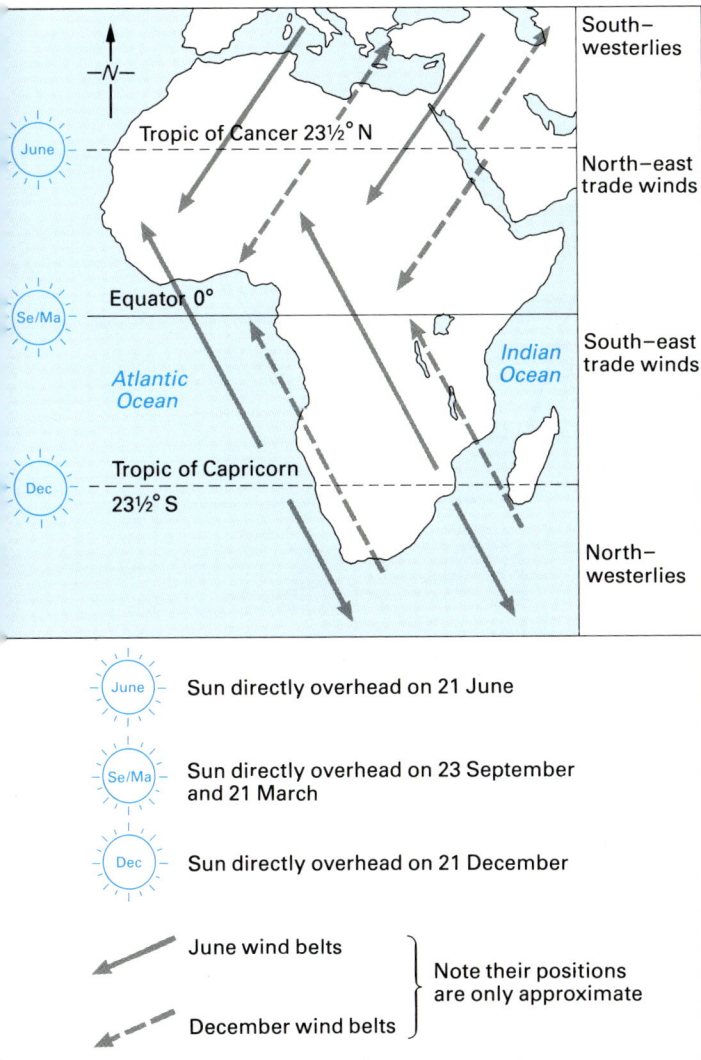

Climate region	Description of temperature in:		Rainfall in:*	
	January	July	January	July
Equatorial rain forest				
Hot desert				
Savanna				
Mediterranean				

*Blue shading = rainfall above 40 mm
Red shading = rainfall 40 mm or below

Mediterranean region climate graph (northern hemisphere)

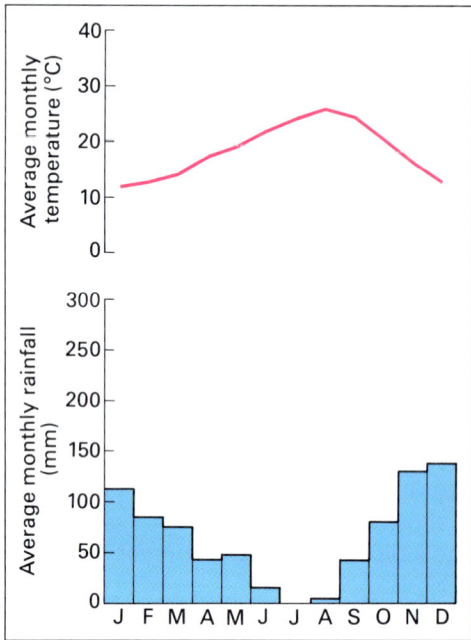

Hot desert region climate graph (northern hemisphere)

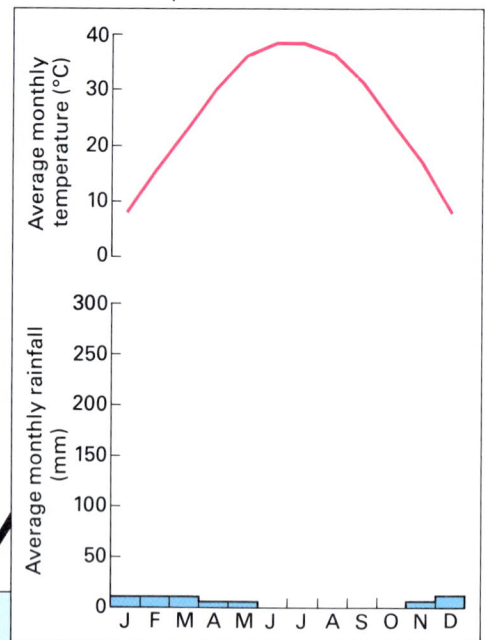

Tropic of Cancer — 23½° N

Equator — 0°

Atlantic Ocean

Indian Ocean

Tropic of Capricorn — 23½° S

Figure 1.15 Africa's four major natural regions

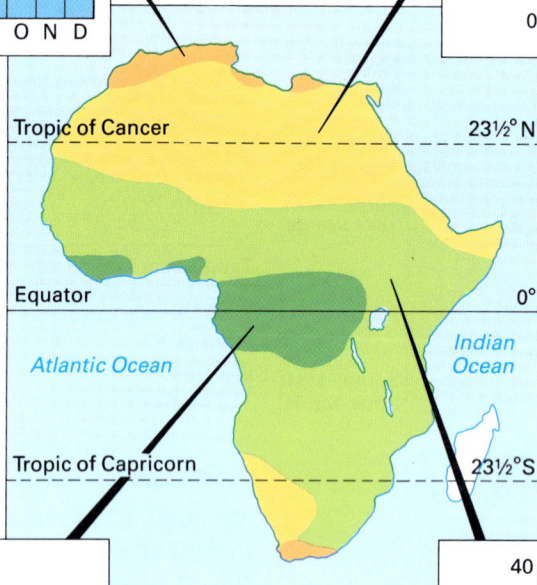

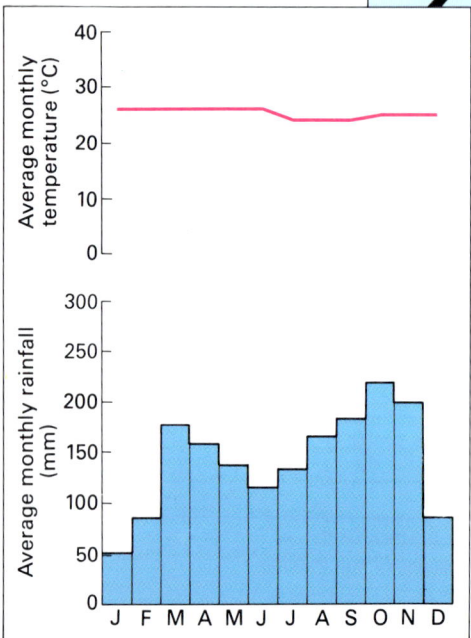

Equatorial rain forest region climate graph

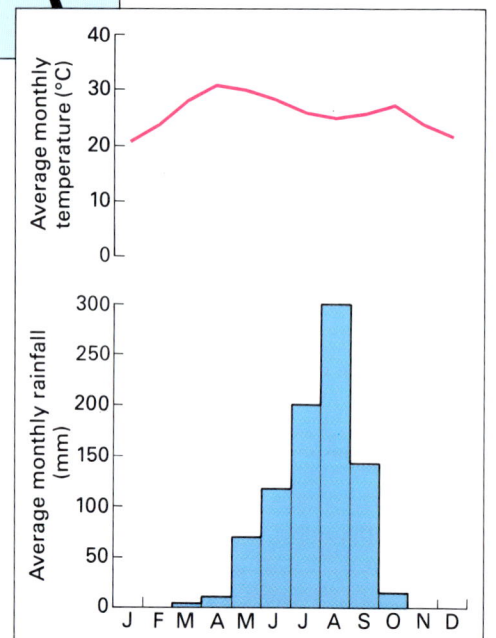

Savanna region climate graph (northern hemisphere)

▲ **Figure 1.16** Savanna landscape (wet season)

▲ **Figure 1.17** The same scene during the dry season

3 With the help of the table of the wind direction information in Figure 1.14, explain why these four natural regions have the rainfall patterns shown in your completed table. In each case you will need to say:

– whether the winds are constant or variable over a whole year
– which direction(s) the winds blow from, and whether they have already passed over large areas of land or sea. Name these areas with the help of an atlas.

4 a Copy out the following landscape description which is based on Figure 1.16.

'The landscape is a deep green colour. The trees are in full leaf and the ground is covered by long grass; one kind – called elephant grass – is 3m high! A rich variety of animal life flourishes in this type of natural region.'
(If time permits) sketch the scenes in Figures 1.16–1.18, and add labels to highlight their key features.
b (After discussion in pairs, then openly in class) write down your own descriptions of the scenes in Figures 1.17 and 1.18.

▼ **Figure 1.18** Mediterranean region landscape

1.4 Perception of tropical regions

Unit 1.3 explained how global temperature and rainfall patterns have combined to produce Africa's four contrasting regions. This unit examines two of the tropical regions which also occur in South America and certain other parts of the world (Figure 1.19). It does this by examining some of the most common **misconceptions** (mistaken ideas) which people have about these regions.

Equatorial rain forest

Four such misconceptions about these heavily forested areas are:

'It rains constantly.'
'Crops grow extremely well there; it is simply a matter of cutting down some trees, then planting the seeds.'
'There is dense undergrowth throughout these areas.'
'Equatorial rain forests are inhabited only by small tribes of primitive indians.'

Figures 1.20–1.23 will help you to understand why these statements are incorrect. Look at Figure 1.20 first. It shows you that the rain usually falls in the mid-afternoon, by which time the sun has heated up the land surface sufficiently to cause heavy rain to fall.

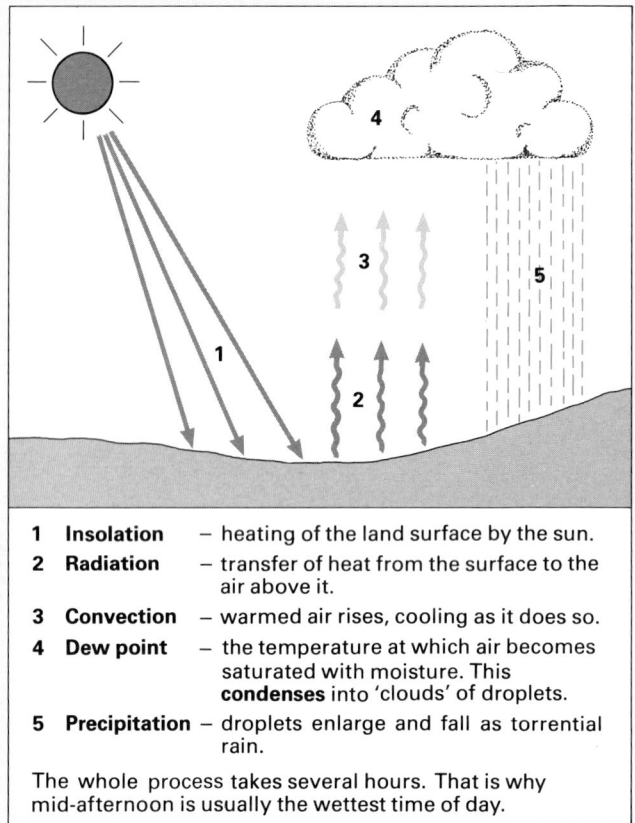

1	**Insolation**	– heating of the land surface by the sun.
2	**Radiation**	– transfer of heat from the surface to the air above it.
3	**Convection**	– warmed air rises, cooling as it does so.
4	**Dew point**	– the temperature at which air becomes saturated with moisture. This **condenses** into 'clouds' of droplets.
5	**Precipitation**	– droplets enlarge and fall as torrential rain.

The whole process takes several hours. That is why mid-afternoon is usually the wettest time of day.

▲ **Figure 1.20** Stages in the formation of convection rainfall

▼ **Figure 1.19** The world's equatorial and hot desert regions

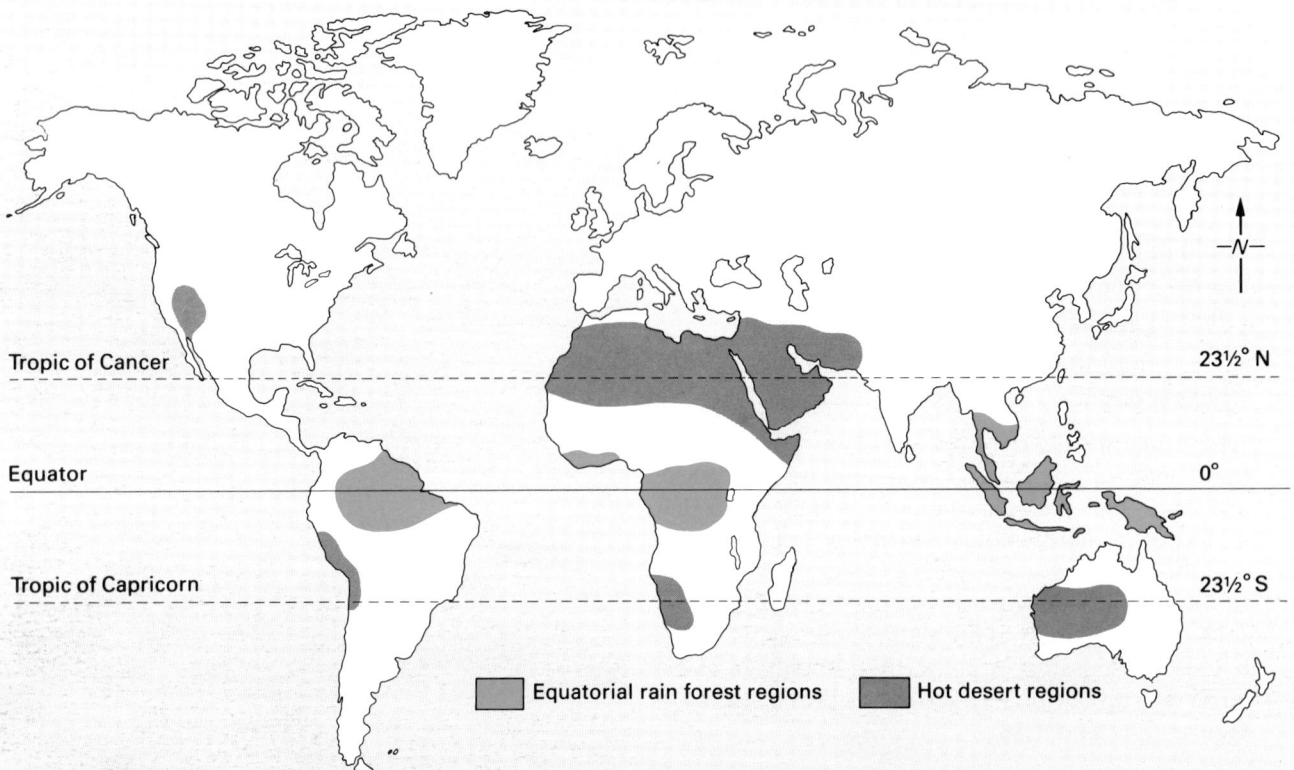

Figure 1.21 shows the kind of nutrient cycle which occurs within equatorial rain forests. Plants grow very quickly due to the humid (hot and wet) climate and the richness of the topsoil. The soil is so fertile because the leaf litter from the trees rots down very quickly. If the trees are cut down, however, this efficient cycle is broken because the soil no longer receives any goodness from the leaves. The bare topsoil is then affected by heavy rain in two different ways. Some of the rainwater seeps downwards through it, dissolving vital nutrients (plant foods) as it does so and taking them deep below the surface. This process also makes the topsoil infertile, and is called **leaching**. Any rain which cannot penetrate the already saturated soil flows over the surface, **eroding** (removing) and transporting (carrying) it to the rivers and then to the open sea. Millions of tonnes of precious soil are lost in this way every year.

Dense undergrowth does occur on river banks, along roadsides and in clearings (Figure 1.22) – in fact anywhere where the strong sunlight can reach the ground. The third misconception arises because this type of forest (called 'secondary' jungle) grows on the edges and is therefore most easily seen by explorers and visitors. 'Primary' jungle occurs much deeper within the forest, where the highest layer of leaves forms an almost continuous canopy. This cuts out much of the sunlight, making it dark and gloomy lower down. It is fairly easy to move about the primary jungle, which is rather like the inside of a great cathedral with its high vaulted roof and towering upright columns.

▼ **Figure 1.22** Secondary jungle grows in clearings and on river banks. This is the Rio Napo in Ecuador

▶ **Figure 1.23** The Trans-Amazonica Highway

▼ **Figure 1.21** Equatorial rain forest nutrient cycle. The cycle is broken if trees are cut down, which means the soil rapidly becomes less and less fertile

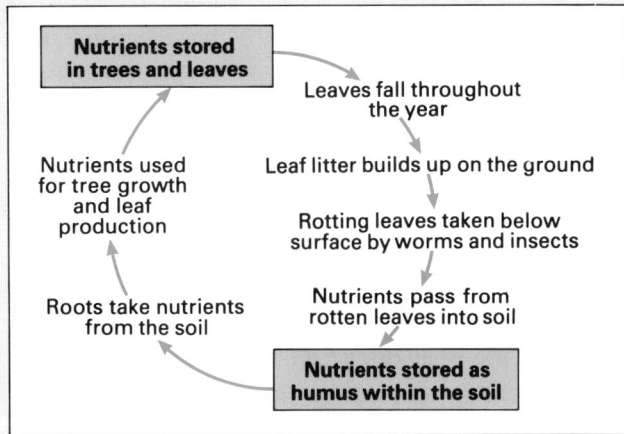

Ancient tribes of people still inhabit the more remote areas. They are however becoming fewer and smaller each year as outsiders clear the land to build new roads and mine valuable raw materials. Figure 1.23 pictures one of the major new roads built across the **selvas**. The Trans-Amazonica Highway is the longest of these and stretches some 5000 km inland from the Atlantic coast. Bauxite (from which we get aluminium), iron ore, lead and gold are some of the minerals being mined within the original but now greatly reduced area of the selvas.

Hot deserts

True deserts receive less than 250mm of rainfall in an average year. Although places like the Sahara Desert in North Africa are being visited by increasing numbers of tourists, many people still have misconceptions of what a fairly typical hot desert is like, e.g.:

'It is always scorching hot in these areas.'
'Hot deserts are completely waterless.'

Figures 1.24 and 1.25 will help you to correct these misconceptions. There is no printed text to help you this time, but you may discuss the diagrams openly in class before attempting question 3. You should note that some desert areas do *not* have artesian basins!

1 a Copy Figure 1.19 onto an outline map of the world.
b Use an atlas to label the shaded areas on your map with these names:

Equatorial rain forests	Hot deserts
Amazon Basin	Arabian Desert
Indonesia	Arizona Desert
Zaire Basin	Atacama Desert
	Australian Desert
	Kalahari Desert
	Sahara Desert

c Also with the help of an atlas, write down the most northerly and the most southerly latitudes between which:
– equatorial rain forests occur
– hot deserts occur.

2 a Copy out the four common misconceptions about equatorial rain forest areas.
b Write a paragraph to explain why each of these misconceptions is false. You must include all the key words printed in bold letters in your answer.

3 a *Correct* both of the misconceptions about hot desert areas.
b Write detailed reasons for your amendments to the original statements.

4 a Discover for yourself whether these statements are true or false:
'Equatorial rain forests are important producers of "softwoods" (e.g. from pine and spruce trees).
'Hot desert landscapes are only of the "erg" (sand-dune) type.'
'Hot deserts are of little economic value.'
b Write down any other useful information which you discovered while investigating these statements.

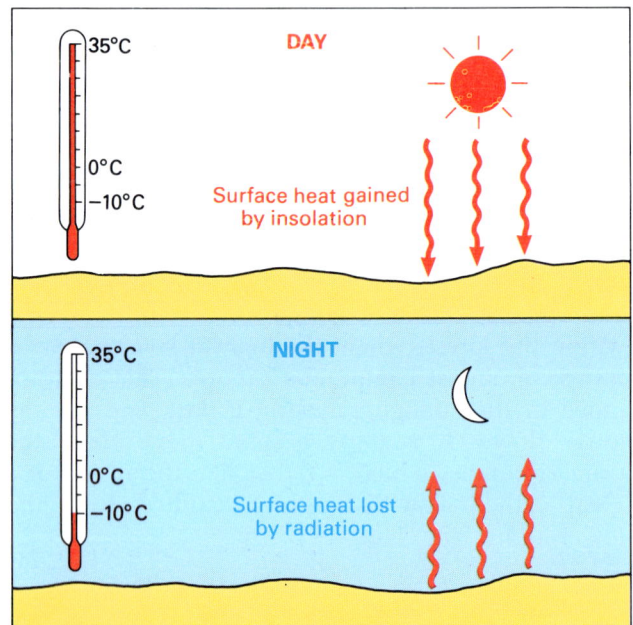

▲ **Figure 1.24** Cloudless skies mean that night time temperatures in hot desert areas are much lower than those during the day

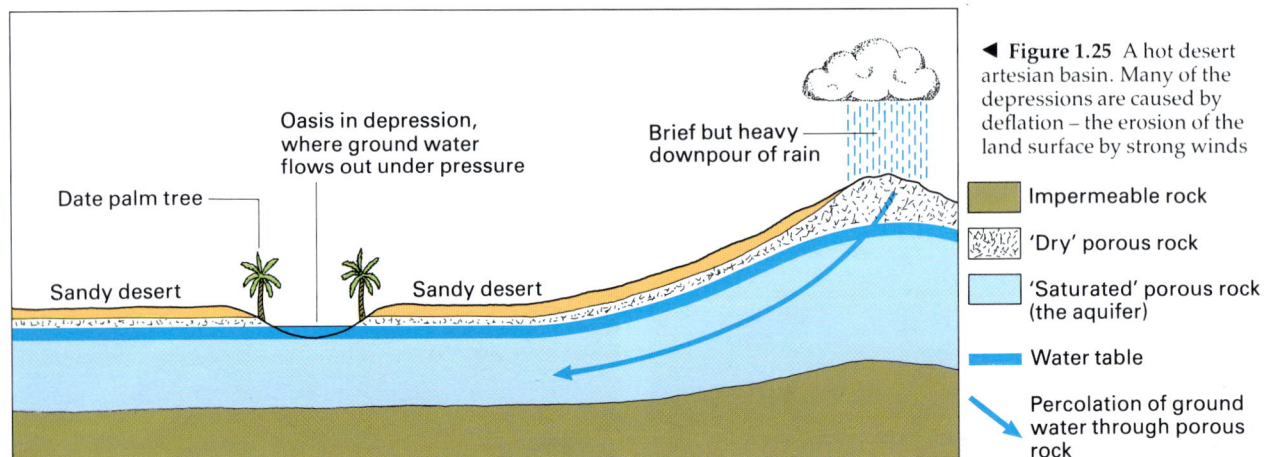

◄ **Figure 1.25** A hot desert artesian basin. Many of the depressions are caused by deflation – the erosion of the land surface by strong winds

2

Ecosystems and Resources

2.1 Introduction: the biosphere

The **biosphere** is 'all those parts of the Earth where life can exist'. It includes places where plants, insects, animals and human beings live. Although a vast area, it is really very small when compared with the whole world and the atmosphere which surrounds it. Figure 2.1 shows the location of the biosphere. It is not drawn to scale but the labels for the different layers put the thickness of the biosphere in its true perspective.

1 Copy out the definition of the biosphere shown in inverted commas.

2 **a** List the four major 'life' groups listed in the text.
b If you can think of any other important 'life' groups, add these to your list.

3 Suggest reasons why the biosphere:
a is rarely deeper than 3 metres under the land surface.
b is deepest in the oceans.
c only occupies the lowest 100 metres or so of the atmosphere.
d is very unlikely to rise higher than 8848 metres above sea level.

4 **a** Copy Figure 2.1.
b How can you tell that this cross-section of the Earth has not been drawn to scale?
c How does the maximum thickness of the biosphere compare with:
i the radius of the 'solid' Earth?
ii the combined radius of the solid Earth and the atmosphere which surrounds it?

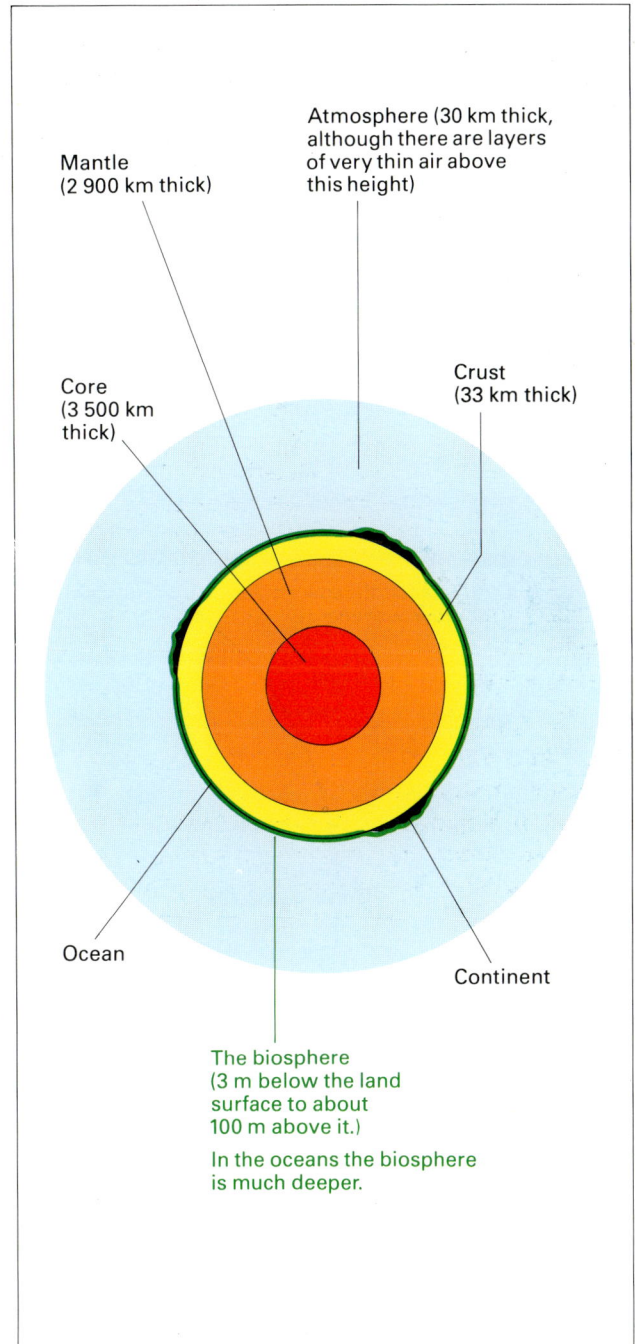

Mantle (2 900 km thick)

Atmosphere (30 km thick, although there are layers of very thin air above this height)

Core (3 500 km thick)

Crust (33 km thick)

Ocean

Continent

The biosphere (3 m below the land surface to about 100 m above it.)

In the oceans the biosphere is much deeper.

▶ **Figure 2.1** The biosphere, in relation to the Earth's major layers

2.2 What is an ecosystem?

All forms of life have certain basic needs. Plants, for example, cannot survive without oxygen obtained from the air. Some animals (the herbivores) eat plants while carnivores are flesh-eaters. **Ecosystems** are useful and interesting because they show how certain forms of life have come to be dependent on each other. They also help us to predict what is likely to happen if one of the essential links within them is affected and the chain breaks down.

Now look at the ecosystem in Figure 2.2, and compare it with the cycle on page 15. Although these diagrams contain different information, they do look quite similar. This is because they share two basic components (parts), which are:

Stores – the labels on the diagrams. Energy and essential foods are held within the bodies of the plants, animals, etc. named in the labels.

Flows – the arrows between the labels. These show how the different forms of life depend on each other and exchange vital food material.

1 Write down the meanings of these key terms:
   a ecosystem   **d** herbivore
   b store   **e** carnivore.
   c flow

2 List at least five different examples of:
   a herbivores   **b** carnivores.

3 **a** Copy the ecosystem in Figure 2.2.
   b Shade all the stores in one colour, then use a different colour for the flows between them.
   c Devise a simple key to show the meanings of your two chosen colours.

4 **a** What would you understand by a pair of stores linked by *two* flow arrows pointing in opposite directions?
   b Try to think of at least two pairs of stores which may be double-linked in this way.

▼ **Figure 2.2** Simplified energy-flow ecosystem based on a cow grazing in a field. This does not include energy transfers between sun and grass, or energy losses through the cow's milk

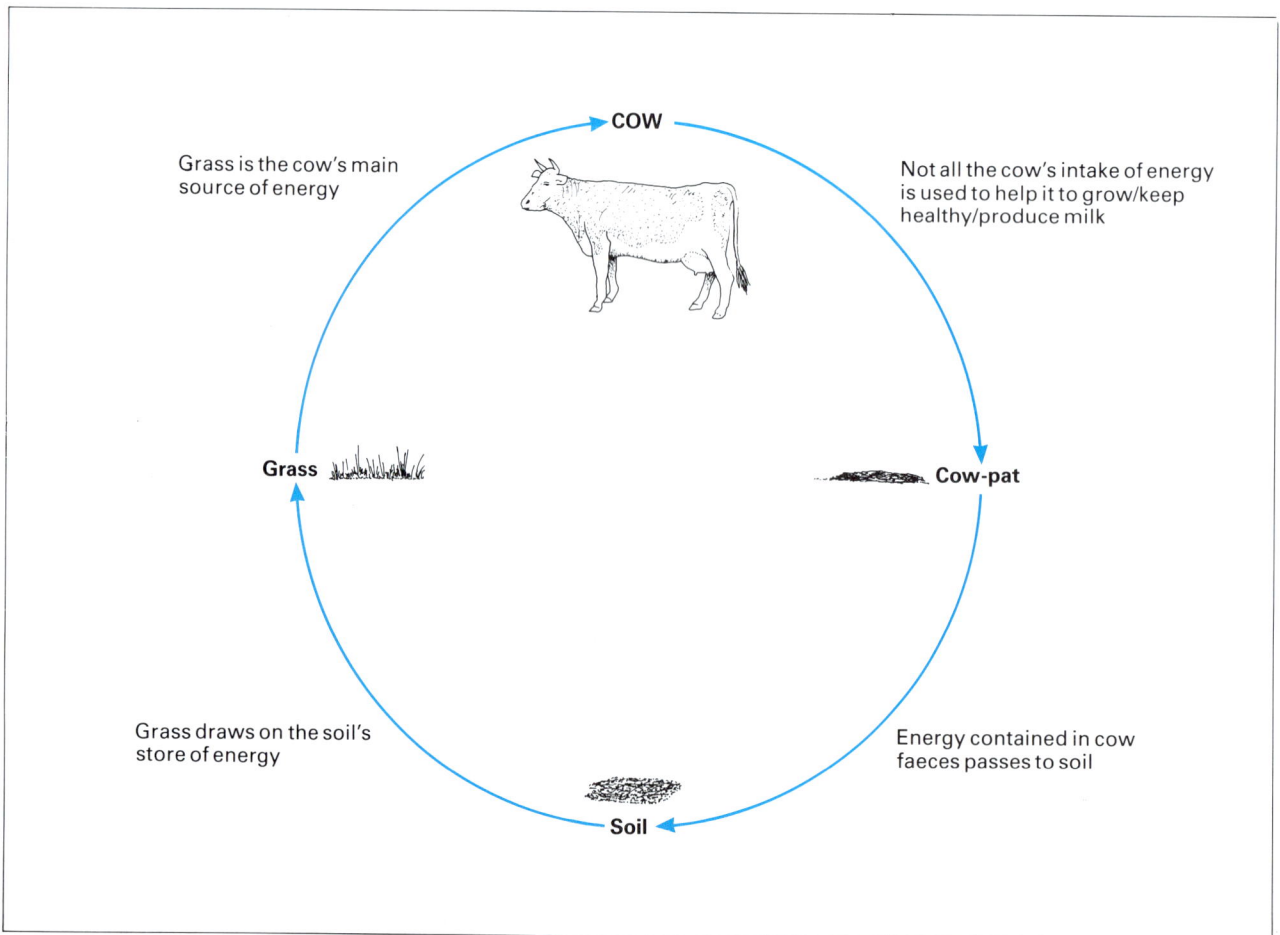

COW

Grass is the cow's main source of energy

Not all the cow's intake of energy is used to help it to grow/keep healthy/produce milk

Grass

Cow-pat

Grass draws on the soil's store of energy

Energy contained in cow faeces passes to soil

Soil

2.3 Local ecosystems

This unit will help you to design simple ecosystems based on wildlife in your local area. The first question can be completed in the classroom, but the others require you to make observations out of doors.

1 a Copy out the 'five-store' ecosystem diagram (Figure 2.3).

b Pair up the information in these two columns. These will give you the five entries to write in your store boxes.

Main entries:	Examples:
decomposers They break down dead material.	caterpillars
large predators They eat smaller birds.	hawks
primary producers All life forms above ground depend on them.	plants, trees and leaves
small herbivores They eat plants	robins
small predators They eat insects, etc.	worms

c Explain why a line has been drawn down the right side of the ecosystem linking the decomposers to the other four stores. Add an arrow to this line to show its correct direction of flow.

2 Design an ecosystem to show how these life forms rely on each other for survival: bushes, cats, flowers, foxes, mice, rabbits and worms. (Note: your teacher may ask you to add to this list.)

3 a Choose one or more of these types of location which you can visit easily: farmland (arable or pastoral), hedgerow, marsh or pond, park, playing field.
b At each location, keep a careful record of the different forms of wildlife and name as many individual animals, birds, fish, etc. which you have been able to identify (you will probably need to take some reference books to do this properly).
c For each location, design an ecosystem which shows how the wildlife you have observed is linked together as a natural community. Your reference books should tell you what each type usually eats.

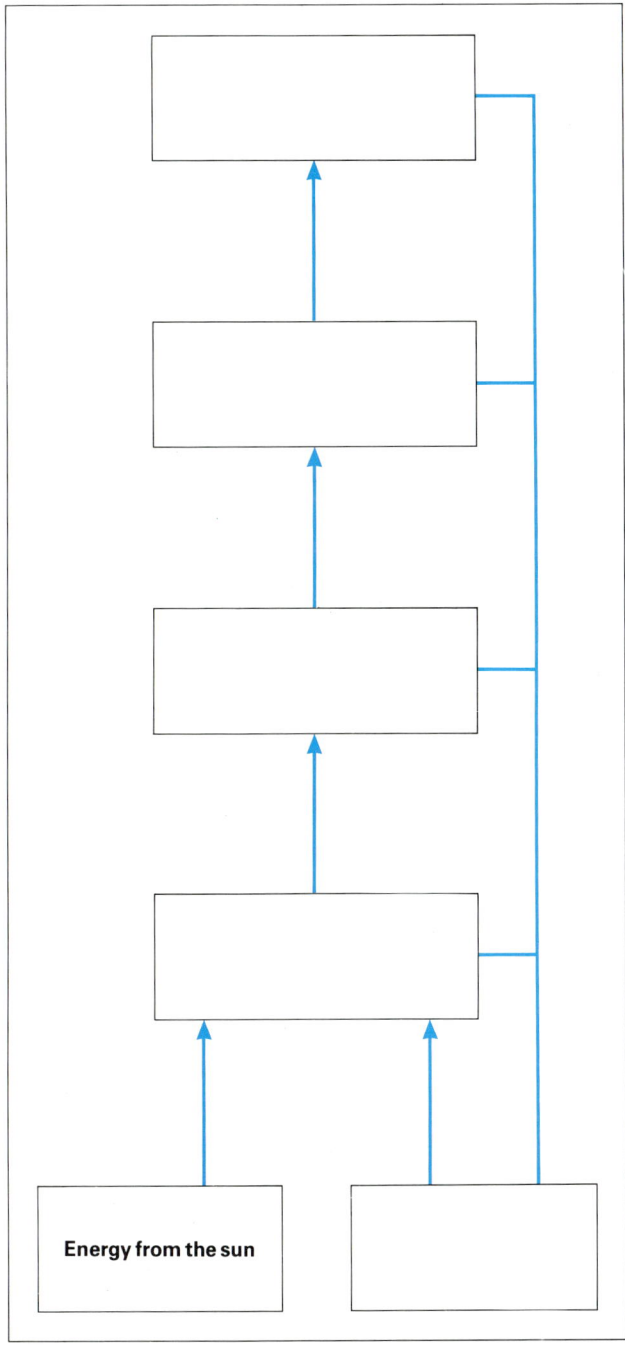

Energy from the sun

◀ Figure 2.3

◀ **Figure 2.4** 'Controlled' burning to clear land for farming in Laos

▼ **Figure 2.5** Erosion rates at five locations in the USA

Location	Land use	Erosion rate
Detroit	Construction work	17 000
	Urban	741
Maryland 1	Construction work	38 610
	Forest	39
	Grassland	250
Maryland 2	Countryside	22
	Urban	337
Maryland 3	Cultivation	550
	Urban	830
Virginia	Construction work	18 764
	Cultivation	1 876
	Forest	9
	Grassland	94

▼ **Figure 2.6** Soil erosion rates in four North American woodlands

Location	Total annual rainfall in mm	Description of cover	Rate of soil loss
Missouri	1 600	Burned	0.83
			0.26
North Carolina	1 160	Burned	7.7
			0.1
Oklahoma	765	Burned	0.3
			0.0
Texas	2 020	Burned	0.9
			0.1

2.4 The human factor

The *human* impact on natural environments has been enormous. Here are just three ways in which parts of Britain have been changed for better or for worse:

☐ Ancient woodlands felled or burned down to increase the area of farmland. In Cambridgeshire, 87% of all land is now under the plough.
☐ Upland valleys flooded to create new reservoirs.
☐ Large surface areas sealed off by building new roads and the constant outward growth of towns and cities.

1 List eight ways in which the natural environment is being changed by large-scale developments. Include the three examples given above.

The impact of burning

Fire has been used as a means of controlling the natural environment for at least 6 000 years. It proved effective in scaring wild animals into the open and is a convenient way of disposing of unwanted vegetation. The fertile ash provides extra food for next year's plants. The effects of burning are closely linked to the intensity of the fire (Figure 2.4), for 'ground' fires penetrate much deeper into the soil than 'surface' fires.

2 a Revise Figure 2.5 to show the land uses *in order of severity of soil erosion*.
  b Suggest reasons why:
    i heavily forested areas suffer little soil erosion.
    ii cultivation soil erosion rates are significantly higher.
    iii construction work produces very high erosion rates in the short term.

3 Summarise the key facts about soil erosion due to burning which are shown by Figure 2.6.

4 What are the most likely effects on different types of natural vegetation (trees, grass, etc.) of:
  a surface fires?
  b ground fires?

Deforestation

About one-third of the Earth's total land area is covered by forests. Unit 1.4 introduced you to the equatorial rain forests, but these are only one part of this enormous area. That unit mentioned some of the ways in which the tropical jungles are proving very helpful; they also provide:

- fuel for many millions of people.
- large quantities of house-building materials.
- a valuable source of income for some of the poorer countries.
- extra land for growing crops and rearing animals. These can be eaten at home or sold abroad for profit.
- essential ingredients for some of our most useful drugs. Both quinine (used in the fight against malaria) and aspirin come from trees. Other medicines are obtained from animals living inside the forests.
- more than 10% of the total oxygen in the Earth's atmosphere; they do this after absorbing the carbon dioxide which animals breathe out.
- the raw materials needed to make a variety of goods. The equatorial rain forests contain some valuable hardwoods such as teak and mahogany. These are hard-wearing and are ideal for building boats and high-quality furniture. The coniferous forests much nearer the Poles grow evergeens (e.g. pine and spruce). These grow more quickly and produce softwoods used in paper-making and house construction.

All of the world's main forested areas are now under threat. Although still covering vast areas of land, they are not limitless and the rate of **deforestation** (cutting down of the trees) is both high and increasing rapidly (Figure 2.7–2.9). Britain provides a good example of this – and what might be done to replace some of the timber already lost.

The Ancient Britons started to have an effect on our forests about 6 000 years ago. Their stone axes weren't very efficient, but could meet the small demand for timber at that time. As Britain's population grew, so did its need for timber. As its society became more advanced, it discovered new uses for the wood from its forests. The building of a wooden battleship such as the 'Mary Rose' at Portsmouth required the felling of hundreds of mature trees. The nineteenth

▼ Figure 2.7 Continental land areas

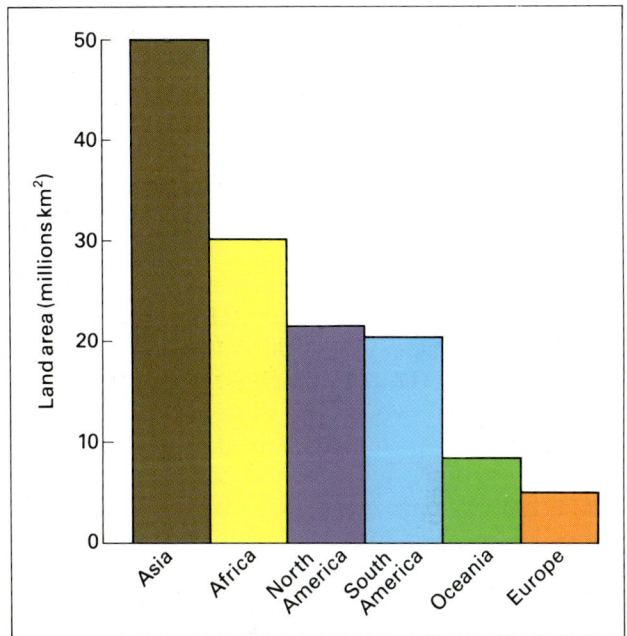

▼ Figure 2.8 The world's total forested area by continent

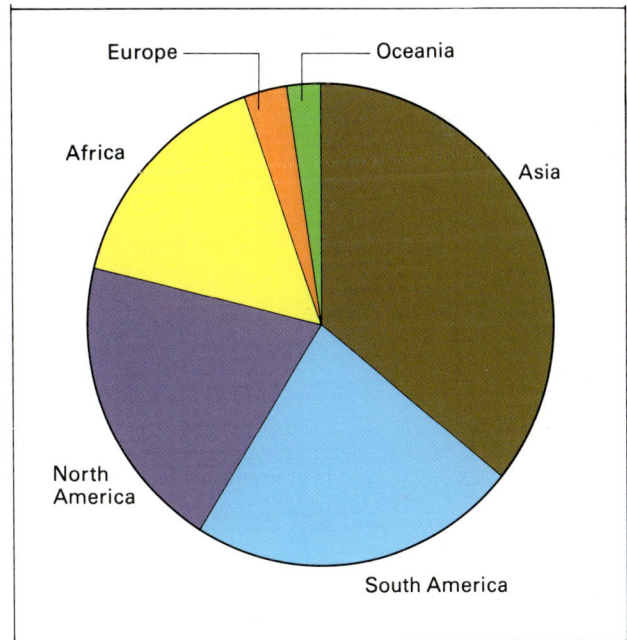

▶ Figure 2.9 Deforestation rates

Continent	Area of forest cut down in a recent year – *in sq km*
Africa	13 000
Asia	18 000
Latin America	42 000

century was especially timber-hungry, but it was the First World War which really brought the plight of our forests into the public eye. The war effort used vast quantities of timber, and German submarine activity meant that shipments of food and weapons had to take priority. The burden of providing timber therefore passed onto our own forests.

By 1919, Britain's reserves of home-grown timber were at an all-time low and the government responded by establishing the Forestry Commission. Its main work is partly **afforestation** (tree-planting in 'new' areas) and partly **reafforestation** (tree-replacement). In both cases, most of their trees are of the coniferous type (Figure 2.10). Other organisations are also involved in woodland management, e.g. the National Trust which owns almost three-quarters of the 38 000 sq km New Forest in southern England. Tax incentives have persuaded many British companies and individuals to become involved in forestry; some of our most successful sportspeople now regard it as one of their best long-term investments and have bought and afforested large **wilderness areas** in the far north of Scotland. (Figure 2.11).

Many foreign countries have similar programmes to increase their stock of home-grown timber. Even Brazil – which still has vast areas of 'virgin' (intact) forest in the Amazon Basin – is becoming more aware of the seriousness of unrestricted deforestation. Unfortunately, many of the measures it has proposed seem to be ineffective.

5 What do these key terms mean:
a afforestation?   c reafforestation?
b deforestation?   d virgin forest?

6 a According to Figures 2.7–2.9, which of the three continents (Latin America, Africa and Asia) has:
i the largest area of land?
ii the largest area of forest?
iii the highest rate of deforestation?
b Comment on your answers to a above.

7 Suggest reasons why the Brazilian government has experienced opposition to its measures for controlling deforestation in the Amazon Basin:
a from tribes of indians inhabiting the region?
b from business companies?

8 What measures would *you* propose to safeguard the *world's* timber resources?

9 a What measures has Britain taken so far to reverse the decline of its native forests?
b What are the likely advantages of increasing the quantities of home-grown timber to:
i companies and private individuals?
ii the government?
c Why is the area shown in Figure 2.11 described as a 'wilderness' area?
d What arguments might be used both for and against large-scale afforestation programmes in such areas?

▶ **Figure 2.10** Coniferous trees such as pine and spruce can grow under quite harsh conditions

Shallow roots avoid the layers of frozen soil deeper in the ground.
Springy branches can bend to let heavy coverings of snow slide off.
Narrow, needle-like leaves do not lose much water to the air.
Thick bark protects the tree trunk against the very cold winters.
The tree can grow in poor, stony soil.
The tree does not shed its leaves in winter. This means that it doesn't have to waste time and plant food producing a new set of leaves in the short summer growing season.
The cone-shape of the tree prevents too much snow collecting on the branches and breaking them.

◀ **Figure 2.11** The 'flow country' of north-west Scotland

The impact on the soil

Plant life of all kinds is very sensitive to soil conditions. It is therefore important to know how soils are formed and what conditions may hinder their development. Soils are highly complex but delicately balanced structures and take hundreds of years to reach maturity. Most are made up of different horizons (layers) and the one nearest the surface is most important to the farmer. This contains **humus**, decomposed plant material which is a sticky black substance and gives the soil its familiar dark colouring. The key functions performed by humus, vegetation cover and animal life within the soil are listed in Figures 2.12–2.14.

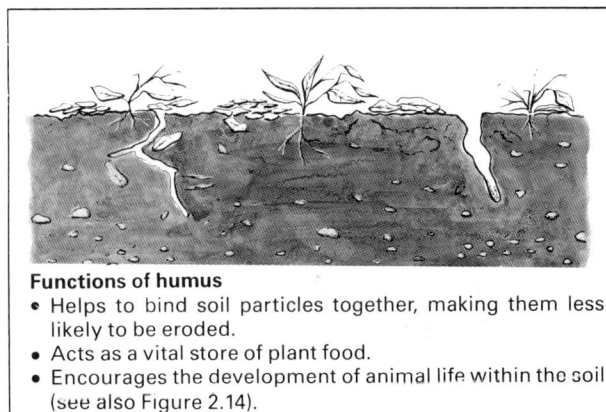

Functions of humus
- Helps to bind soil particles together, making them less likely to be eroded.
- Acts as a vital store of plant food.
- Encourages the development of animal life within the soil (see also Figure 2.14).

▲ Figure 2.12

◀ Figure 2.13

▼ Figure 2.14

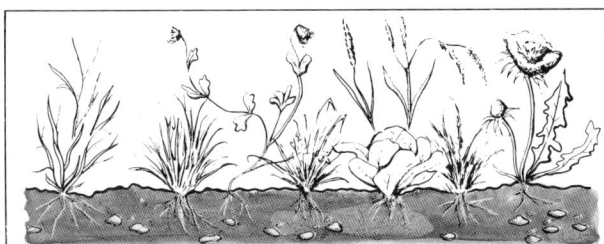

Functions of vegetation cover
- Traps particles of soil transported by run-off water from higher land.
- Protects the surface from wind erosion.
- Also gives protection from heavy rain and the sheet (surface) erosion which it causes.
- Reduces the leaching of dissolved minerals (such as calcium and gases e.g. nitrogen) from the surface downwards below the depth of most plant roots. Both minerals and gases vital to plant growth.
- Roots draw water and nutrients nearer to the surface, making them more accessible to the plants.
- Reduces evaporation – the loss of surface water due to insolation (the heating of the topsoil by the sun's rays).

Functions of animal life within the soil
- Animal life (especially earthworms) decompose plant debris into humus.
- Animals mix this debris evenly within the soil.
- Aerate the soil – create passages through which oxygen can reach the lower levels of the soil and keep it 'healthy'.

10 Write your own definitions of the following key terms:

decomposition   soil horizon
humus   soil profile
parent rock

11 Using the information in Figures 2.12–2.14, draw two labelled flow-diagrams to show how the functions of humus, vegetation cover and animal life within the soil are linked

a in the *formation and preservation* of a rich, balanced soil

b in the *conservation* of soil (i.e. how it is able to withstand leaching and erosion).

12 **a** Draw the profile in Figure 2.15 of a typical low-land soil.

b Describe how the soil profile in Figure 2.16 differs from that in Figure 2.15.

c Give reasons which help to explain the differences you described in **b**.

▼ **Figure 2.15** Profile of a chernozem (black-earth) soil

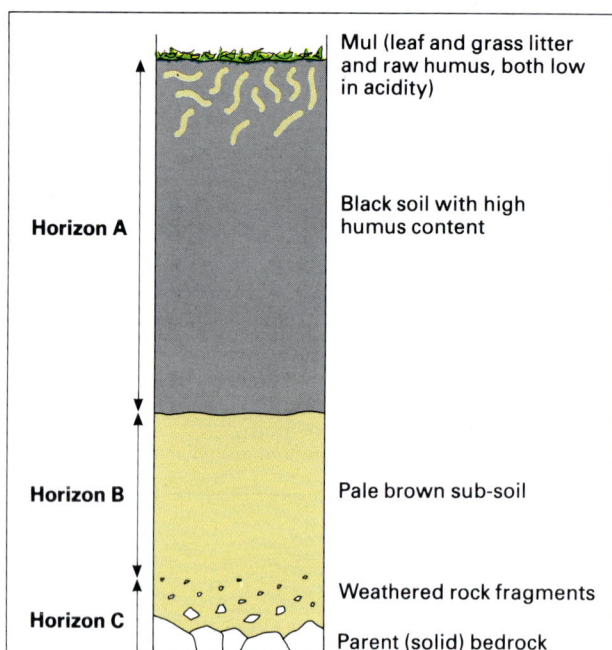

Horizon A

Mul (leaf and grass litter and raw humus, both low in acidity)

Black soil with high humus content

Horizon B

Pale brown sub-soil

Horizon C

Weathered rock fragments

Parent (solid) bedrock

Background information

Found in mid-continental regions (e.g. central Russia)
Low precipitation, mainly in summer
Very warm summers; cold winters
High evaporation rate for much of the year
Natural vegetation cover: grass

Hints

Is water more likely to seep downwards or upwards through the soil?
How has this movement helped to produce the distribution of humus shown in the profile?
Why is the surface litter/raw humus likely to decompose quite rapidly?

▼ **Figure 2.16** Profile of a podzol soil

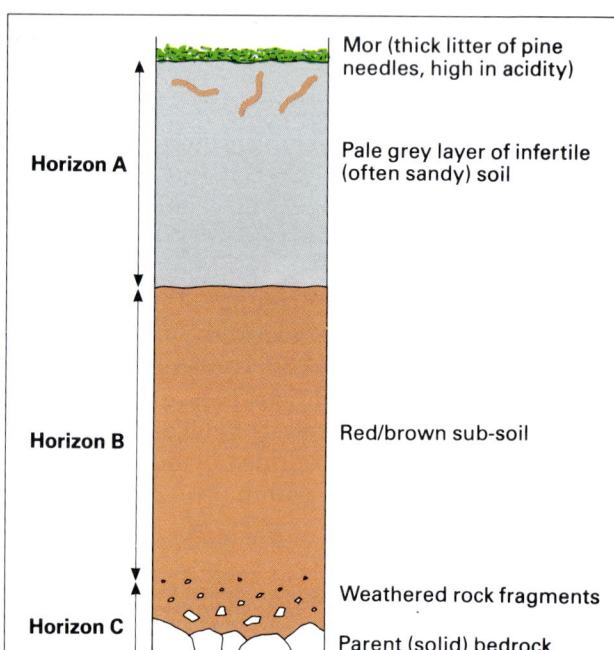

Horizon A

Mor (thick litter of pine needles, high in acidity)

Pale grey layer of infertile (often sandy) soil

Horizon B

Red/brown sub-soil

Horizon C

Weathered rock fragments

Parent (solid) bedrock

Background information

Found in coniferous forest regions (e.g. northern Sweden)
Low precipitation, hence needle-shaped leaves to reduce trees' water loss through transpiration
Cool summers; very cold winters
Poor drainage in soil above permafrost (permanently frozen sub-soil)
Few worms in topsoil to reduce the acidity caused by decaying pine needles

Hints

Is water more likely to seep downwards or upwards through this soil?
How are the very cold conditions likely to effect the earthworm and bacteria populations with the soil?
How does the thickness of horizon A compare with that of the chernozem soil?

2.5 Wildlife protection

People are increasingly worried about our natural environment and the wildlife it supports. The Wildfowl Trust is just one of many organisations dedicated to voicing this concern and actually doing something about it. Its main aims (Figure 2.17) are similar to those of the Royal Society for the Protection of Birds (RSPB), but concentrate on *wildfowl*. These are the birds which inhabit marshes and fens – the **wetlands** around our rivers and coasts. These areas are under great pressure from planned forms of land use, e.g.:

– *farmland*, because they are flat and have deep, rich soils.
– *industrial areas*, because they are usually some distance from major built-up areas and pollution is less likely to cause offence.
– *refuse tips*, also because of their remoteness from urban areas.

Martin Mere was once the largest lake in Lancashire,

and until the eighteenth century was about 8 km across at its widest point. Drainage schemes and constant refuse tipping reduced it to a peat bog capable of grazing sheep in summer; there were no deep pools like the artificial ones shown in Figure 2.19.

The Wildfowl Trust bought 140 hectares of the original Martin Mere site and immediately set about modifying the area in keeping with its main aims. The area has been completely transformed and further changes made since it was officially opened to the general public in 1975. Probably the most outstanding new feature is the network of 'waterfowl gardens' covering 10% of the total area. The birdlife on these ponds is fascinating to watch and can be seen from outdoor paths or specially-built 'hides'. The birds are encouraged to breed at Martin Mere, and even the roof of the main building has been covered so as to make it look natural from the air (Figure 2.20).

▼ **Figure 2.17**

▼ **Figure 2.18** The seven Wildfowl Trust sanctuaries

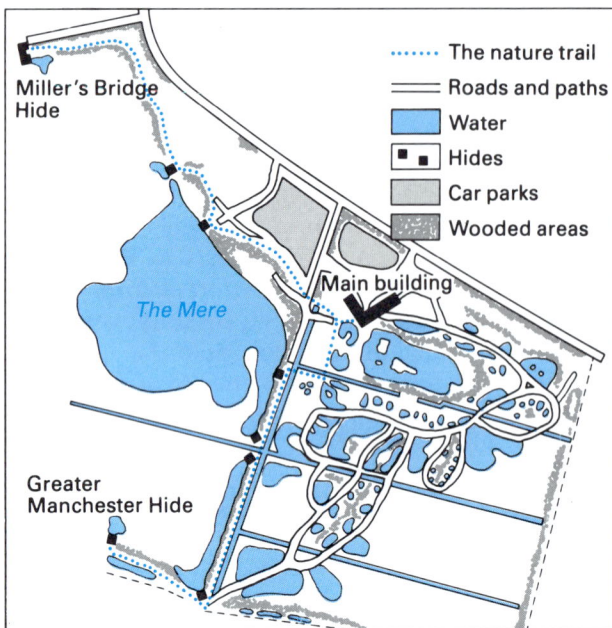

▲ **Figure 2.19** Layout of the Martin Mere sanctuary

Legend for Figure 2.19:
- ······ The nature trail
- —— Roads and paths
- Water
- Hides
- Car parks
- Wooded areas

Map labels: Miller's Bridge Hide, The Mere, Main building, Greater Manchester Hide

▼ **Figure 2.20**

1 a What types of bird does the Wildfowl Trust try to protect?
b How many bird sanctuaries does the Wildfowl Trust operate at present, and how are they distributed within Britain?

2 a List the main aims of the Wildfowl Trust.
b How did the Trust's development of the Martin Mere site help it to fulfil these aims?
c Note down any ways (apart from attracting large numbers of wildfowl) in which this type of development might affect the natural environment.

3 The following projects have been suggested to the Wildfowl Trust team at Martin Mere. Their proposers think they might help to improve the site and bring in more money from visitors.
– a museum of stuffed birds.
– a small-scale railway which will enable visitors to cover the site much more quickly.
– a small fairground in which children can play while their parents study the birdlife.
– allow limited fishing (in season, of course) from the deeper ponds on the site.
– increase the size of the shop so as to increase its range of souvenirs, books, etc.

For each proposal:
a (After class discussion, if necessary) state whether the proposal is generally 'in keeping' with the Trust's aims.
b State fully the reasons for your decision in **a**.

2.6 Selby – the caring coalfield

The Selby area is at the northern tip of Britain's largest and most productive coal mining region – the Yorkshire, Nottinghamshire and Derbyshire Coalfield. It lies around the small towns of Selby (population 12 000) and Tadcaster (6 000) and includes some extremely attractive lowland farming country (Figure 2.21).

It was almost inevitable, however, that the coal there would be extracted sooner or later. Selby's main seam is 3½ metres thick, which is well above the average and provides ideal conditions for the large coal-cutting equipment now available. Output per man-shift is expected to be about fives times greater than that achieved by most British coalfields (4 tonnes is the present figure). Experts believe Selby's coal reserves exceed 600 million tonnes and that about 10 million tonnes of high-quality coal can be mined every year. The total output will be used in three modern power stations further south (Figure 2.22).

1 Complete this 'fact-list' for the Selby coalfield:

    Estimated total reserves of coal: . . .
    Greatest thickness of seams: . . .
    Quality of coal: . . .
    Planned annual output of coal: . . .
    Likely output per man-shift: . . .
    Use of coal extracted: . . .
    Size of coalfield area: . . . (west-east)
                                            . . . (north-south).

Important town

Village

River

Existing railway line

Diverted railway line

Closed railway line (coal can now be mined under this route)

Coal-fired power station

Drift mine (where coal is brought to the surface)

Shaft mine (used only by miners and for maintenance)

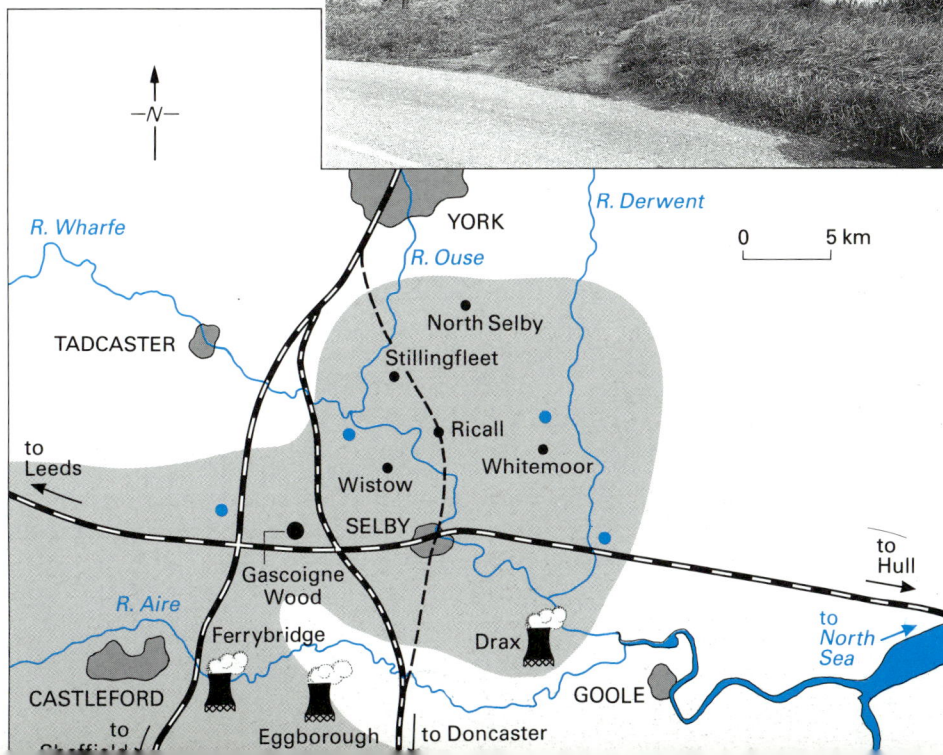

► **Figure 2.23** Gascoigne Wood drift mine on the Selby coalfield

2 The Selby Coalfield has been developed with environmental and social needs very much in mind. Pair up each half-statement below with its best-fit second half from the sentences which follow. The link-word 'therefore' is to be added every time.

A huge pillar of coal under the heart of Selby will be left untouched

Any waste material from under the ground will be tipped around the six mines, landscaped and planted with trees

The four thousand miners who come into the area from exhausted pits in West Yorkshire and elsewhere will be housed throughout the area

The coal will be brought to the surface only at one site (Gascoigne Wood)

The mine at Gascoigne Wood is a drift mine and has gently sloping tunnels instead of vertical shafts

The National Coal Board has agreed to raise the level of the banks of the Rivers Ouse and Wharfe

The seams are much thicker than usual and the coal is of a high quality

Stock-piles of reserve coal within the area will not normally exceed 12 metres in height

Therefore:

avoiding the need to erect the tall winding gear needed to operate vertical shafts.

modern underground mining machinery can be used and little waste material is produced. This avoids the need for large coal-washing plant to remove unwanted shale and dirt.

much less countryside is disfigured by railway sidings and coal stock yards.

only in emergencies will they become an eyesore.

preserving distant views of the attractive countryside.

the beautiful eleventh century abbey there is protected against land subsidence due to coal mining.

there is less chance of farmland being flooded.

the social impact of in-migration is not concentrated in just one or two towns.

3 Explain why the Gascoigne Wood site was chosen for coal extraction. You should consider any advantages of the site itself as well as its more general situation.

4 For each of the following, **i** state whether they were more likely to be for or against the development of the Selby coalfield, and **ii** give reasons for your choice of answer in **i**:

a The Secretary of State for the Environment.

b A retired couple living exactly mid-way between Selby and York.

c A farmer with agricultural land close to the River Ouse.

d The chief sales manager for the National Coal Board.

e A shop-keeper in Selby.

f A lorry driver who has just started up his own business in Tadcaster.

g An official of the National Union of Mineworkers (West Yorkshire Branch).

5 Suggest any measures you believe the National Coal Board should take when developing new resources in areas similar to Selby, but which are not described in this unit.

2.7 The impact of tourism

Tourism and recreation are big business, and the table in Figure 2.24 is proof of the increasing demand for leisure facilities. Like most growth industries, they can be thought of in different ways. They have certainly created thousands of extra jobs and brought new 'life' to areas of high unemployment. Others view tourism and recreation with concern, particularly those who live in the **honeypots** – the most visited areas – where litter, traffic jams, noise and environmental damage are all too common.

During the nineteenth century most tourist activity was concentrated in the coastal holiday resorts such as Blackpool, Brighton and Scarborough. They encouraged tourists, and welcomed the prosperity they brought to the local people. The pattern today is somewhat different as increasing affluence, leisure time and above all car ownership have enabled tourists to travel much further afield. The growing number of foreign tourists has added to the pressures imposed on the country as a whole, and in certain areas has had a dramatic effect on the landscape and the wildlife within it.

Many tourists seem content to drive around, sightsee, have a meal and then leave. But every year an increasing number choose to do ,something more energetic, and it is they who pose the greatest threat to the natural environment. The ordinary family intent on enjoying a pleasant afternoon stroll may not think of themselves in this way, but the total number of walkers, ramblers, hikers, nature-lovers. campers, etc. adds up to a sizeable army which assaults our rural areas for weeks on end. The effect of thousands of feet grinding constantly on the most popular routes is shown all too clearly in Figure 2.25.

	Annual membership of			
Year	Camping and Caravan Club	National Trust	Royal Society for the Protection of Birds	Royal Yachting Association
1950	14 000	25 000	6 000	2 000
1960	51 000	95 000	14 000	11 000
1970	110 000	278 000	53 000	34 000
1988	186 000	1 500 000	540 000	60 000

▲ **Figure 2.24** Membership trends in four societies concerned with recreational outdoor activities

▶ **Figure 2.25** Path surgery on Ingleborough!

► **Figure 2.26** Modern pleasure cruisers often disturb nesting birds, although their speed is usually limited to only 5 kph

An even greater threat is posed by those who come 'equipped' for a holiday. Fishing has obvious disadvantages for marine life, campers increase the fire-risk to woodlands and boating enthusiasts wreak havock on the banks of rivers and lakes. One area under extreme pressure from tourists is the Norfolk Broads. Already greatly reduced by the constant demand for arable land (see Unit 3.4), this rich wetland area is now only a fraction of its original size. The wakes of cabin cruisers erode the soft banks of silt and make life impossible for nesting birds (Figure 2.26), their oil **pollutes** the water and special anti-fouling compounds painted on the hulls are highly **toxic** (poisonous). Many stretches of waterway have been 'improved' by replacing their reed beds (which trap silt) with concrete retaining walls. Doing this helps the Broads to cope with more boats and visitors, but further reduces one of our richest wildlife habitats. Waterfowl (see Unit 2.5), beetles, dragonflies, moths, butterflies and spiders thrive within this sheltered, rich yet dangerously fragile miniature natural world.

1 a Un-jumble the names of these British coastal holiday resorts, and say whether each one is in England, Scotland or Wales. (Hint: there are two resorts in each country.)

    BENYT   NABO   RAY
    LYHR   QUOTARY   RUNBOUTHERD

b In which century did these resorts grow very quickly?

2 When answering these questions, try to add your own information to that given in this unit.
a Why is there a constant demand for more recreational facilities?

b Why are much larger areas of the country now affected by tourism and recreation?

3 a Write down the total membership of all four societies in Figure 2.24 for each of the five years.
b Plot your five yearly totals as a line graph.
c Describe the trend shown by your completed graph.
d In what ways are the members of each society likely to endanger the natural environment? (Take each society in turn.)

4 a What effects are recreation and tourism having on the Norfolk Broads?
b What measures would *you* introduce to limit environmental damage to this area?

5 These questions are based on the Ordnance Survey map extract on page 144.
a List the different types of recreational facility (e.g. car parks) in the area, and add their six-figure grid reference positions.
b Comment on the location of the nature reserve in the north-east corner of the extract. (i.e. What are its likely advantages and disadvantages?)
c You have been asked to investigate other stretches of water within the area, the idea being to create another nature reserve south of Nottingham. Choose what you consider to be the most suitable and the least suitable sites for such a purpose, then summarise your reasons for choosing them both. You should do this with the help of fully labelled sketch maps.

2.8 Resource management

We can only make the best use of the Earth's resources by thinking of them as precious and in very short supply; also by recognising that they have to meet not just our immediate needs but those of future generations.

Unfortunately, most of us are concerned only with the present! We like to take the easy way out – the one which demands the least effort from us. A classic example is that of litter. How often have you seen rubbish thrown from a passing car, to be left for someone else to pick up and dispose of properly?

Selfishness and lack of concern for others are particularly common amongst organised groups of people, e.g. companies striving to make a profit, but political bodies are also often accused of putting their own interests first. Both are in a position to wield considerable power and it is quite difficult for ordinary individuals to influence what they do. Fortunately, not all groups or individuals are blind to the needs of others, both present and future. Figure 2.27 proves that this is so. Study the articles carefully before attempting the questions on the next page.

▼ Figure 2.27

Call for early tax cut on unleaded petrol

By JOHN LANGLEY Motoring Correspondent

AS THE FIRST unleaded petrol went on sale at Esso stations around London yesterday, the AA called for an early cut in the tax on it to bring the price into line with leaded fuel.

Chancellor Mr Lawson, has already promised to create a tax differential between the two types of petrol to offset the higher production cost of unleaded.

"Now the unleaded fuel is becoming available, motorists should not have to wait until the next Budget for a cut in the tax," an AA spokesman said last night.

"As 10 per cent of cars in Britain can run on unleaded fuel already our view is that as the whole community will benefit from the use of unleaded petrol, the extra cost of using it should be born by the community and not the individual motorist".

Cars that can already run on unleaded petrol include many German and Japanese models and some of the latest British cars like the new Rovers.

But in many cases their ignition settings would need to be adjusted.

A Volkswagen GB official said last night: "If the cars normally run on two-star petrol no adjustment would be needed but if they operate on 98 octane (four-star) they need to have their ignition retarded."

Unleaded petrol is costing between 4p and 5p a gallon more than ordinary fuel. The total tax on a gallon is around 110p.

BNFL fined £10,000 over radiation leak

By JOHN WILLIAMS

THE Government-owned British Nuclear Fuels Ltd was fined a total of £10,000 with costs up to a limit of £60,000 last night after being found guilty of charges relating to a leak of radioactive material from the Windscale nuclear reprocessing plant at Sellafield, Cumbria.

The jury returned its 10—1 majority verdicts on two of the charges after retiring for $5\frac{1}{2}$ hours on the 34th day of the trial at Carlisle Crown Court and on the third, also by a 10—1 majority, after being sent out again by the judge, Mr Justice Rose.

The company was found guilty of failing to ensure that discharges of radioactive material were kept as low as reasonably achievable and failing to take all reasonable steps to minimise the exposure of persons to radiation.

It was also found guilty of failing to keep records of the disposal of radioactive materials in the Irish Sea.

BNFL had denied the three charges arising from radioactive contamination along more than 20 miles of the coastline in November 1983.

The discharge came to light when a diving crew employed by the environmental group Greenpeace happened to be in the area and discovered a highly radioactive slick floating in the sea. A geiger counter on board their inflatable dinghy went off the scale.

The judge said that in deciding the appropriate sentence, he had in mind that the primary purpose of the prosecution — "namely the public investigation by a jury of the events in November 1983" — had been achieved.

Most polluted river 'now 75pc cleaner'

Daily Telegraph Reporter

THE MERSEY, once the most polluted river system in Britain, is slowly being cleaned up, according to the North West Water Authority, which announced yesterday that it planned to spend £2 billion on further cleansing over the next 25 years.

A conference at Daresbury near Warrington yesterday was told that in the 200 miles of water courses joining the Mersey, pollution in the "nuisance" class had been cut by 45 per cent, and in the Mersey itself it had gone down 75 per cent.

Despite it's still poor reputation, the Mersey estuary had become a haven for wildfowl and birds while the number of species of fish in the waters had increased dramatically from seven to 36.

Mr Ridley, Environment Secretary pledged the Government's continuing support for the programme.

Campfield Marsh in Cumbria which the RSPB is acquiring to make it safe for the birds.

Bird haven bought for £70,000

By Robert Bedlow
Estates Correspondent

THE 200-acre Campfield Marsh site on the Solway saltmarshes in Cumbria, has been bought for £70,000 by the Royal Society for the Protection of Birds.

More than 10,000 pink-footed geese use the area during winter and oystercatchers and bar-tailed godwits during the autumn moult.

One of Britain's top 10 estuaries for wild birds, the saltmarshes and mudflats are internationally important for wintering wildfowl and waders. They attract large flocks of curlew, dunlin, knot and grey plover.

But there is growing concern that a tidal power station may be built on the Solway estuary. The department of Energy has already carried out a study of the estuary's potential.

"Estuaries all over Britain are under threat and we are determined to protect them," said Mr Ian Prestt, director-general of the RSPB.

Fifty per cent of the purchase price has been met by the Government's own Nature Conservancy Council "watchdog" on conservation issues.

Three new reserves have also been acquired by the RSPB which is spending between £1 and £1½ million each year to save sites of national and international importance from development and to provide long-term protection.

▲ **Figure 2.27** *Continued*

1 For each article in Figure 2.27:
   a Describe briefly what is being done to protect the environment and/or meet the needs of other people.
   b Which of the following is most likely to have taken the·decision to carry out this action?
   a private individual
   a group of private individuals
   a company
   a local council
   a government or government department
   another (give details)
   c What benefit(s) is each individual or group in **b** most likely to have obtained from doing this work?

2 **a** Discuss openly in class whether the 'doers of good works' such as those in Figure 2.27 should be rewarded publicly in some way.
   b Similarly discuss what kinds of public reward are:
   i currently available.
   ii suitable for this kind of work.
   c Now write down your own reactions to **a** and **b**. You may find it helpful to refer to the examples in this unit.

2.9 Waste not, want not

Unit 1.1 introduced the idea that most of the Earth's natural resources are not inexhaustible, meaning that they must run out at some time in the future. Resources which cannot be replaced are also called **finite resources**. Unit 4.7 is concerned with the rates at which natural sources of energy such as coal are being used up, but the same principle applies equally to all minerals. This unit shows how the demand for 'new' copper can be greatly reduced by recycling scrap metal.

Copper is one of the world's most useful metals. It first became important during the Bronze Age (2000–500 B.C.) when it was mixed with zinc to produce a useful alloy. Being harder, it proved much more suitable for making weapons. Iron later replaced bronze as the chief 'industrial' metal but inventions during the nineteenth century found a new use for it – in electrical circuits. About half of all the copper now produced is taken by the electrical and electronics industries. This metal's most important properties are listed below:

☐ It is the best conductor (carrier) of electricity.
☐ It is also a very efficient conductor of heat.
☐ It is very resistant to corrosion.
☐ It is smooth and pleasant to handle.
☐ It is malleable (easily moulded into the required shape).
☐ It is easily drawn (stretched into long, fine strands).
☐ It is an attractive, warm-coloured metal.

Copper occurs naturally in two different ways. A small proportion occurs in a completely pure form, with the metal ready for use. Most however has to be smelted to extract it from the ore and this lower grade source usually has a copper content of less than 20%. The smelting is quite a complicated process, part of which requires the use of large quantities of electricity.

Much of the demand for copper is now met by recycling scrap. About 40% of total needs is satisfied in this way, and scrap merchants throughout the industrial world welcome supplies of the metal because of its high value. In Britain, the gathering was traditionally carried out by 'tatters', who plied the streets on horse and cart and called out aloud to attract the attention of householders. It is now usual for people to take unwanted goods direct to the scrap merchant, thus cutting out the middle-man. The number of merchants' advertisements in Yellow Pages and Thompson Directories is proof of the intense competition within the trade (Figure 2.29).

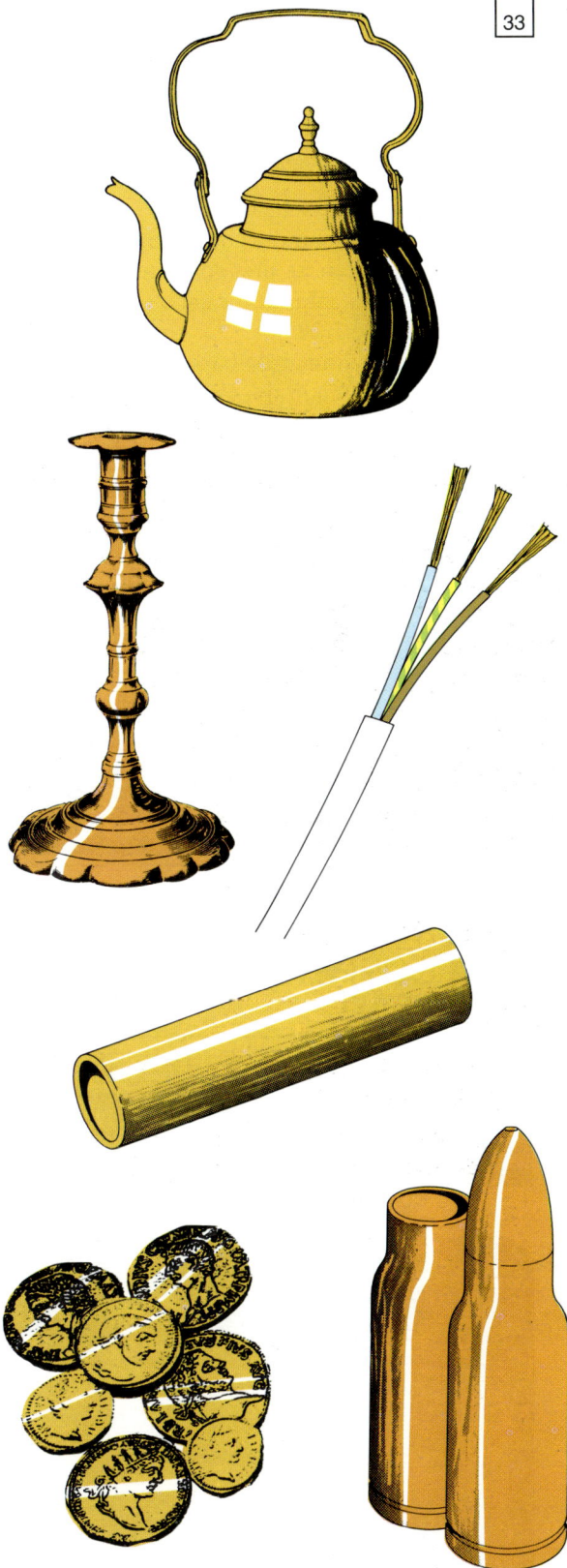

▲ **Figure 2.28** Copper is used to manufacture a wide range of goods

1 What is meant by each of these terms?
a alloy c scrap
b re-cycle d smelt

2 a Devise a table which has:
– the seven important properties of copper listed down its first column.
– one extra column for each of the items shown in Figure 2.28.
– a 'totals' line at its base.
b Tick the boxes in the table to link the items with the relevent properties (e.g. 'coins' and 'It is smooth and pleasant to handle.').
c Enter along the bottom line the tick-totals for every column.
d Add and complete this title: 'A table to show . . .'
e Comment on the information shown by the table. (e.g. Do *you* feel that the property with the highest total is likely to be the *most* important one as far as industry is concerned?)

3 Answer these questions with the help of Figure 2.29 *and your own enquiries*.
a Which *pure* metals are most sought after by scrap merchants?
b What are the chief uses of these metals (except copper, which has already been covered by question 2)?
c Name the *alloys* mentioned in the advertisements.
d Which pure metals does each of these alloys contain? What proportions of these metals are used in each case?
e What is meant by the term '*non-ferrous* metals'?
f What *manufactured products* are welcomed by scrap merchants?
g Why are these products in great demand for the scrap metal trade?
h What evidence is there in Figure 2.29 that scrap metal dealing is a highly competitive business?
i How have individual dealers tried to increase their share of the trade?

▼ Figure 2.29

Figure 2.30

WE KEEP SUPPLY AND DEMAND IN BALANCE, SAY WASTE PAPER PEOPLE

WASTE paper is a "secondary" raw material supplied to the paper and board manufacturing industry and its supply and demand need to be delicately balanced, particularly in the short and medium term. "Primary" raw material demand cycles are easier to deal with since the raw material can be left in the ground or standing in the forest.

In the waste paper industry, the periods of high and low demand seem to operate in four or five years cycles – a good year followed by three or four lean ones. In a lean year either the raw material requirement decreases, sometimes with little warning, or prices are so depressed that collection and processing becomes uneconomic. Throughout these peaks and troughs, the waste paper industry attempts to keep supply and demand in some sort of balance – a difficult exercise when emotive and environmental pressures often clash with market forces.

Consumption of waste paper by the UK paper and board mills is more than two million tonnes a year and constitutes 55 per cent of mill intake of fibrous raw material; a larger proportion than in most countries, including West Germany, France, Japan and the USA (a mere 22 per cent). Even after an inevitable yield loss in manufacturing from waste paper, UK mill usage of "secondary" fibres equates broadly with the tonnage of "primary" wood pulp consumed, most of which is imported. The waste paper industry exports as well – 248,000 tonnes in 1986 and is on target for 280,000 tonnes in 1987.

There are, of course, a number of barriers to recycling waste paper, including manufacturing capacity, technical factors, economics, product specifications and consumer resistance to using waste-based products.

In the UK, we annually consume 8m tonnes of paper and board. A substantial quantity clearly cannot be recycled – tissues, wallpaper etc. Our total manufacturing capacity is 4m tonnes – and growing. Many paper products cannot technically be made from recycled fibre, so the balance cannot be used by paper mills. However, other uses can be found for waste paper as long as it can be collected and processed economically. Examples are fuel, animal bedding, insulation and building materials.

Consumer resistance to some waste-based products naturally inhibits growth in waste paper recycling. Industry, commerce, government and the general public can assist by reviewing paper and board products they purchase, with a view to using recycled products wherever they are adequate for their use and economical. Continual demand for products containing secondary materials would motivate the mills to produce even more waste-based products – if technically possible and economically competitive. If consumers don't demand them, the mills won't make them!

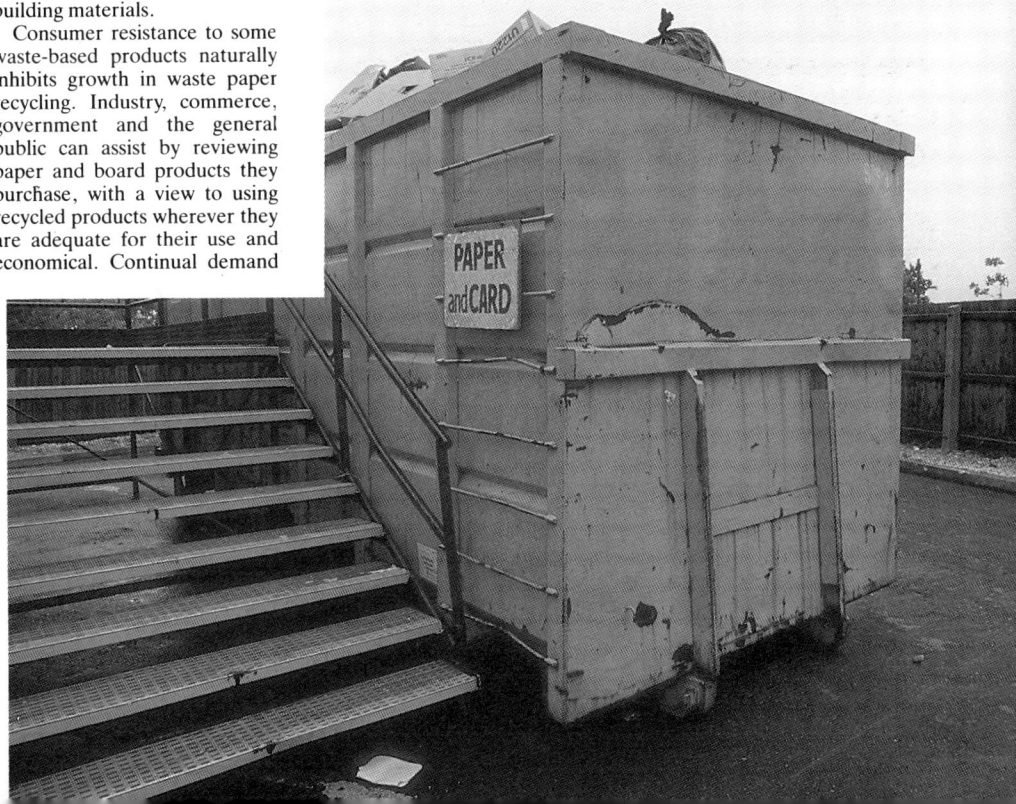

4 Use the information in Figure 2.30 to:
  a assess the importance of re-cycling to the British paper industry.
  b give reasons for its importance.
  c identify any factors which *limit* the contribution of re-cycling to this industry.

5 a Draw a bar graph to show the amounts of copper produced by these *named countries* in a recent year. Use a different colour to shade each country's column in your graph.

▼ Figure 2.31

Country	Annual output of copper in tonnes
USA	1 529 000
Chile	1 079 000
Philippines	923 000
Zambia	701 000
Canada	693 000
Zaire	505 000
Poland	310 000
Mexico	231 000
Australia	217 000
Rest of world	2 524 000

  b On an outline map of the world, shade in the land areas of these countries – using the colours chosen for the graph.
  c Copy this table, then write in the total world production of copper (based on the information listed in **a**).

▼ Figure 2.32

Metal	Total world production in a recent year (tonnes) (excluding recycled metal)
Aluminium	12 320 000
Copper	
Zinc	6 133 000
Lead	3 472 000
Tin	237 000
Silver	11 175
Gold	1 200

6 a Copy Figure 2.33.
  b Complete the second column in your table by writing 1 by the name of the most common metal (according to the table you drew for question **3 c**, 2 by the next most common, and so on.

c Ask one or more local scrap metal dealers to list the same seven metals in order of scrap value. The second rank order can then be entered in the third column (i.e. with a 1 for the most sought-after metal).
d In the next column, write down the difference in rank orders in columns 2 and 3 for each metal. There is no need to add a + or − sign.
e The last column requires you to 'square' each of these rank order differences.
f Total the seven entries in the last column and write this number in the box provided.
g Use this formula, and the information in the table you have just completed, to investigate the relationship between the two rank orders in columns 2 and 3.

$$\text{The rank correlation coefficient} = 1 - \frac{6 \times \Sigma d^2}{n^3 - n}$$

where: Σd^2 is the sum of all the d^2 added together (from the total box at the bottom of the table)
  n is the number of entries in each rank order

Your answer should lie between 1.0 (which shows a perfect positive correlation) and − 1.0 (a perfect negative correlation).

h Write down the answer you obtained, then add which of the following kinds of relationship this number indicates:
a strong relationship (correlation coefficient greater than + or − 0.8).
a significant relationship (between ± 0.6 and ± 0.79).
an insignificant relationship (lower than ± 0.59).
i Suggest reasons for this strength of relationship between the two sets of information.

▼ Figure 2.33

Metal	Rank order of world production	Rank order of scrap metal value	d (difference in rank order)	d^2
Aluminium				
Copper				
Gold				
Lead				
Silver				
Tin				
Zinc				

Σd^2 (total) = _____

3
Agriculture

3.1 Introduction: the self-sufficient Aborigines

This unit looks at the life-style of a race of people whose main aim is to be **self-sufficient**, that is to satisfy their various needs without the help of others.

Australia's Aborigines are one of the world's most interesting and talented peoples. They first came to Australia about 50 000 years ago – from the islands of Java and New Guinea to the north (Figure 3.1) – and have since evolved a life-style which is very well suited to their natural environment. It is their store of knowledge about this environment, and the way their community is organised, which have enabled them to become *totally* self-sufficient.

In the 'happy years' before the Europeans first settled in Australia in the late eighteenth century, most Aborigines lived in forested areas near the east

▲ **Figure 3.2** An aborigine man in the Northern Territory of Australia

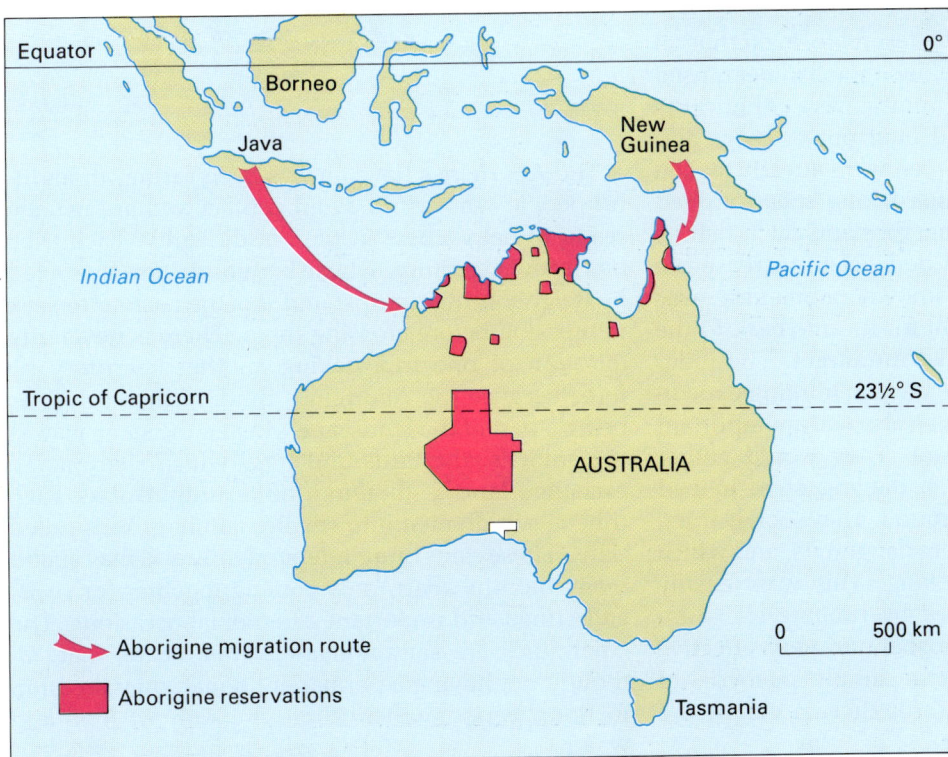

◀ **Figure 3.1** Aborigine migration routes and reservations

◀ **Figure 3.3** An Aboriginal family beneath a shelter built to provide shade

▼ **Figure 3.4** The 'woomera' helps a hunter to throw the spear much further. Its effect is to lengthen the thrower's arm and so make it more powerful

coast. Food was plentiful and their tribal territories were quite small. However, they soon learned to fear the newcomers, who were greedy for land and would use guns to obtain it. A few Aborigines were killed as a result but *many* more died of the diseases (e.g. small-pox) which the White Man brought and against which their own bodies had little defence. The survivors fled into the dry heart of the continent – the Outback – where some of their descendents still live.

The traditional way of life

The migrants soon adapted to desert life, even though it was much harder than the one they had been used to in the forests. Their new 'homes' were either caves or shelters against the wind built out of twigs and long grass (Figure 3.3). The men were already skilled in hunting for food. They used long spears tipped with sharp stones to kill kangeroos and catch fish. A woomera (Figure 3.4) could be used to increase the thrower's range. The well-known boomerang was ideal for killing birds in flight for it came back to the thrower after failing to strike the target. The older boys were allowed to join the men on hunting expeditions into the bush. The women also had an important role to pay in obtaining food. They would gather berries, insects and grubs; a digging stick helped them to get roots out of the ground. They soon learned which plants and animals were dangerous, and which could be made safe by cooking. This was usually done on an open fire started by rubbing sticks together, but they had an unusual and very effective way of cooking turtles – they simply pushed hot stones inside their bodies through slits cut in the throat!

The Aborigines have always been caring, thoughtful people who try to avoid conflict and are usually ready to help others in time of difficulty. Each tribe has its own territory, whose boundaries are respected by neighbouring groups, and it is the custom to seek permission before crossing them. There is never any question of one tribe taking another's territory by force because the Aborigines think of themselves as being a part of the landscape – in just the same way as the animals, the birds and trees which share it. To exchange land is therefore quite unthinkable. Each tribe is sub-divided into smaller family-groups called clans. These clans hunt independently and may spend many months apart, only coming together for social gatherings and important ceremonial occasions. The Aborigines are semi-nomadic. This means that, although not having a permanent home, they do camp for long periods where there is plenty of food and water.

◀ **Figure 3.5** Ayer's Rock is sacred to the Aborigines

▶ **Figure 3.6** An Aborigine reservation in northern Australia. Many of the people who live here work for a local bauxite mining company

Very few Aborigines still lead the traditional life-style described above, and follow the ways of their respected ancestors. It has always been difficult to follow the desert code, but they have taken great care to kill only for food – never for sport. This has usually ensured enough food for future years, even in times of prolonged drought. They are a deeply religious people and often meditate (think very deeply) about their beloved land – especially the sun and the sky, which they believe will always give them hope and courage. This meditation is called The Dreaming. It is not easy for us to understand exactly what this means, but one way of describing it is 'being at peace with nature' – the ability to love the tribal territory and everything about it (Figure 3.5).

The present situtation

There are now only about 20 000 pure Aborigines, out of a total population of 16 000 000 Australians. Most of these full-blooded Aborigines live in villages with modern houses, shops, schools and clinics. Some work on the huge cattle ranches in the north and western parts of Australia, while others have found jobs in the cities. The Australian government has created special reservations (Figure 3.6) for those who wish to keep to the traditional ways and it is not un-common for Aborigines who have spent their working lives with White People to return to the tribal territory and spend their remaining years just as their ancestors would have wished.

1 **a** List at least ten ways in which the Aborigines' traditional life-style is completely self-sufficient.
b Why is it reasonable to describe the Aborigines as a race of 'hunter-gatherers'?

2 Suggest reasons why Aborigine groups:
a divide into family-sized clans for most of the year.
b occupy very large tribal territories.
c do not wish to get involved in territorial disputes.
d do not feel the need to use footwear or wear many clothes.
e now form less than 1% of Australia's total population.
f provide stockmen who are ideally suited to the work and conditions on large cattle ranches.

3 Imagine that you are an old and respected Aborigine hunter! You have been elected to tell the tjitjes (young people) in your tribe about the importance of The Dreaming to life in the Outback. Write down what you would say to your pupils, having first discussed possible ideas openly in class.

3.2 Farming systems

Successful farmers think very carefully about local conditions before deciding what type(s) of food to produce, and what methods are best suited to do this. They are also greatly influenced by the general wealth and technology of the country in which they live. Every farm, however, can be thought of as a **system** with its own individual sets of inputs, outputs and the processes which link them. Figure 3.7 outlines the system of a typical British farm which rears animals as well as growing crops. This flow diagram has some blanks in it, because question 1 invites you to add the missing items!

1 Draw Figure 3.7, then write these extra items in the twelve blank spaces in it.

barley	harvesting	milking
buildings	labour	planting
eggs	land	soil
feeding	milk	sugar beet

2 Write a sentence about each of the following sets in a farm system – without quoting examples from Figure 3.7 (e.g. barley).
a Inputs.
b Processes.
c Outputs.

Every farm is unique (totally different) in some ways. Although this is so, it is usually possible to describe it quite accurately by using just a few key words. The main ones, and their meanings, are listed below.

Set 1

Arable: concentrates on growing crops (mainly cereal crops).
Horticultural: grows certain types of specialised crops such as vegetables, fruit, vines and flowers.
Pastoral: concentrates on rearing animals.
Mixed: where arable and pastoral are both important to the success of the farm.

▼ **Figure 3.7** A typical British farm system

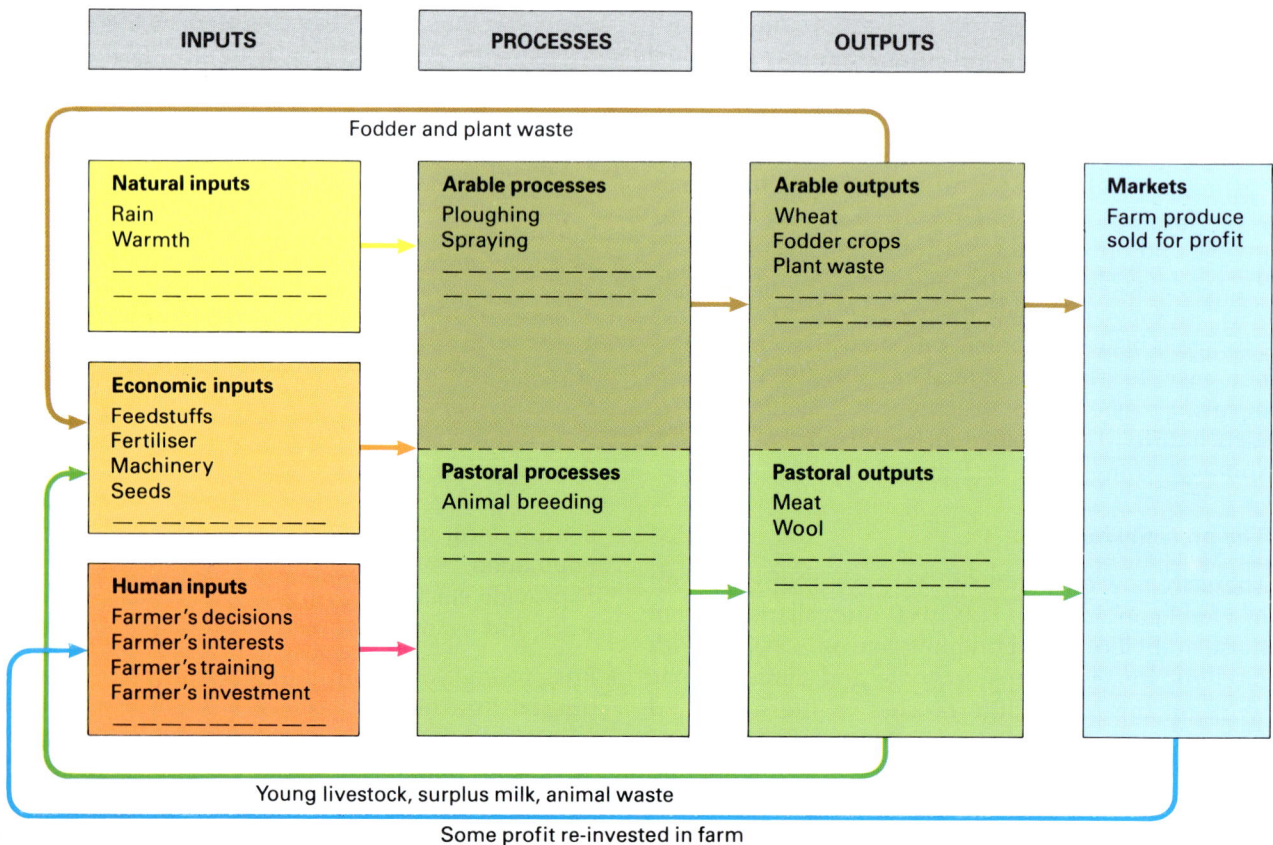

▲ **Figure 3.8** A farm in a developed country

▼ **Figure 3.9** A farm in a developing country

Set 2

Commercial: describes a farm which exists to sell its produce and so make a profit. Crops grown for sales are also referred to as cash crops.

Subsistence: describes a farm which hopes to produce enough to feed the farmer and his family but cannot guarantee to produce a surplus every year.

Set 3

Extensive: describes a very large farm which employs very few workers. The land is not very productive, and so a large area is needed to support the owner

Intensive: the opposite of extensive; i.e. a much smaller farm which produces high yields of food per unit area.

Set 4 (these terms may not apply)

Nomadic: the farmer does not work one particular area of land, but moves about from time to time to meet the needs of his animals.

Irrigation: putting extra water on the land in areas where the normal rainfall is too low.

3 For each of the scenes in Figure 3.8 and 3.9:
   a describe the type of farming being carried out. Use the appropriate 'key words' from Sets 1–4.
   b suggest one area/country where this type of farming is probably quite common.
   c give reasons for your choice in **b**. Your atlas may help you to do this.

◀ **Figure 3.10** Sowing seed in the nineteenth century

SVSLADER

▼ **Figure 3.11** The three-field crop rotation. Oats, peas and beans were sometimes grown instead of barley

3.3 Britain's first agricultural revolution

A 'revolution' is said to take place when important events change rapidly. The word is often used to describe a sudden change of government brought about by force but it can also refer to changes in the nature of work or any other aspect of everyday life. This unit studies Britain's first *agricultural* revolution; the next considers the ways in which our farming methods have changed dramatically during the present century.

The first agricultural revolution took place in the eighteenth century and affected both arable and pastoral farming. Before 1750, most of our farmers were illiterate, which means that they couldn't read or write. Their methods were quite basic, and not very efficient (Figure 3.10). Many of the fields were small by modern standards and some of the land was shared by a number of farmers. The arable land was usually divided up into long strips separated by grass-covered banks called balks. These acted as boundaries between each farmer's land and were never ploughed up. This system not only wasted some of the best land but allowed weeds to grow and spread onto cropped areas on either side. Some farmers had more than one strip, and it was quite usual for their strips to be some distance apart. A simple form of crop rotation was in common use (Figure 3.11). After harvesting had taken place,

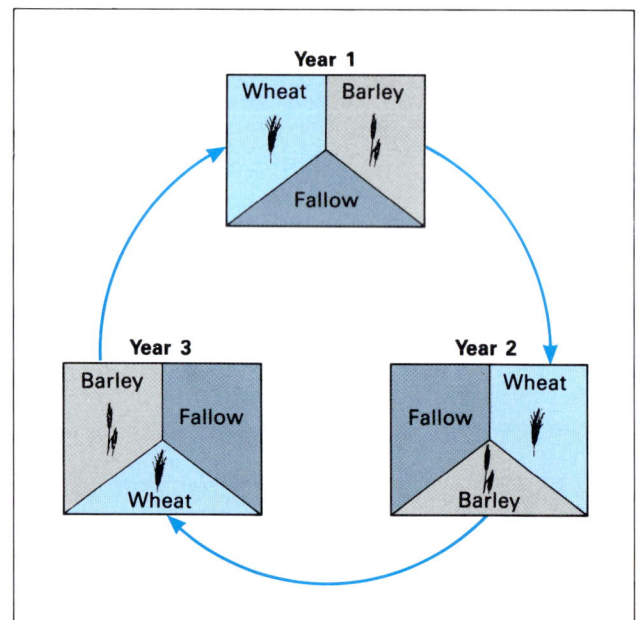

animals were allowed to graze on the arable land as their manure would fertilise its soil ready for sowing after the winter. This was called the open-field system. Most villages had at least one very large field which was used solely for grazing. As many farmers shared these common grazings, they took far less interest in them than their own strips. They also found it impossible to keep weak or diseased animals apart from the healthy ones.

I

Fig. 22.

B   C

E   a a a   b b   F
     c   d

Fig. 21.

◄ **Figure 3.12** Jethro Tull and the seed drill he invented

▼ **Figure 3.14** The Norfolk System – a four field crop rotation. The beans (or clover) restored the fertility of the soil ready for the next crop of wheat

▼ **Figure 3.13** Viscount Thomas Townshend was a wealthy landowner who thought it wasteful to leave land fallow every third year. He developed a new four-year rotation using root crops to return goodness to the soil. He was later nick-named 'Turnip' Townshend'

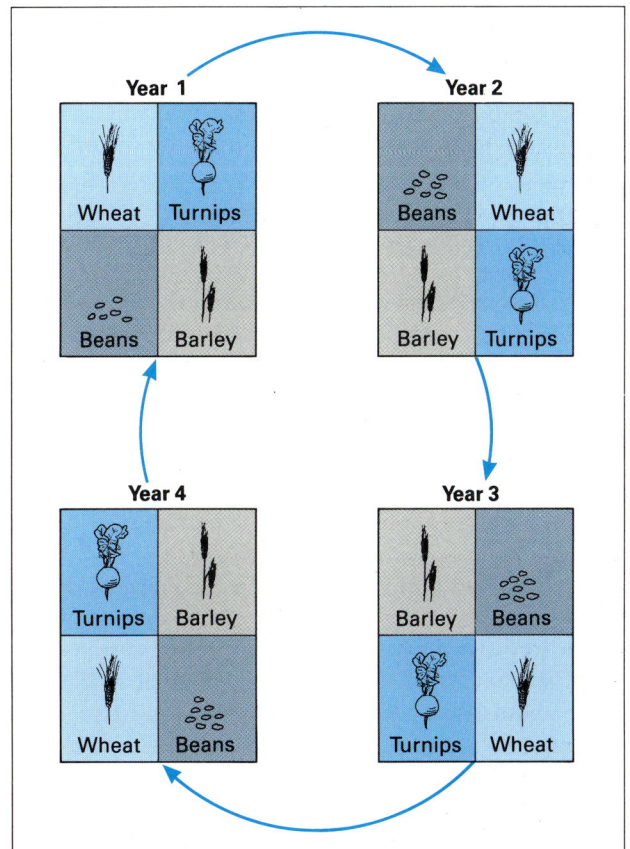

Year 1

| Wheat | Turnips |
| Beans | Barley |

Year 2

| Beans | Wheat |
| Barley | Turnips |

Year 4

| Turnips | Barley |
| Wheat | Beans |

Year 3

| Barley | Beans |
| Turnips | Wheat |

▼ **Figure 3.15** Robert Bakewell concentrated on improving the breeding of animals. The 'New Leicester' breed of sheep carried more flesh and provided much needed meat for Britain's growing population

By 1760, a number of important changes were beginning to make British agriculture a more efficient producer of food. However, as we shall see, not everyone gained by these changes. The most obvious effect on the landscape was the use of ditches, fences and hedges to enclose the fields. Providing these created a good deal of network, but only the wealthier landowners could afford to pay for them. Many farmers left the land to find work in the growing industrial towns, but some were able to rent more land than they had before and benefited greatly from the new field system. Enclosure became so popular that even village greens were threatened with enclosure, until the government stepped in and passed special Acts of Parliament to make this illegal!

Farming methods also changed very rapidly during the second half of the eighteenth century – due mainly to the efforts of three reforming landowners (see Figures 3.12–3.14). Not all kinds of work on a farm changed, of course; ploughs continued to be horse-drawn and long sharp scythes were used for harvesting well into the present century. But the first argicultural revolution did mean that we could feed the growing populations of our towns during the first part of the Industrial Revolution (approximately 1760–1850). It was not until the nineteenth century that our urban (town-dwelling) population grew faster than our ability to produce more food, and we became dependent on additional supplies imported from abroad.

1 Compare the 'open field' (strip) and 'enclosed field' systems.

2 **a** When did Britain's first agricultural revolution take place?
   b State the main effects of this revolution on:
   i the size of the average farm.
   ii employment and unemployment.
   iii the migration (movement) of people.
   iv farming efficiency (see Figures 3.12–3.15)
   v the nation's ability to feed its growing urban population.
   vi our need to import food.

3 Write a discussion between a rich landowner and a poor peasant farmer of the mid-eighteenth century who are arguing about the 'good' and 'bad' points of the enclosed field system.

3.4 Agribusiness: Britain's second agricultural revolution

Farming is now as highly competitive as any other industry in Britain, hence the use of the term **agribusiness** to describe the way in which it operates. Our farms have certainly become far more efficient and profitable since the Second World War, but achieving this has tended to put the natural environment at risk. The effects on the rural landscape have been clear for some time, and it is the threat of *unseen* damage which is now causing the greatest concern.

Machinery and the landscape (Figure 3.16)

Tractors outnumbered farm horses in Britain as long ago as 1950. The first generation of tractors were quite small and could work efficiently within the fields of that period. As the size of tractors and other types of farm machinery increased, so did the fields in which they had to operate. Machines work best on long, straight runs with gradients well below 20%, and the fewer the turns they have to make, the better. Increasing the size of fields to cope with them has meant 'grubbing-up' (removing) thousands of hedgerows and copses (small woods). Many ponds have been filled in because they 'waste' land and get in the way of the machines. The changes which machines have brought to the landscape are most noticeable in arable farming areas such as East Anglia, where large sections of the Fens have been filled in and drained to increase the area of prime agricultural land. Eliminating hedgerows, copses and ponds has not only produced a very different farming landscape but has also affected the balance of those wildlife communities which are so dependent upon them.

▲ **Figure 3.16** Wildlife endangered by hedge removal

Impact on the soil (Figure 3.17)

Some of the latest farm machinery is very heavy, and has much the same effect as an army tank moving across the land. Its weight compacts (compresses) the soil and destroys its natural structure. Even healthy, balanced soils cannot withstand this kind of treat-

▶ **Figure 3.17**

► **Figure 3.18** The strength of colour shows the concentration of DDT in each level of this food chain. All levels, apart from the one at the base, are called trophic levels. This means that they have consumers in them

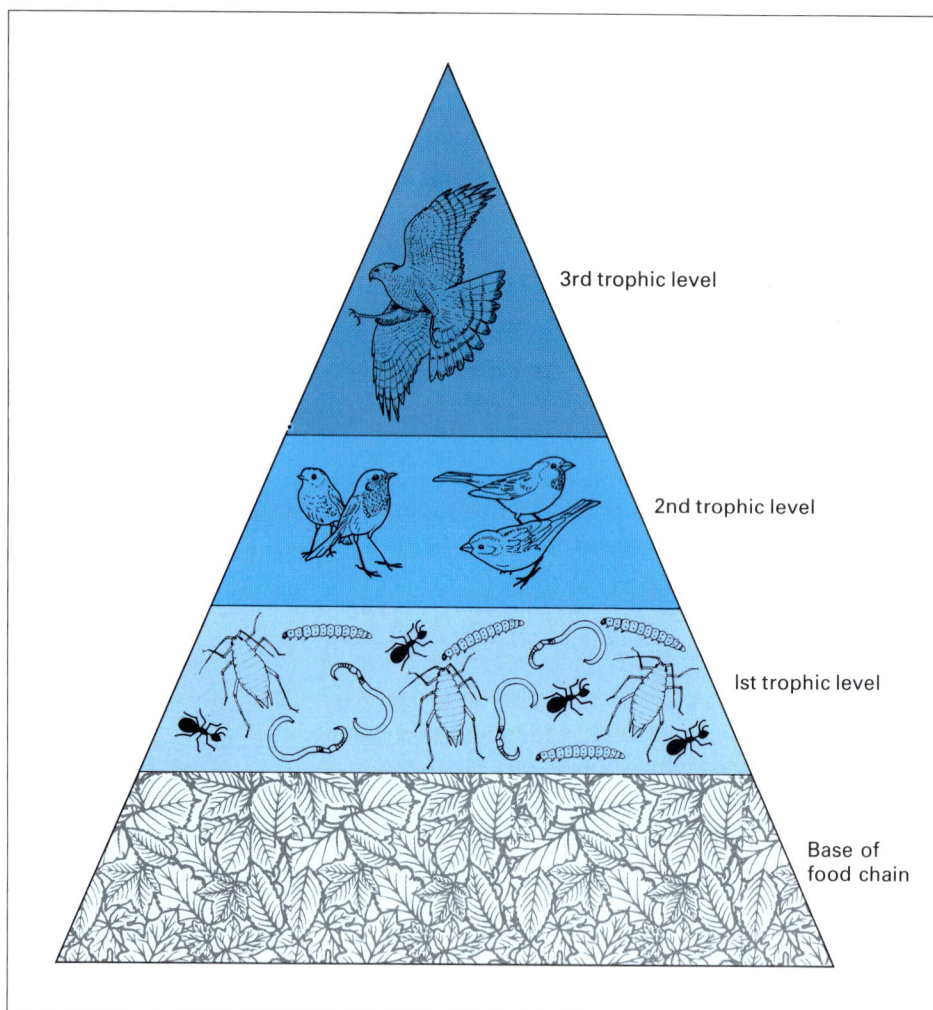

3rd trophic level

2nd trophic level

lst trophic level

Base of food chain

ment, but those with small amounts of humus – the decayed remains of grass and crop stubble – face the greatest risk. Unfortunately, modern farming techniques mean that less humus is produced. Top quality arable land is under constant pressure to achieve the maximum yield and so is rarely given the chance to recover naturally; today's farmer would much rather see a field of wheat or barley than one lying fallow and grazing animals, even though they produce the finest kind of fertiliser.

Another problem brought about by heavy machinery concerns naturally moist soils such as clay. Modern ploughs bite deeper and create a compact, **impermeable** layer which moisture and plant roots cannot pass through easily. The result is stale, waterlogged soil on the surface which encourages the spread of plant diseases. The farmers' response: spray fungicides on the crops!

The rise and fall of DDT (Figure 3.18)

Dichlor-di-phenyl-trichlorathene, (better known as DDT!) was one of the first pesticides designed to help the farmer. It was developed during the late 1930s and initially produced some remarkable results. In fact Paul Muller, the Swiss chemist who invented it, was awarded the Nobel Prize for his pioneering work. Unfortunately, DDT did not prove to be as safe as people had hoped. What the food chain in Figure 3.18 does *not* show is how the pests DDT was designed to kill gradually became immune to its effects. This meant that a new generation of stronger pesticides had to be invented to replace it. The demand for artificial aids has also been increased by the use of new, high-yielding varieties of cereal, for they are very prone to disease. It seems that people are fighting a never-ending war in which we win the occasional battle, but the insects can never be totally defeated!

Straw burning (Figure 3.19)

Straw was once a vital by-product of farming. It could be used for thatching cottages, feeding cattle and providing bedding material for them. The present trend is for large farming areas to specialise in growing crops *or* rearing animals so, while considerable amounts of straw are still being produced, it is becoming increasingly expensive to transport it to the farms which need it most. Arable farmers avoid leaving straw on their land because it shelters insects which could harm next year's crops. It has therefore become usual to burn the straw rather than sell it, and no fewer than 5 000 000 tonnes of it are destroyed every year in Britain alone. This invariably produces an unwelcome crop of complaints from a general public annoyed by the way smoke from the fires soils washing and blackens paintwork. Far more serious is the way straw-burning endangers both motorists and property when the operating gets out of hand, and fire engines are quite a common sight in arable areas after harvest time.

Waste disposal (Figure 3.20)

Farm animals used to be grazed out of doors throughout the year. This meant that their waste was recycled naturally by worms and other creatures in the soil. The modern approach is to keep cows and pigs under cover for much longer periods. This creates a serious dung disposal problem. (Note: every cow produces more waste than 50 adult people!) Surplus waste is usually stored in special lagoons until it can be sprayed on the fields as fertiliser. Keeping it in this way makes it much stronger, as passing motorists know! It can be so strong that leakages may damage the soil. Animal waste now accounts for over 10% of all the pollution incidents affecting British streams and lakes.

▲ **Figure 3.19** Straw burning can be annoying!

▼ **Figure 3.20**

▶ and ▼ **Figure 3.21** Black grass and couch grass are just two of the weeds which thrive on artificial fertilisers

The effects of constant cropping (Figure 3.21)

Crop rotation is the traditional way of replacing lost goodness in the soil (see previous unit). The modern farmer believes this practice is wasteful as it means growing some crops which are less profitable as well as leaving the land fallow for long periods. His answer has been to apply artificial fertilisers at regular intervals, especially those rich in nitrates and phosphates. Although this by-passes the crop rotation system, it can have some curious side effects, e.g. the more rapid growth of weeds such as black grass as well as the food crops! The farmer then returns to his catalogue and orders the herbicide which best meets his need.

1 Which of the following have increased or decreased as a result of recent changes in British farming?
a The number of ponds.
b The total length of hedgerows.
c The size of farm machinery.
d The number of tractors.
e The risk of cereal crops being damaged by disease.
f The total area of 'dead land' around the edges of fields and ponds.
g The likelihood of insect pests being controlled naturally.
h The chances of soil structures being damaged by great heat.
i The profits obtained by farm owners.
j The need for unskilled labour.

2 Answer these questions in full sentences:
a What do the letters DDT stand for?
b When was DDT invented, and by whom?
c What evidence suggests that DDT was extremely successful in its early years?
d What was the main problem with using DDT?
e What action has been taken to limit the use of DDT?
f How do the concentrations of DDT change up the food chain shown in Figure 3.18?
g Why is the DDT concentration in the highest **trophic level** so great?

▲ **Figure 3.22** The battery hen system of egg production

3 Write your own definitions for these important words (listed in text order):

agribusiness   grubbing-up
compact (the *verb*)   herbicide
copse   immunity
fungicide   pesticide
generation

4 You are a dedicated environmentalist, which means you can't bear to watch the natural environment suffer just because people want to make more money. What words of complaint and/or advice would you feel bound to give the farmer in Figure 3.22?

5 Now write the modern *farmer*'s response to the points raised by the environmentalist in question **4**. No doubt the farmer will mention all the pressures he is under, as well as the many benefits which an efficient farming industry can bring to the community as a whole.

6 Figure 3.22 shows one type of agribusiness. Reread Unit 3.2 then devise a systems diagram to show its component inputs, outputs, flows and stores.

7 Think very carefully before answering this question. Is it generally true to say that Britain's second agricultural revolution was:

a inevitable?

b an obvious sequel to the first revolution in the nineteenth century?

3.5 Europe's Common Agricultural Policy

The European Community (the EC for short) was formed in 1957. It had six founder members: the Netherlands, Italy, Luxembourg, Belgium, West Germany and France. The phrase 'Never Include Little Bunnies With Ferrets' might help you to remember their names, as each word shares the first letter of one of these countries! Denmark, the United Kingdom and the Irish Republic joined the EC in 1973; Greece joined in 1981; Spain and Portugal did so in 1985.

One of the main aims of the Common Market, as the EC is usually called, was to make its farmers more efficient and to improve their standard of living. It hoped to achieve this by means of its **Common Agricultural Policy** (the CAP) – a system of guaranteeing the prices which farmers receive for the food they produce. These prices are reviewed and agreed each year. The CAP has proved so successful that the member countries have now been told to reduce their production of certain items of food! They have produced more food than can be sold and these surpluses are kept in large 'intervention stores' (Figure 3.23). The cost of keeping all of this unwanted food in good condition is very high indeed, and many people object to some of the taxes they pay being spent on food which will never be eaten.

Shoppers are also annoyed at the way food prices have risen since Britain joined the EC. We used to import much of our food from other parts of the world, especially Commonwealth countries such as Australia and New Zealand. High import levies were then charged on these goods which increased their cost, making them less competitive within the European Community.

▼ **Figure 3.23 a** A European Community intervention store of milk powder in Britain. Britain has 250 grain stores holding 3 million tonnes of surplus wheat and barley. Other British intervention stores contain 25 000 tonnes of skimmed-milk powder.

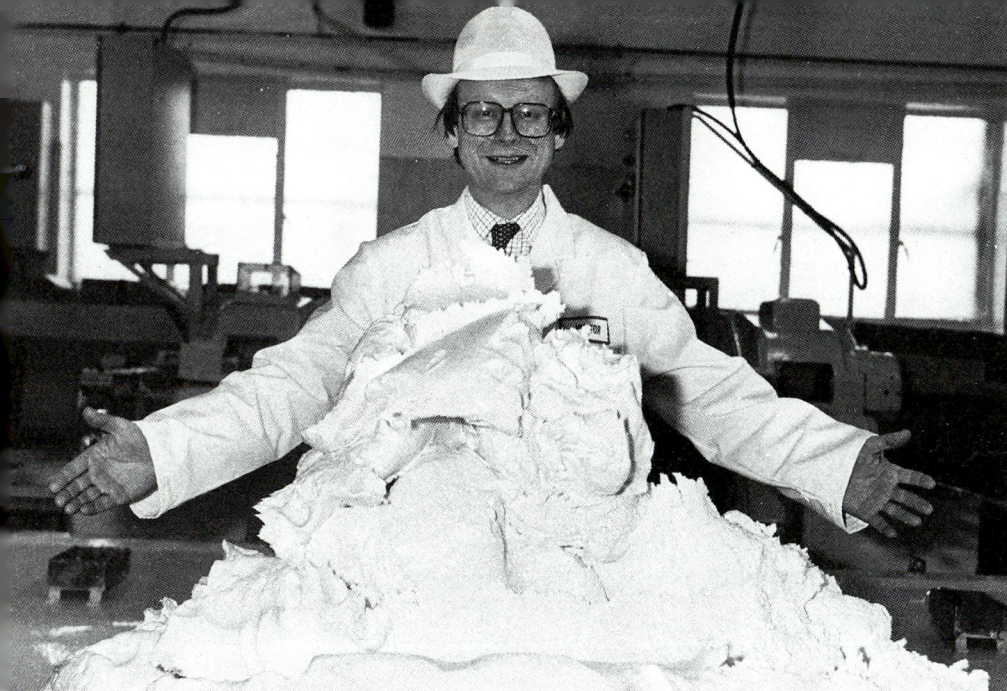

b John Gummer, then Britain's Agriculture Minister, watches the first batch of 250 000 tonnes of surplus butter which was given to the needy in early 1987. There are 100 cold stores in Britain containing 50 000 tonnes of beef and 250 000 tonnes of butter.
Liquid intervention stores throughout the EC hold enough wine to fill 700 Olympic-size swimming pools! It costs £200 million *every week* to maintain Europe's intervention stores; this represents half of the European Community's total annual budget.

1 On an outline political map of Western Europe, shade and name all the member countries of the European Community.

2 What were the main aims of the Common Agricultural Policy?

3 Write down your own definitions of these important words:
a surplus
b intervention store
c levy
d competitive
e budget

4 a What are Britain's surpluses of these items of food according to the captions for Figure 3.23a and b:
beef?
butter?
skimmed-milk powder?
wheat and barley?
wine?
b What means are used to store large quantities of surplus food?
c How much does it cost the EC *every year* to maintain its intervention stores?
d State one fact which proves that Common Market farmers are much more efficient than they used to be.

5 Describe the most likely feelings of the following people towards Europe's Common Agricultural Policy:
a A British housewife.
b A French pig farmer.
c The owner of beef cattle ranch in Australia.
d An old age pensioner in Scotland.

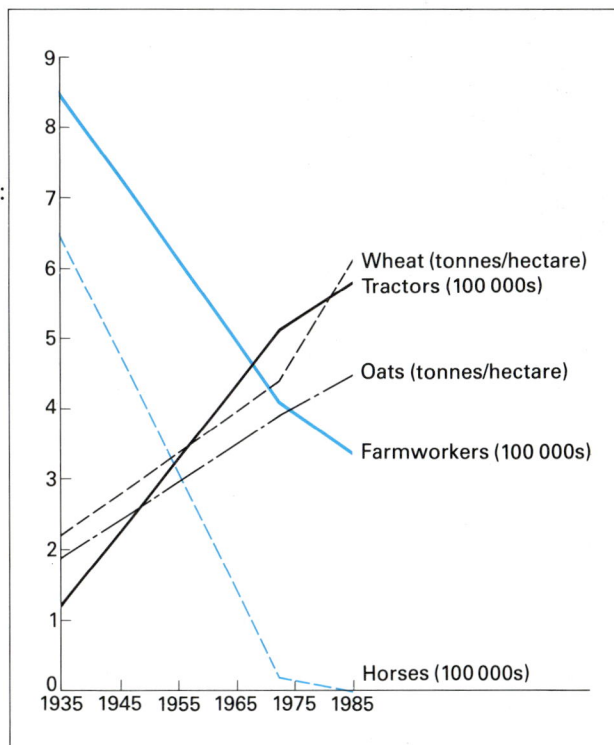

▶ **Figure 3.24** Agricultural trends in the UK, 1935–1985

3.6 Choice foods

Farmers are greatly influenced by the demands of both shopper and food retailer. The traditional trading pattern included wholesalers who bought in bulk from the processors or direct from the farmers, then supplied numerous small retailers as required. The present arrangement is very different. Two-thirds of all food sales are now made by superstore chains (e.g. ASDA), while groups of individual traders such as Spa and Mace dominate the remainder. These trading groups are large enough to carry out the wholesalers' role themselves, which of course gives them a greater share of the total operating profit. The direct purchasing power of these nationwide groups – and through them the influence of the individual shopper – is clearly shown by the demand for certain types of beef product.

Most people now prefer to buy small joints of tender, lean meat. A pinky red colour is another strong selling point. The large trading groups employ expert full-time buyers to make sure that only the 'right' kinds of meat find their way to the counter. These buyers regularly visit the abbatoirs to pass on up-to-date information about their companies' requirements. The abattoir buying staff then give this vital information to local farmers, who in turn devise ways of meeting the groups' needs as cheaply and efficiently as possible.

Knowing that tender, lean meat is likely to sell well and that fatty meat will not because of the wastage involved, the farmers once used barley to speed up the fattening process (young animals produce the tenderest meat). This rich diet worked well and barley-fed animals were in prime condition after only twelve months. In the 1970s, however, the price of barley rose sharply and threatened the profit margins of the farmers at the base of the food chain. They have since discovered that processed straw and certain by-products of the brewing industry are just as effective!

Shoppers are now far more concerned about 'healthy' eating, and this has affected the demand for certain products and ingredients. The outstanding example of this is sugar, which is very high in calories but has no vitamins or other dietary value; others are considered in the illustrations here and on the next page.

▶ Figure 3.25

Fifteen Diet Tips That Can Change Your Life

BY SYBIL FERGUSON

1 Select your weight goal. Write it down. Now pin this note *where you'll see it every day.*

2 Weigh yourself every morning for the rest of your life.

3 Drink several glasses of water a day. Water is essential to every bodily function. It is also inexpensive and calorie-free, making it the perfect drink for dieting.

4 When you're under stress, you may want to eat. Break the stress cycle with exercise and a hot bath.

5 *Always* be aware of calories. Sugar, for example, is a leading additive in foods. Read all labels carefully for any sugars ending in *ose*: lactose, sucrose, dextrose, maltose and fructose.

6 Decrease red meats which are high in fat: increase fish and poultry.

7 Avoid excessive amounts of caffeine-filled beverages. They may be bad for your blood pressure; they may also make you nervous, and many people eat more when they get the jitters.

8 Eat a balanced diet that includes lean meats, raw fruits and vegetables.

9 Stick to a set schedule each day and eat on time. Most dieters starve all day to indulge at night. If no food has been eaten, the

READER'S DIGEST

blood-sugar level drops, you crave food, and you may lose control.

10 Never shop for food when you're hungry.

11 Limit your salt intake. The more salted food you eat, the more you want.

12 Don't take less than 20 minutes to finish a meal.

13 Avoid foods that are served with sauces. Sauces are often rich in butter, sugar, salt and flour, adding to your calorie count.

14 Learn to relax before a party. It will fortify your self-control when snacks are offered.

15 Remember: you are learning a "way to live," not just a way to diet.

CONDENSED FROM "100 DIET TIPS THAT CAN CHANGE YOUR LIFE." BY SYBIL FERGUSON © 1987 DIET CENTRE INC. PUBLISHED BY DIET CENTRE INC, REXBURG, IDAHO. ILLUSTRATIONS: DIET CENTRE INC

800 g MEDIUM SLICED WHOLEMEAL BREAD

RECOM

NUTRITION INFORMATION

TYPICAL VALUES

	Per 100 g	Per daily serving of 4 slices — 130 g
Energy	913 kJ/215 k cal	1191 kJ/280 k cal
Protein	9·5 g	12·4 g
Carbohydrate	41·2 g	53·6 g
Fat	2·5 g	3·3 g
Salt	1·2 g	1·6 g
Dietary Fibre	8·6 g	11·2 g
Vitamins/Minerals		
Thiamin (B1)	0·26 mg	0·34 mg
Niacin	3·9 mg	5.1 mg
Calcium	73·0 mg	94·9 mg
Iron	4·1 mg	5·3 mg

PROTEIN Essential for good health. Important for growing children. 4 slices provides 22% of R.D.A.

Why ASDA
Asda who
wholeme
artificial pr
of dietary
which are

FREEZING

For freezing, place in deep freeze on day of purchase. Use within one month. Defrost slowly.

"G

Food firms cause salt problems

EFFORTS to limit increases in blood pressure by reducing the amount of salt in food should be aimed at the manufacturers, according to research by three experts.

They point out the "substantial" health benefits to be gained by curbing the development of coronary artery disease and they say that previous studies have failed to take sufficient account of salt losses in the cooking process.

Our Medical Consultant writes—Men in this country consume twice as much salt as they require. Salt is essential for health but too much may increase the risk of coronary heart disease and strokes.

The average daily salt intake in Britain is 10.7grms for men and 8grms for women, while international committees have suggested that this average should be reduced by 5grms daily.

Campaign's coffin-shaped pie angers meat traders

By Peter Pallot
Health Staff

MEAT traders are furious over the drugs industry's healthy eating campaign. Advertisements, designed to support the Government's £2.5 million "Look After Your Heart" drive, depict a coffin-shaped meat pie.

Last night Mr Keith Roberts, chairman of the Government-appointed Meat and Livestock Commission, asked the Association of the British Pharmaceutical Industry to scrap its "scurrilous" advertisements.

He condemned the £750,000 campaign — which will include television commercials from tomorrow—as "misleading, unreasonable and highly offensive."

The British Pharmaceutical Industry advertisement which has angered meat traders.

Plans laid for 'healthier' egg

By Our Agriculture Correspondent

In an attempt to reverse the steady fall in egg consumption by a health-conscious public, Britain's biggest animal feed manufacturer yesterday launched a new range of chicken feeds claimed to produce eggs that are rich in vitamins and low in calories and saturated fat.

The Farmgate feeds from the giant Unilever subsidiary, B O C M-Silcock, are said to contain no drugs, antibiotics or hormones, and only natural pigments to produce eggs with a rich yolk colour.

ED DAILY AMOUNT		
IRON Required to keep blood healthy.	VITAMIN B1 (Thiamin) Needed to keep the nerves & muscles healthy.	NIACIN (Part of B Group) Needed for a healthy skin & nervous system.
4 slices provides 44% of R.D.A.	4 slices provides 27% of R.D.A.	4 slices provides 27% of R.D.A.

MEAL BREAD is good for you.

read is produced with 100%
t contains no animal fats, no
es, and is an invaluable source
otein, vitamins and iron, all of
to keep you, and your family,
and healthy.

and enjoy your bread".

1 Ask your parents/milkman/local shopkeeper to help you answer these questions.
   a What types of milk are indicated by bottle tops coloured blue, red, silver and yellow?
   b Which of these types of milk have proved increasingly popular/unpopular in recent years?
   c Suggest reasons for the trends you noted down in b.

2 With the *help* of the illustrations in this unit, write an essay entitled 'Changing eating patterns'. You will need to state how *and why* the demand for each type of food is changing.

3.7 Plantation farming

Plantations are very large farms. They usually specialise in growing just one crop and most of what they produce is exported abroad. It is quite common for some processing to be carried out on plantations, and for the owners to provide accommodation for their workers. Some also provide schools, shops and other services. Figure 3.26 lists some of the most common plantation crops and the areas where they are chiefly grown.

The first plantations grew sugar cane, and were laid out in Brazil and the West Indies during the sixteenth century (Figure 3.27). Most of them, however, date from the nineteenth century, when the British, the French and the Dutch were creating large empires from the overseas territories they had discovered. Their plantations grew crops which couldn't survive the cooler European climate. Most of these colonies are now independent countries. Very conscious of their new freedom, they tend to be resentful towards the old plantations. They particularly don't like the way in which much of the wealth they create goes overseas to the European companies which own

them. This has led to some of the larger plantations being broken up into small plots which can be farmed by the local people. This is a popular, vote-winning idea, which can increase the quantity of home-grown food and reduce the need for expensive imports. It has however destroyed some very efficient businesses which generated wealth – if only for their owners, many of whom were multinational companies with interests in many countries.

1 Write down this definition of the plantation system of farming, using the best-fit word(s) to fill in each blank.

'Plantations are farms which usually grow . . . (a few crops/only one crop). Their aim is to produce crops which can be (eaten by the local people/exported for profit). They are generally . . . (large/small) enough to have their own processing factories, as well as villages to house . . . (any visitors/the workers). Most plantations lie in the . . . (cooler/warmer) parts of the world . . . (between/outside) the Tropics of . . . (Africa and Asia/Cancer and Capricorn).

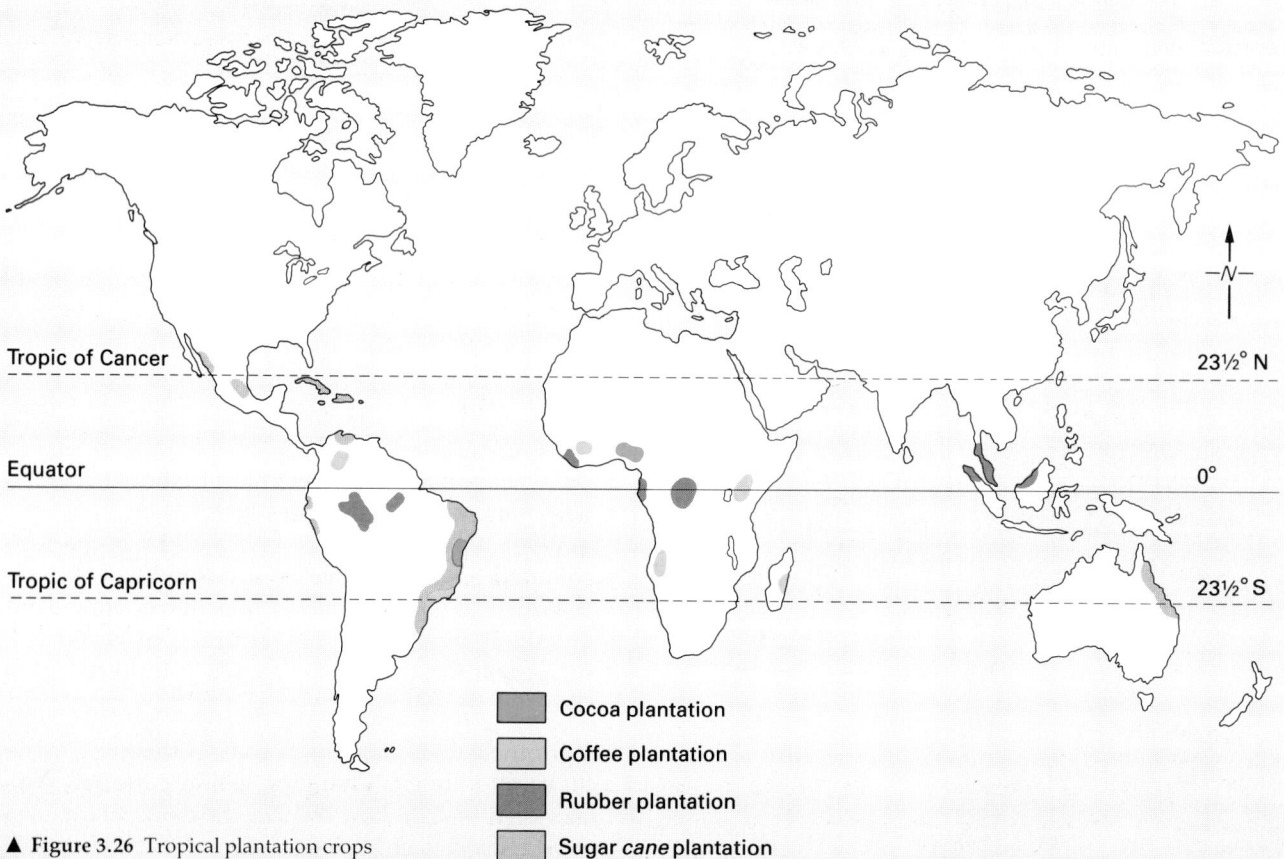

▲ Figure 3.26 Tropical plantation crops

Cocoa plantation

Coffee plantation

Rubber plantation

Sugar *cane* plantation

◀ **Figure 3.27** An early sugar cane plantation in the West Indies – planting the cane

2 a Write the following statements under the most appropriate of these two headings: **Advantages of the plantation system** and **Disadvantages of the plantation system**.

'A disease may wipe out the entire crop for a whole year; farms which grow more than one crop greatly reduce the chance of this happening.'

'Large plantations can afford to carry out research into the crops they grow.'

'Dependence on just one crop makes a plantation very senstive to its changing value on the world market.'

'Plantations can afford to buy their own vehicles and up-to-date farm machinery.'

'Plantations often provide housing for their workers. It may not be of a very high standard, but it is often free or cheap to rent.'

'Plantations pay regular wages to their employees. Many Third World countries have too few "permanent" jobs of this kind.'

'The demand for a particular crop may be greatly reduced as a result of changing attitudes and "tastes" (e.g. the use of sugar in drinks and in food processing).'

b Add at least two more statements of your own to *each* list.

c Highlight (e.g. by underlining) the five statements which you consider to be most important. Your choices are not restricted in any way, so it is *possible* to make all five from one list.

d According to your now complete and 'highlighted' lists, do the advantages of the plantation system appear to outweigh its disadvantages? Try to include some comments in your answer rather than just a 'yes/no' response!

3 a Put the information in Figure 3.26 on to an outline map of the world.

b Describe the main distribution pattern features for each plantation crop shown in Figure 3.26.

c With the help of an atlas, suggest reasons for any differences in the patterns you have just described.

4 State whether the following are likely to be 'for' or 'against' the plantation system of farming, and give reasons for your choice in each case.

a The owner of a shipping line.

b The British Prime Minister of 1890.

c The present Prime Minister of a typical Third World country which has many large, well-established plantations.

d An unemployed labourer in Cuba.

e A French share-holder in a multi-national company which owns many plantations abroad.

5 Why are most plantations:

a located in tropical lands?

b sited near the coast?

c linked to the ports by their own railway lines?

6 a Discover as much as you can about each of these two important plantation crops (e.g. where they are grown, what they are used for):

i palm oil

ii jute.

b write up your findings, adding any illustrations which appear necessary.

▲ Figure 3.29 Harvesting sugar cane the easy way!

◀ Figure 3.28 Harvesting sugar cane by hand

Sugar plantations in Cuba

Sugar can be found in most plants, but only sugar cane and sugar beet produce it in commercial quantities. The beet grows best in cool regions such as Western Europe, and looks very like a turnip. Cane on the other hand is a tropical crop which can grow where the temperatures are constantly above 20°C and the total annual rainfall exceeds 2 000 mm. It grows up to 4 metres high and is a bulky plant with the sugar forming only 10%–20% of its total weight.

Sugar cane is a perennial crop, which means that each plant grows for a number of years. After harvesting either by machete (Figure 3.28), the old, back-breaking method, or modern machinery (Figure 3.29), the cane is taken to a nearby processing factory. There it is crushed between heavy rollers. These squeeze a sugary juice out of the cane. The juice is then boiled until crystals form. The remains of the crushed cane have many uses and provide a very useful second source of income when sugar prices on the world market are lower than usual.

Sugar has always been one of Cuba's main exports and sources of income. It used to be grown on large, privately-owned estates called latifundia. Many of these have been taken over by the state since the revolution of 1959 when President Fidel Castro came to power. The plan has been to keep the most efficient plantations intact and under state control, but subdivide the other 'nationalised' areas as discussed earlier. Each peasant farmer may buy up to 67 hectares of land with the help of cheap loans from the government. In keeping with the communist tradition, the state-run farms (which total over 78% of the transferred land) are well equipped with schools, clinics and other basic facilities. Their workers are not rich, but are much better off than those working on certain privately-owned plantations in other parts of the world.

7 **a** State briefly where sugar beet grows best.
   b What are the basic growing requirements of sugar cane?

◀ **Figure 3.30** Sugar cane plantations on Cuba

Map legend:
- Sugar cane plantation
- High land, rising above 2 500 m
- ■ Capital city
- ● Large town
- → Prevailing winds (summer)
- ⇢ Prevailing winds (winter)

▼ **Figure 3.31** Layout of a typical state-owned sugar cane plantation in Cuba

8 Draw simple sketches to illustrate these by-products of the sugar cane processing plants: cattle food, fertiliser, rum, treacle, fuel, paper and cardboard.

9 Draw a flow-diagram to show the various stages in the handling and processing of sugar cane.

10 Contrast the two harvesting methods shown in Figures 3.28 and 3.29 in terms of:
  a efficiency
  b labour force
  c cost.

11 a Describe the distribution of sugar plantations on the island of Cuba.
   b Give reasons for this distribution pattern.

12 Suggest reasons why:
   a Weeds are a far more serious problem on cane growing plantations than beet farms.
   b The sugar plantation in Figure 3.31 has its own processing plant.
   c The same plantation is only 42 km from the nearest port.
   d There is a range of services provided for the benefit of workers on this plantation.
   e Large areas have been set aside for the plantation workers to grow their own vegetables.
   f Crop rotation methods cannot be used for growing sugar cane.
   g Soil on the older plantations may be less fertile than those used for other types of farming in Cuba.

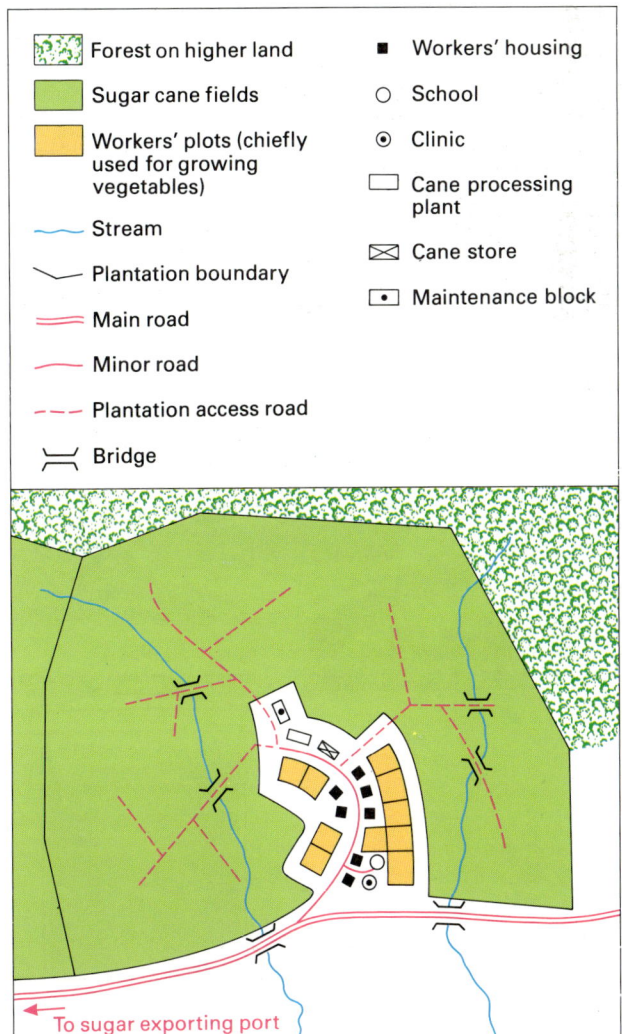

Legend:
- Forest on higher land
- Sugar cane fields
- Workers' plots (chiefly used for growing vegetables)
- Stream
- Plantation boundary
- Main road
- Minor road
- Plantation access road
- Bridge
- ■ Workers' housing
- ○ School
- ◉ Clinic
- Cane processing plant
- Cane store
- Maintenance block

To sugar exporting port

4

Pollution of Land and Air

4.1 Introduction: refuse disposal

Disposing of our waste is an increasingly difficult task. Every community – no matter how small or primitive – produces waste of some kind; it is the *quantity* and *nature* of modern waste which makes it so much harder to cope with.

Figure 4.1 gives you some idea of the scale of the problem. This barge was loaded up with 25 000 tonnes of New York's ordinary domestic refuse, and the captain of its towing barge ordered to cruise up and down the east coast of North America in search of a town willing to dispose of the load safely. The captain was authorised to offer a substantial sum of money in return for this service. After sailing many thousands of kilometres without success, he was recalled by the New York refuse department. The ultimate fate of this unusual load wasn't known at the time this book was written but, interestingly, only a fraction of it had been affected by the long cruise. The waste food had started to rot, but everything made out of plastic or glass, for example, was quite unchanged. Like much of today's refuse, it was not **biodegradable** (able to rot naturally).

◀ **Figure 4.1** An American refuse barge in search of a tip

▶ **Figure 4.2** Household refuse has changed in many ways over the last few decades

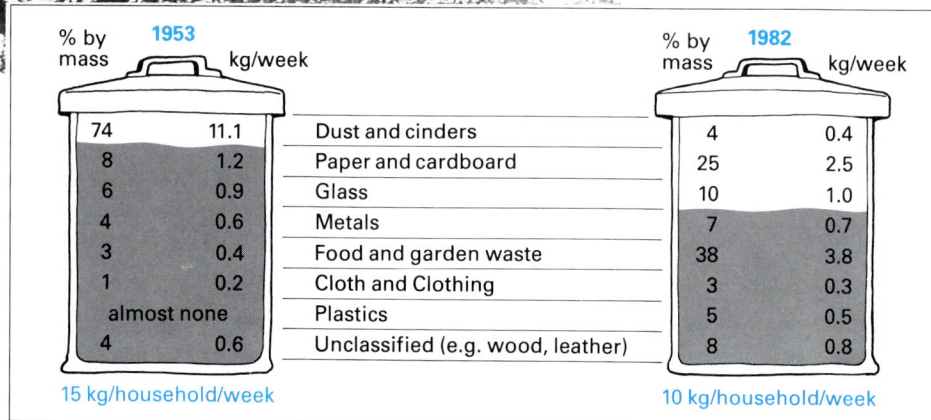

% by mass 1953	kg/week		% by mass 1982	kg/week
74	11.1	Dust and cinders	4	0.4
8	1.2	Paper and cardboard	25	2.5
6	0.9	Glass	10	1.0
4	0.6	Metals	7	0.7
3	0.4	Food and garden waste	38	3.8
1	0.2	Cloth and Clothing	3	0.3
almost none		Plastics	5	0.5
4	0.6	Unclassified (e.g. wood, leather)	8	0.8
15 kg/household/week			10 kg/household/week	

▲ Figure 4.3 View from the tower of Longridge Church looking west over the town's HWDC

1 Explain why the waste produced by groups of people like the Aborigines (see Unit 3.1) is unlikely to present serious environmental problems. Include the word 'biodegradable' in your answer, and show that you understand what it means.

2 Imagine that you live in one of the ports visited by the captain of the tug towing the barge in Figure 4.1.
a Would you recommend acceptance or rejection of the offer described in the text?
b Give reasons for your decision, remembering that acceptance is likely to lead to similar offers in the future.

3 Describe and explain any differences you can see between the contents of the two refuse bins in Figure 4.2.

A dump on the doorstep

Britain's domestic rubbish tips are now called 'Household Waste Disposal Centres' (HWDCs, for short). Their new name is a little more subtle, but they still make very unwelcome neighbours. The HWDC shown in Figure 4.3 is at Longridge, a mid-Lancashire country town of about 7 000 people. Although located in a beautiful lowland farming area, the town itself has few noteworthy buildings. One of these is the sturdy stone-built church at its south-eastern corner. You may therefore be surprised to learn that the town's 'tip' is immediately to the west of it! In all fairness, the site had already been spoiled by three quarries which were very active in the late nineteenth century. These provided the stone to build many of the town's terraced houses, and one reason for granting planning permission for the tip was so that the unsightly quarries might eventually be filled in, levelled, and then put to a different use.

4 a At which times of the year are HWDCs likely to be busiest? Give reasons for your answer.
b Why do local residents often complain about HWDCs after a spell of windy weather?
c What measures can be taken to reduce this particular problem?
d What other problems might HWDCs create for the people living near to them?

5 Carry out an investigation of the HWDC nearest to your home or school, then:
a Draw a map to show its location and any land uses in the neighbouring areas.
b Summarise the advantages and disadvantages of your chosen HWDC's location.
c Explain what measures have been taken by the operators of this HWDC to reduce the problems you noted down in answer to Questions 4 b and d.

▶ **Figure 4.5** *Vulcanus II* – the waste burning ship

▼ **Figure 4.4**

4.2 Hazardous waste

Factory waste has also changed a good deal during the present century. Some of our modern processes are very complicated and make some remarkable things. Unfortunately they also create some very unpleasant forms of waste which are expensive to dispose of safely. Some companies have taken the easy way out and allowed them to pollute the environ-

ment; they have used the biosphere as their own personal **sink** – a place to dispose of unwanted matter quickly and cheaply, without worrying too much about what happens to it afterwards. Others pollute the environment unwittingly, but their accidents can create just as much pollution.

Most of this dangerous industrial waste is taken to **landfill** sites which are also used for disposing of ordinary domestic rubbish. They are adapted by digging deep trenches at intervals across the site (Figure 4.4), and quantities of the harmful waste pumped into them at safe intervals.

The noxious waste then seeps slowly through layers of refuse, giving the natural bacteria within them time to render it harmless. Cadmium and lead, both by-products of electrical battery manufacture, are often disposed of in this way. Because they are so highly toxic (dangerous to health), they can only be taken to sites which are specially licensed by local councils. These materials take much longer than the two years which ordinary household refuse needs to rot down naturally. This allows them to infiltrate much deeper within the underlying rocks and eventually pollute nearby streams, lakes and possibly reservoirs. Soil and water samples are taken regularly from around the controlled sites and then laboratory tested for signs of pollution.

Legend

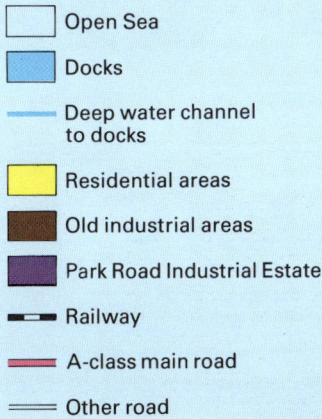

- Open Sea
- Docks
- Deep water channel to docks
- Residential areas
- Old industrial areas
- Park Road Industrial Estate
- Railway
- A-class main road
- Other road
- **T** Town hall
- **B** Site of British Cellophane's factory

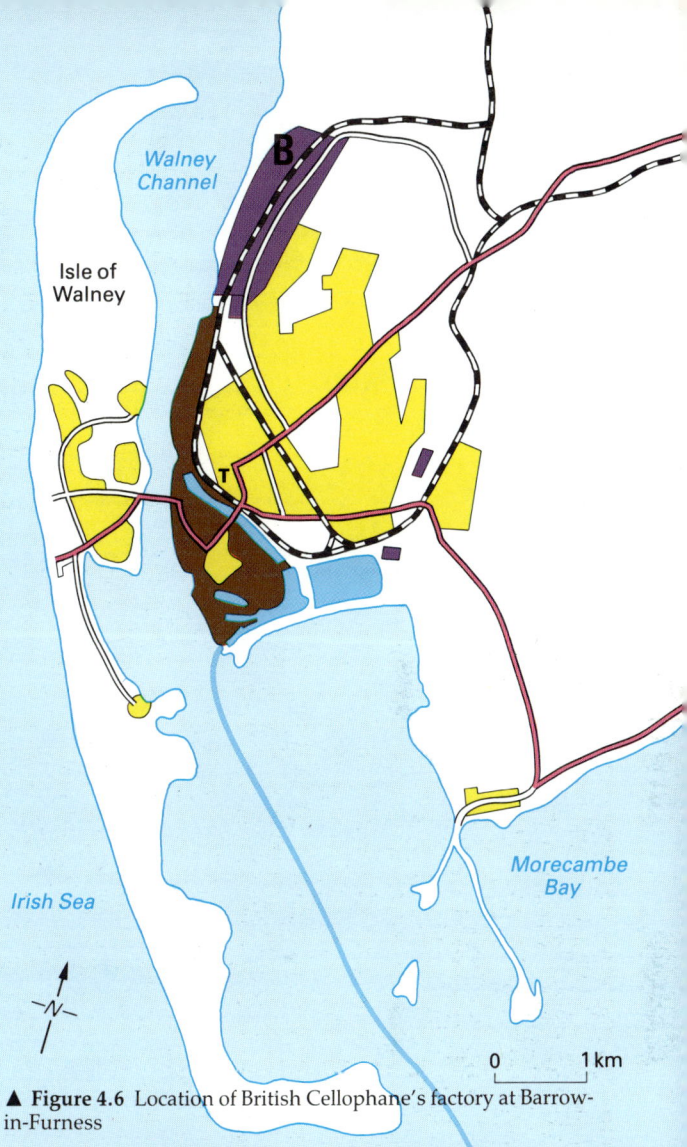

▲ **Figure 4.6** Location of British Cellophane's factory at Barrow-in-Furness

Another possible 'solution' is to use waste-burning ships such as *Vulcanus II* (Figure 4.5). She has special boilers which can burn 300 tonnes of highly toxic industrial waste a day. Waste-burning must not take place within 80 km of the nearest coast, but many environmentalists are still worried by this disposal method and the ship was disabled by members of Greenpeace in 1987.

1 a Name two highly toxic metals which require special disposal facilities.
b Which industry produces these two metals as waste materials?
c What special arrangements are necessary before ordinary landfill sites can be used for the disposal of toxic substances? (Mention arrangements both within and outside the sites).
d Find out what arrangements exist in your local area for the disposal of toxic waste, and whether there are any firms which specialise in rendering it safe.

2 a Write down at least five facts about *Vulcanus II* (e.g. her appearance and operations).
b Write down your own considered opinions about this method of toxic waste disposal.

Leaks of toxic waste usually make the headlines. The following article describes a small but worrying leak at Barrow-in-Furness, in Cumbria.

'Grassland near one of Britain's most important nature reserves has been polluted by chemicals from British Cellophane's Park Road factory in Barrow.

The leaks are into part of Sandscale Haws National Trust Reserve, home to the endangered natterjack toad and several orchids. The firm denied knowledge of chemical leaks.

The leakage was spotted last week by National Trust warden Peter Carty, a qualified biologist. There were two leaks, he said, "one caustic soda and the second a mixture of acetic acid and acetone".

Contacted by the Evening Mail, British Cellophane's works manager Mr. David Smith expressed surprise. "The National Trust have been talking to us about some water seepage, but I knew nothing of any caustic soda leaks, and we do not use acetone. We talk to the National Trust all the time and we are not aware of any problem", he said.

Peter Carty said he had been in touch with British Cellophane – with a chemist who confirmed what the chemicals were. "I was told the acetone leak was caused by a 'blocked-up' drain". Mr. Carty was told that it was not known how long it would be before the problem could be dealt with but the leaks stopped the day after the Evening Mail spoke to the firm.'
(From: *North-West Evening Mail*, 5th May, 1987)

▲ **Figure 4.7** The spillage from British Cellophane's plant at Barrow-in-Furness

▲ **Figure 4.8** Chernobyl's nuclear power station after the disaster of 1976

3 These questions are based on the newspaper article.

a Suggest reasons why British Cellophane decided to build their Barrow Factory on the Park Road Industrial Estate to the north of the town's main built-up area.

b What evidence is there that a leak definitely took place?

c How did the National Trust become involved in the affair?

d What was the company's official reaction to the alleged leak?

e Which version of the story (the company's or the warden's) are you inclined to believe?

f Give reasons for your choice in **e**.

4 (Possibly after class discussion) summarise all the reasons which people might have for:

a reporting leakages of toxic waste.

b deciding it might be better not to report a leak like the one described in the newspaper article.

Nuclear waste

Nuclear power stations and the waste they produce create special difficulties. This is because the **radiation** emitted from disintegrating nuclear particles is highly dangerous to living tissue and can trigger off cancers and other serious medical problems. These rays are able to pass through all but the densest materials (e.g. lead) and so are very hard to contain.

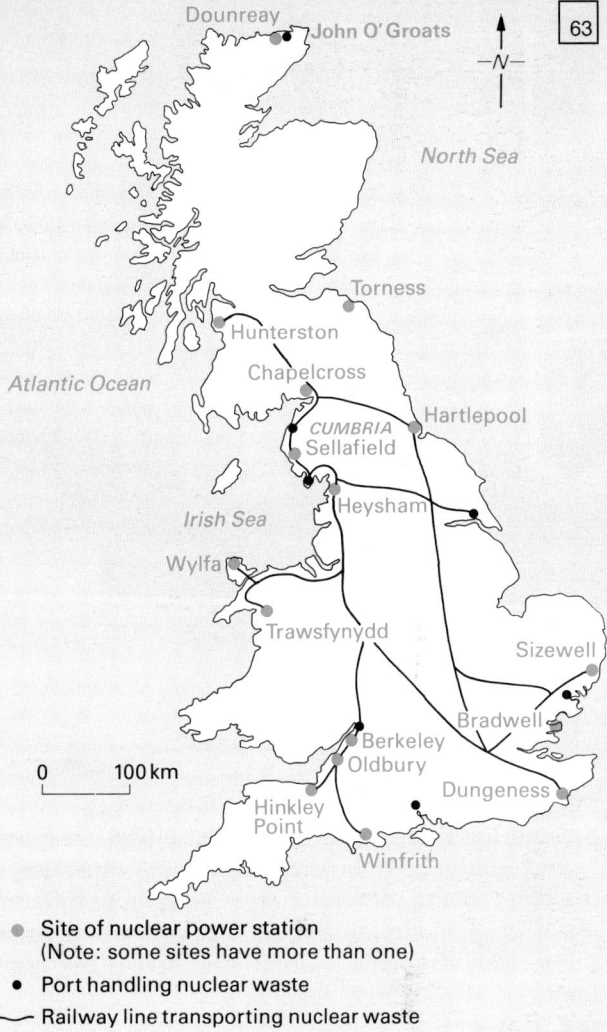

▲ **Figure 4.9** The British nuclear power industry

Site of nuclear power station
(Note: some sites have more than one)

Port handling nuclear waste

Railway line transporting nuclear waste

Escaping radioactive particles are scattered in a number of ways. They may be carried down-wind as 'dust' and/or contaminated raindrops. After being deposited on the surface they very quickly affect food chains and ecosystems, being absorbed by all forms of plant and animal life. Contaminated areas may be unfit to live in for hundreds of years, but the long-term effects of leakages are only just becoming clear as experts monitor the aftermath of the Chernobyl reactor disaster of April, 1986 (Figure 4.8).

High-level waste from our own reactors (Figure 4.9) is taken by rail to Sellafield, on the Cumbrian coast north of Barrow-in Furness. There it is processed and then stored in double-walled stainless steel containers. These are then encased in several metres of concrete. There have been several leaks of radioactive waste from the Sellafield plant, but never from one of these special containers! Sellafield has only a limited amount of space for storage of this type, and eventually additional sites will have to be found.

5 **a** What are the main problems associated with the use of nuclear power?
b What *kinds* of areas are likely to be most affected by leakages of radioactive material?

6 Suggest the possible *advantages* of dumping high-level nuclear waste:
a deep under the ground at John O'Groats (see Figure 4.9).
b in disused coal workings under the seabed off the Cumbrian coast.

7 What are the possible *disadvantages* of dumping *low-level* nuclear waste at these two places on the Ordnance Survey map extract on page 144:
a site A at G.R. 511329?
b site B at G.R. 461268?

▼ **Figure 4.11** The London smog of December 1952

4.3 Local air pollution

Most of us are not aware of pollution in the air we breathe; it is there all the time and its effects are usually very gradual. We become much more conscious of it when moving into other areas with quite different levels of air pollution (Figure 4.10), or when something really dramatic happens and makes the headlines.

Smog

The scene in Figure 4.11 was all too common in British cities until the mid-1950s. The eerie darkness of the picture was cause by **smog**, an unpleasant mixture of smoke and fog. Some of London's worst smogs were so thick that they became known as 'pea-soupers'. It was quite usual for visibility to be reduced to only four metres, and for even the most experienced taxi drivers to get completely lost.

The worst London smog took place early in December, 1952. The first few days of the month had been unusually mild and calm, due to an **anticyclone** of high pressure which 'sat' over the British Isles. On the 6th, the temperature suddenly dropped several degrees to well below freezing. The moisture in the air condensed into thick fog and millions of Londoners lit their coal fires. The chimney smoke combined with the fog which by nightfall had turned completely black. Many people contracted acute bronchitis that month and some already suffering from a weak heart couldn't stand up to the constant coughing and retch-ing caused by the foul air, and died. Over 4 000 sudden deaths were reported in London as a result of that smog.

In 1956, shocked by what had happened, the British government passed the first of a series of Clean Air Acts. These created smokeless zones in most urban areas; in future, houses would have to burn smoke-less fuel and factories drastically reduce their emis-sions of smoke. The results of these acts can – quite literally – be seen today. Air pollution generally is still a matter for concern, but at least the quanities of smoke and dirt above our towns and cities are much lower than they used to be.

▲ **Figure 4.13** Los Angeles is notorious for its petro-chemical smogs

Petro-chemical smog

This type of smog also occurs in large cities and is highly dangerous to all forms of life. It is especially serious in Los Angeles, on the Californian coast of the United States, because conditions there are ideal for it to form (Figure 4.12). Normally air becomes cooler with increasing height. But where there is a **temperature inversion** the opposite happens, and a city's polluted air cannot escape into the upper atmosphere where it would disperse and become harmless.

The second vital ingredient, strong sunlight, acts on the trapped vehicle exhaust fumes and factory emissions to produce a grey-green haze. This creates breathing difficulties, causes vomitting and makes people lethargic (feel much lazier than usual); their eyes sting and water a good deal to wash the obnoxious cocktail out. Schools cancel games lessons, and crops and animals on nearby farms suffer lasting damage.

▼ **Figure 4.12** Temperature inversion over Los Angeles. Normally, cold winds from mountains to the east, north and south pass well above the city and this allows its polluted air to rise clear of the ground

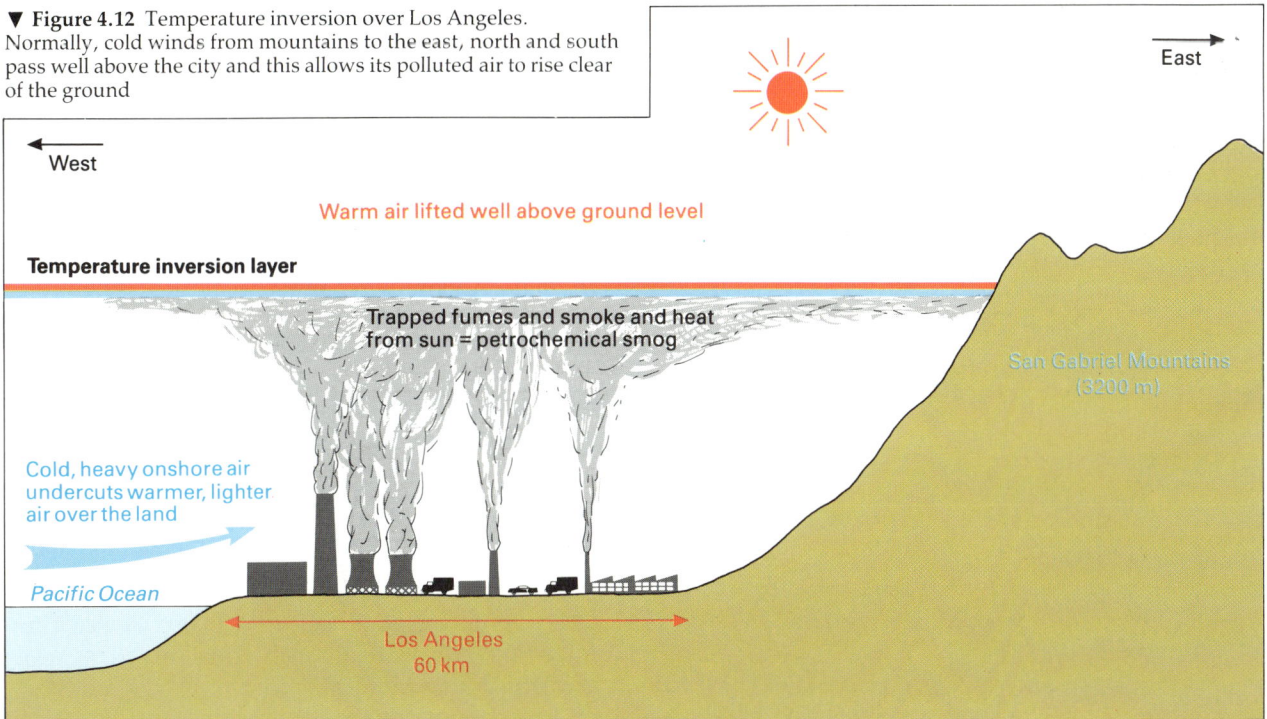

East

West

Warm air lifted well above ground level

Temperature inversion layer

Trapped fumes and smoke and heat from sun = petrochemical smog

San Gabriel Mountains (3200 m)

Cold, heavy onshore air undercuts warmer, lighter air over the land

Pacific Ocean

Los Angeles 60 km

What has been done to reduce these problems by cities such as Los Angeles which are almost completely surrounded by mountains and 'enjoy' a hot, sunny climate? Most issue Petro-chemical Smog Alert Warnings. These are graded according to the predicted levels of pollution and the worst affected cities have issued as many as one hundred Grade 1 warnings in a bad year. They are broadcast by local TV and radio stations as soon as strong temperature inversions seem likely to form.

These measures are beginning to take effect. Although the number of petrol-driven vehicles in Britain continues to rise, the quantity of lead they injected into the atmosphere in 1985 was 10% down on the previous year. Using unleaded petrol is also helpful because lead is one of the chief causes of brain damage in young children.

Car engines also produce carbon monoxide, nitrogen oxides and a wide range of dangerous substances called hydrocarbons. Each has its own particular

▲ **Figure 4.14** Exhaust fumes and driving don't mix!

damaging effect on animals and plants. For example, carbon monoxide reduces the amount of oxygen in the blood. This means that the heart has to work much harder to circulate enough oxygen to the body. It may become so strained trying to do this that a heart attack is the result. Being trapped in dense, slow-moving traffic makes travellers feel drowsy and lose concentration.

▼ **Figure 4.15** Air pollution danger areas' in Britain

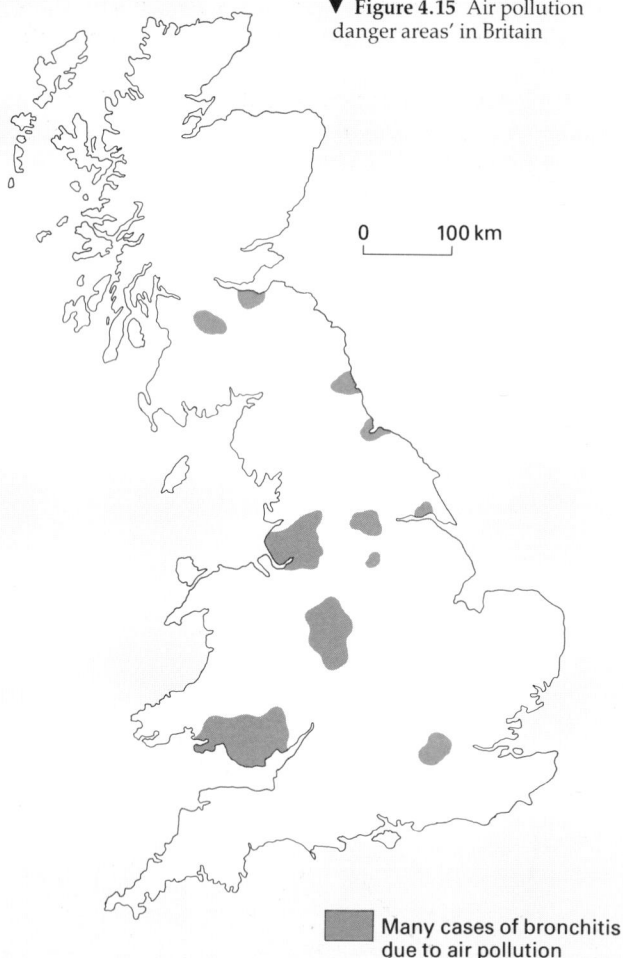

0   100 km

Many cases of bronchitis due to air pollution

1 **a** What is the term 'smog' short for?
b State when, where and why Britain's worst smog took place.
c Describe the immediate effects of this smog and the problems caused by it. Try to add your own ideas to the information given in the text.
d What were the more lasting effects of this particular smog?

2 **a** Copy Figure 4.15.
b Describe how the pattern shown by your map compares with atlas map distributions of Britain's:
i coalfields
ii densely populated areas
iii mountainous regions.

3 **a** What do you understand by the terms 'petro-chemical smog' and 'temperature inversion'?
b Describe the link which exists between them.

4 **a** Explain why temperature inversion might be described as 'unusual'.
b Describe carefully how temperature inversions occur, basing your answer on Figure 4.12.

5 Describe and explain the most likely views of the following groups of people living in Los Angeles towards petro-chemical smog:
doctors   employers   parents

4.4 Acid rain

Most people have heard the term **acid rain** and know that it has something to do with air pollution, dead trees and lifeless lakes. The term was first used as long ago as 1872 – by Britain's first Air Pollution Inspector. Robert Angus had noticed traces of sulphuric acid in the air around Manchester and believed they were linked in some way with the industry of that area.

A Swedish professor revived the term and the idea in the 1950s, but nobody took much notice until 1967 when another Swede – a soil scientist called Svante Oden – voiced concern at the increasing environmental damage in the southern part of his country. He too linked acidity in the air with densely populated and heavily industrialised regions. Figure 4.16 shows why he believed Britain to be mostly to blame.

Here are some of the problems which have been associated with acid rain:

Millions of trees have died or been seriously damaged. In the Black Forest area of West Germany over 50% of all trees were reported to be unhealthy in 1986, compared with only 8% four years earlier. Parts exposed to direct sunlight are affected the most; upper surfaces turn yellow and side branches hang limply from the trunk (Figure 4.17). Coniferous trees shed their pine needles faster than they would normally.

Thousands of fresh-water lakes no longer support any fish life. In southern Sweden over 20 000 lakes are now affected in this way. Salmon and trout are particularly sensitive to pollution, and were the first to disappear.

Many species of lichen cannot cope with the increasing acidity, while others which thrive on it have replaced them.

Bird's eggs have become so brittle that their shells break under the mother's weight.

Avalanches now kill more than 20 people every year in Switzerland. This figure is rising as the number of avalanches increases. Vital road and railway routes through the Alps are becoming much more dangerous to use.

Buildings and statues are being eaten away by acidity in the air (Figure 4.18). Even modern concrete buildings are affected, and some may not survive half their intended life-span.

Domestic water supplies carried in metal piping are far more contaminated than they used to be.

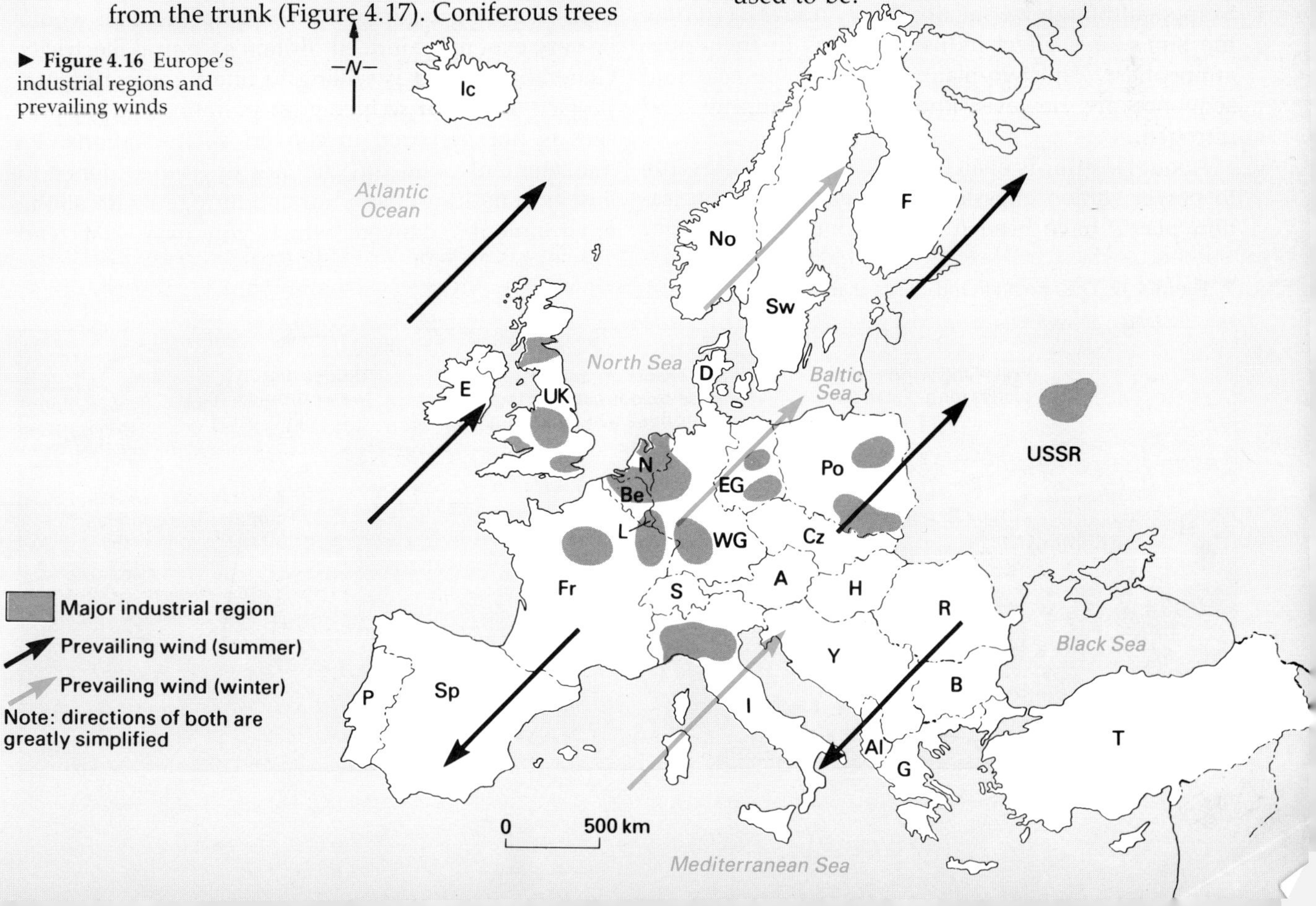

▶ Figure 4.16 Europe's industrial regions and prevailing winds

■ Major industrial region

➤ Prevailing wind (summer)

➤ Prevailing wind (winter)

Note: directions of both are greatly simplified

0   500 km

▶ **Figure 4.17** The Black Forest in West Germany has suffered great damage due to acid rain

▼ **Figure 4.18** Polluted air is the main reason for the serious erosion of this statue on St Paul's Cathedral, London

Figure 4.19 shows how we believe acid rain is formed, although we still don't fully understand how the sun's rays affect industrial gases in the upper atmosphere. The two major inputs in the acid rain sequence are however known to be sulphur and nitrogen.

About two-thirds of all the sulphur in the air is due to power station emissions. Flue-gas de-sulphurisation plants have been fitted to some of our larger stations and are proving a success (the amount of sulphur dioxide emitted throughout Britain fell by 40% during the 1970s and early 1980s). Coal-fired power stations also produce about one-third of all the nitrogen oxide in our air. These emissions are more difficult and certainly more expensive to control, but similar experiments are being carried out at selected power stations.

So far, only the largest stations have been fitted with cleansing equipment. To equip them all would be very expensive indeed. Britain's Central Electricity Generating Board is willing to finance experimental projects aimed at reducing air pollution, but at present is not prepared to convert all its stations. Its management point out the lack of firm evidence to link its emissions of sulphur and nitrogen with all the environmental damage which you have just read

▼ **Figure 4.19** The formation and effects of acid rain

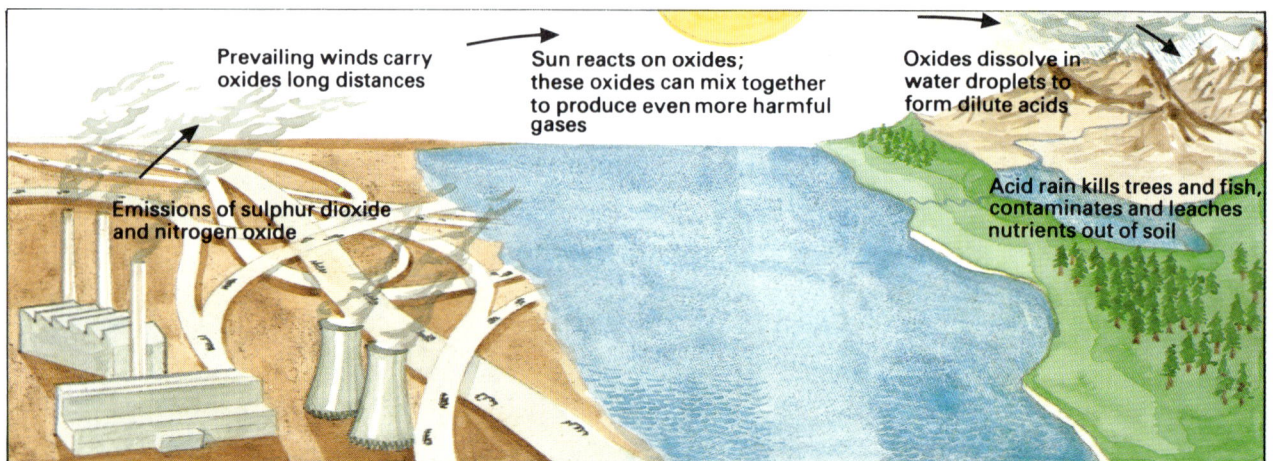

Prevailing winds carry oxides long distances

Sun reacts on oxides; these oxides can mix together to produce even more harmful gases

Oxides dissolve in water droplets to form dilute acids

Emissions of sulphur dioxide and nitrogen oxide

Acid rain kills trees and fish, contaminates and leaches nutrients out of soil about. Here are two of the CEGB's chief arguments for this viewpoint:

Why are some identical, neighbouring lakes in Sweden affected by acidity while others are not? Surely, if acid rain were the cause, lakes so close together would be affected in just the same way? New research suggests that the nature of the topsoil and the underlying rock – and possibly variations in climate too – could explain the puzzle. The CEGB refuses to burden its customers with higher electricity charges (to pay for flue cleansing equipment in all its power stations) just because some lakes in Sweden have granite rather than limestone beneath them, or because the Germans have enjoyed a much hotter summer than usual!

Careful investigations in West Germany reveal that two-thirds of that country's nitrogen oxide pollution comes from vehicle exhausts. This means that not more than one-third of this form of pollution can be blamed on electricity generation.

The CEGB stresses evidence such as this because it helps it to withstand increasing pressure from environmentally active groups such as Greenpeace. The Swedes are not at all convinced by the CEGB's case. They are the ones who have to pay for the lime-spraying of 'dead' lakes to neutralise their excess acidity (Figure 4.20). They feel that Britain and the other offending industrial nations have a moral duty to take all possible steps to reduce atmospheric pollution over Scandinavia. They also say it is only a matter of time before evidence is produced to link acid rain with poor health and possibly higher death rates in humans. They believe the British public would agree to pay that bit extra on their electricity bills to combat the problems described in this unit.

Clearly, a compromise is needed if any progress is to be made. Individual governments have been taking selective action for some time. Acid rain has been a major political issue in West Germany for about 10 years, and even prompted the creation of a new group – the Green Party. The 'Greens' support all forms of environmental protection, and particularly those which could aid the 'waldsterben' (dying forests).

1 a Name four European countries which are likely to be blamed for the 'acid rain problem'.
b Name those European countries which suffer greatly from acid rain, and state what their particular problems are.

2 Explain why there is now some doubt about whether acid rain can be blamed for all the problems you have just described.

3 What action has been taken by the following countries to overcome problems associated with acid rain?
a Britain.
b Sweden.
c West Germany.

4 For both of the following characters:
a state whether they are likely to blame Britain for the acid rain problems of Western Europe;
b give reasons for your answer to a.
The Chairman of the CEGB.
A West German professor who has carried out a careful study of nitrogen oxide sources.

5 Imagine that the Board of Directors of the CEGB is considering installing sulphur and nitrogen filtrating equipment in *all* its power stations. It estimates that this will increase every British householder's electricity bills by 10% for approximately five years. The Board has said it will not approve such a plan without first consulting all its customers.
a Would you vote for or against the proposed plan?
b Give your own personal reasons for making this decision.

▼ **Figure 4.20** Spraying lime on a Swedish Lake. Although expensive, this quickly reduces the acidity of the water and encourages fish to return

4.5 Locating thermal power stations

Thermal power stations burn coal and oil to raise the steam needed to drive their turbines and generators. We now know that they represent a very serious air pollution problem. This and the next unit explain, with the help of two case studies, that large power stations of this type have to be located with great care if they are to operate efficiently. Their main **location factors** are listed below.

1 Firm ground on which to build.

2 A large area of land, especially for coal-fired power stations which need generous storage areas.

3 Good communications to transport their fuel. Coal is usually carried by train or barge; oil by pipeline or coastal tanker.

4 Nearness to large quantities of water. This acts as the coolant which condenses the steam from the turbines back into water. This explains why many thermal power stations are built on river banks.

5 Ideally, some distance away from densely populated areas so as to reduce the chance of them being polluted by the stations' emissions.

6 Relative nearness to the large built-up areas which use their electricity. This used to be very important before the introduction of the national grid and the development of cables which can carry electricity over long distances without much power-loss.

Figures 4.21 and 4.22 show the location of the main coal and oil-fired power stations in England and Wales as well as their chief sources of fuel. The questions which follow are based on these two maps and the Ordnance Survey map extract of the area on the south side of Nottingham (p. 144).

1 a Explain what the term 'location factor' means.
 b Copy down the six thermal power station location factors listed above.
 c Note down any additional location factors which you feel are important.

2 a Draw the information for coal-fired power stations in Figure 4.21 and then either shade in the coalfield areas in Figure 4.22 on the same map or put this information on a tracing overlay. This should be glued down at only one edge so that the two maps can be viewed together or separately.
 b With the help of an atlas, label the coalfields with their correct names, which are:
Cumberland Coalfield (Hint: Cumberland is now in the county of Cumbria)

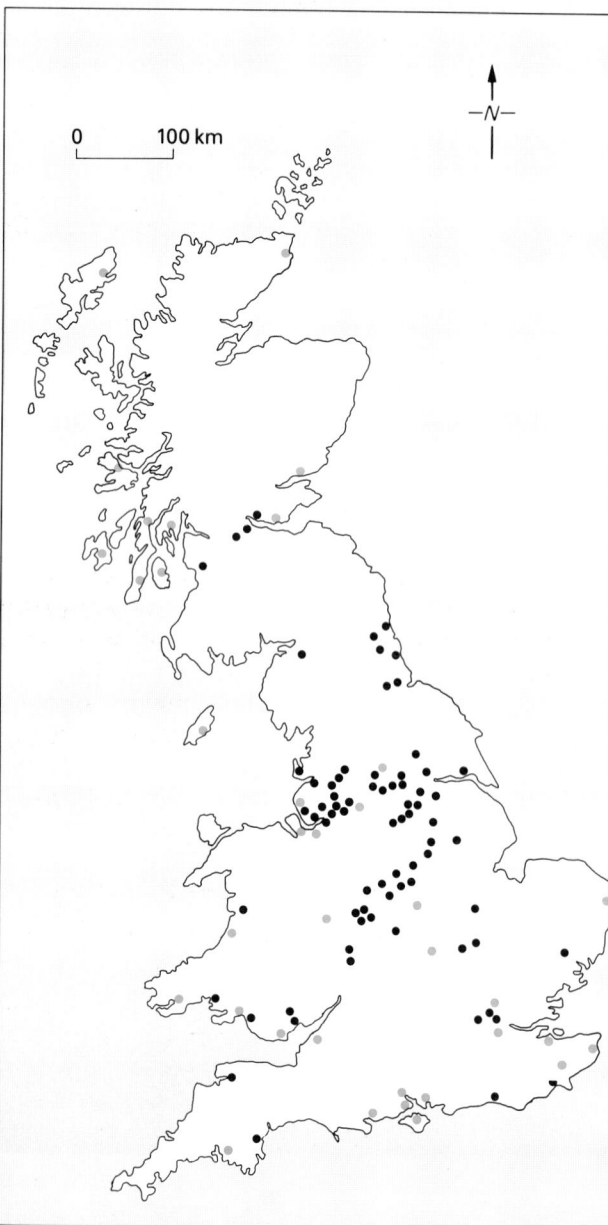

Figure 4.21 Britain's coal and oil fired power stations

• Coal–fired power stations
○ Oil–fired power stations

Durham Coalfield

South Wales Coalfield

Kent Coalfield

Staffordshire Coalfield

Lancashire Coalfield

Warwickshire Coalfield

North Wales Coalfield

Yorkshire, Nottinghamshire and Derbyshire Coalfield.

c Also use the atlas to name all the rivers shown in your maps.

d Repeat a for the oil-fired power stations (in Figure 4.21) and the oil-related developments in Figure 4.22.

3 For each group of thermal power stations:

a describe the general distribution (location pattern) of its power stations.

b suggest reasons for the pattern you have just described.

4 After class discussion, note down the relative advantages of coastal tankers and pipelines as a means of supplying power stations with fuel.

5 Answer the following questions about Ratcliffe-on-Soar coal-fired power station south of Nottingham shown on the map extract on page 144. This station takes its name from the small river which flows to the west of it and is a tributary of the River Trent further north.

a By what form of transport will the station be supplied with coal?

b How will most of the power station staff travel to and from work each day?

c How many cooling towers does the station have?

d What is their approximate width (in metres)?

e Is the power station's stockpile of coal most likely to be in grid reference position 496300, 502296 or 507301?

f Give reasons for your answer to e.

g In which 6-figure grid reference position are the station's own three reservoirs?

h How wide is the whole power station site from west to east (to the nearest 100m)?

i How can you tell that this power provides electricity for a large area?

j From which directions (north and east or south and west) is the power station best shielded from view by woods and small clumps of trees?

k Is the station built on very flat land? If so, how can you tell?

l Do the emissions from Ratcliffe-on-Soar power station blow across or by-pass the southern part of Nottingham when the winds are blowing from their usual, south-westerly direction?

m How high would the station's chimneys have to be for their emssions to clear the ridge of higher land to the north-east of them?

(Hint: assume that the emissions do not change height after leaving the chimney tops.)

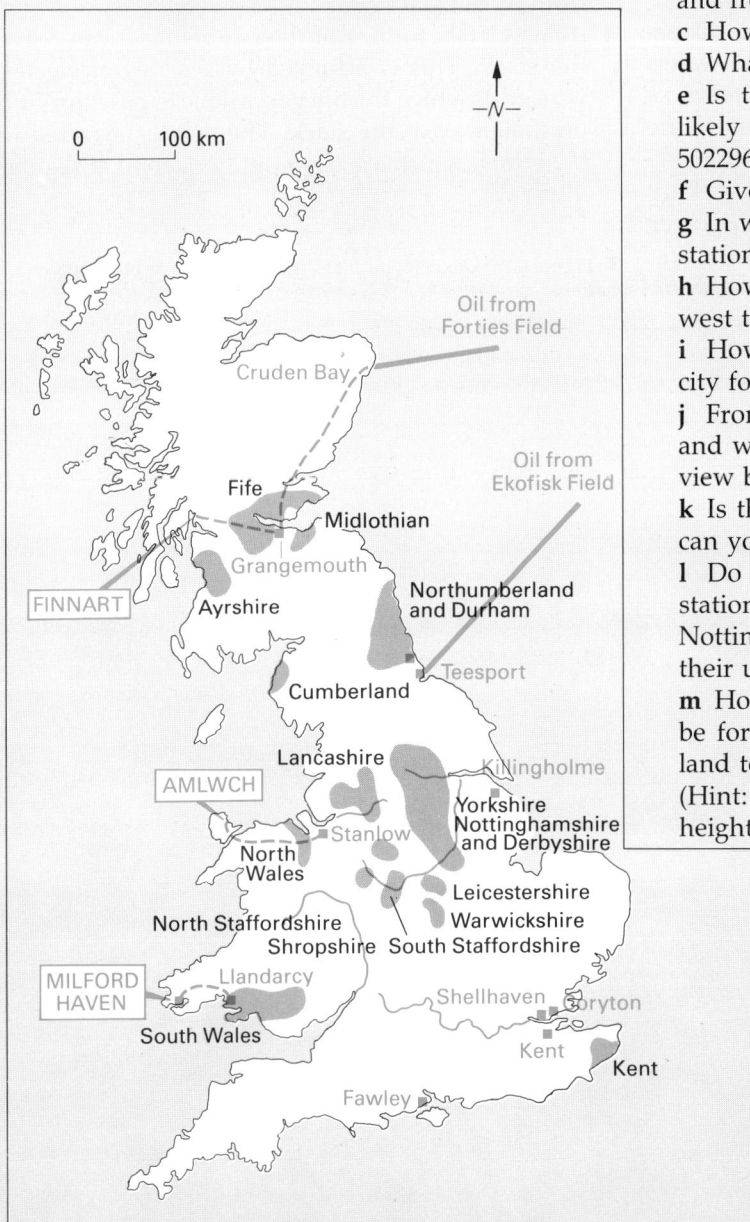

◀ **Figure 4.22** Location factors for Britain's coal and oil-fired power stations

- Coalfield
- River
- Deep–water oil terminal
- Oil refinery(ies)
- Oil pipeline (offshore)
- Oil pipeline (underground)

4.6 Drax: A 'clean' power station

Drax is one of Britain's largest and most modern thermal power stations. It has three giant generators which at full power can meet all the electricity demands of two million people. Drax burns 5 000 000 tonnes of locally mined coal every year. This is delivered from the Selby area (see Unit 2.6) by freight trains operating on a merry-go-round basis, with the same trains constantly running between the coalfield and the power station.

In many ways, Drax's appearance is typical of the thermal power stations built in Britain since the early 1960s (Figure 4.23). It has the usual massive boiler-house in which the coal is burned to raise steam for the turbines, as well as a cluster of cooling towers where the hot steam is condensed back into water. Much of the 200 ha site is taken up by coal reserves and overhead conveyor belts which link them to the boiler-house.

The very tall chimney is easily the most striking feature of the latest generation of thermal power stations. The work force call it the 'stack' and the one at Drax is 250m (750 feet) high. Tall stacks were adopted by the Central Electricity Generating Board (CEGB) because they help the wind to carry emissions well away from the surrounding area. Figure 4.24 shows that this is generally true, and question **3** tests your understanding of the principles involved. A night-time advantage of very tall stacks is shown in Figure 4.25.

It is not easy to say whether Drax is a 'clean' power station or not, but the following information will help you to decide this for yourself. Every day, Drax:

- burns 19 000 tonnes of coal.
- has to dispose of 5 500 tonnes of 'heavy' ash produced by its boilers.
- emits 21 tonnes of 'fly-ash' (fine dust and dirt) from its tall stack.
- collects 3 000 tonnes of fly-ash before it can leave the stack. This is achieved by a series of electric wire grids which the hot gases have to pass through on their way to the stack. The dust is attracted to the wires, which are thoroughly cleaned at regular intervals.

▼ **Figure 4.23** Drax is typical of Britain's latest coal-burning power stations

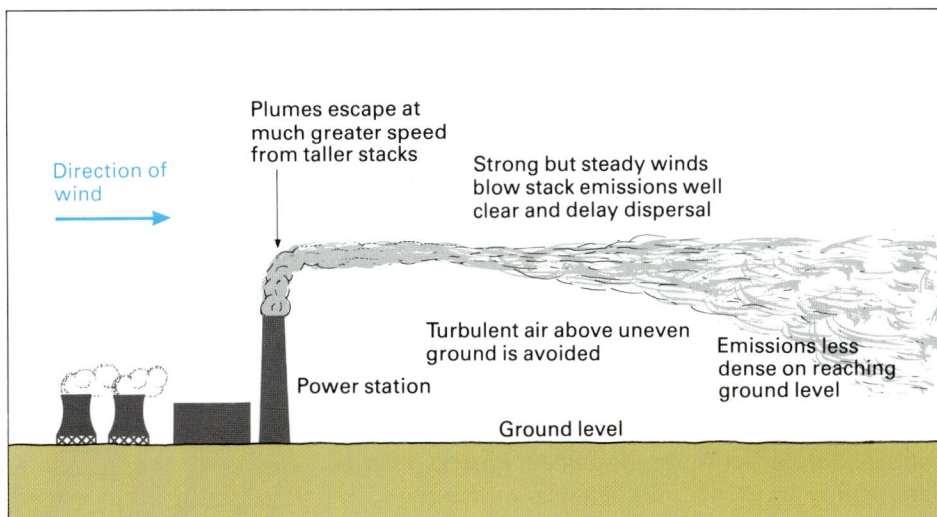

► **Figure 4.24** The effect on emission dispersal of building taller power station stacks

Direction of wind

Plumes escape at much greater speed from taller stacks

Strong but steady winds blow stack emissions well clear and delay dispersal

Turbulent air above uneven ground is avoided

Emissions less dense on reaching ground level

Power station

Ground level

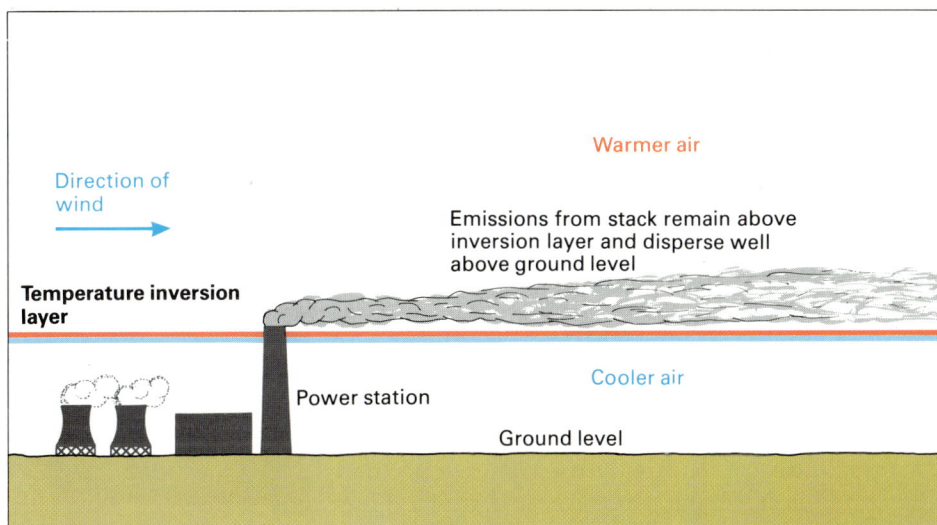

► **Figure 4.25** The effect of an inversion layer on stack emission dispersal

Warmer air

Direction of wind

Emissions from stack remain above inversion layer and disperse well above ground level

Temperature inversion layer

Cooler air

Power station

Ground level

- emits 400 tonnes of sulphur into the air. This is in the form of sulphur dioxide gas, a particularly harmful pollutant whose effects were described in Unit 4.4. It is possible to extract much of the sulphur from the flue gases, but this is very expensive to do.
- uses 5 000 000 litres of water as a coolant. This is returned to the River Ouse – provided its temperature does not exceed 30°C; warmer water would endanger the fish in the river.

1 State how Drax Power Station is well sited in terms of:
   a fuel supply
   b water supply
   c transport
   d land relief
   e density of population in the surrounding area.

2 Design a flow diagram which shows the sequence of operations at Drax Power Station. Figure 4.23 will help you to do this.

3 Describe the effects of increasing the height of power station stacks, and give the reasons for these changes.

4 In which ways do you consider Drax to be:
   a a 'clean' power station?
   b a power station which needs to take greater care over its effects on the natural environment?

4.7 Alternative energy

We have seen that power stations are a major source of air pollution. In fact, electricity may be generated from three types of natural resources:

1 **Fossil fuels,** such as coal, oil and natural gas. They were produced millions of years ago from the remains of dead plants and animals, and this process also took a very long period of time. In other words, we cannot replace any of the fossil fuels we use, and as the total world reserves of all types is only about 500 years, we really ought to be concentrating on other ways of meeting our energy needs. There is another reason too, in addition to the pollution problems described earlier. This is our ability to produce an astonishing range of by-products from fossil fuels, and so it seems very short-sighted to burn such valuable raw materials when they could be saved for manufacture into medicines, soap, man-made fibres and synthetic rubber to name just a few. Perhaps we ought to think of them as fossil *resources* rather than fossil *fuels*.

2 **Renewable resources,** such as wood. These resources can be replaced within a relatively short period of time. For example, fast-growing coniferous trees (e.g. the pine and the spruce) reach maturity in only 30–35 years. Unfortunately:
   • most of the world's wood 'crop' is already required for the construction and manufacturing industries (e.g. furniture and paper making).
   • these industries currently use more wood than the world is planning to replace, and Unit 2.4 has already made the point that large areas of 'virgin' forest are being felled each year.
   • energy demands are now so great that such resources alone cannot possibly meet them fully.

3 **Inexhaustible resources,** such as water, wind and energy from the sun's rays. These pose a dilemma. They are 'free' in the sense that we don't have to mine, grow or refine them, and in global terms they represent a vast reserve of stored energy, *but* they are generally unpredictable, inconvenient and dangerous. The rest of this unit is devoted to some of the most attractive forms of **alternative energy** which have not yet been fully exploited. Hydro-electric power generated from fresh water sources such as rivers and lakes is considered separately in Unit 5.8.

WAVE POWER FOR SCOTTISH ISLE

An experimental shore-based wave power installation is to be built on the Scottish island of Islay. Designed by engineers at Queen's University, Belfast, it will be based on an oscillating water column. If data gathered on the column this winter shows it to be worthwhile then a Wells turbine and generator could be added to produce electricity next year. A low-cost method of construction has been devised, and it is estimated that 1 MW stations based on this concept might achieve generating costs between 3–4.5p/kWh.

The installation is designed to operate in shallow water sites and will be located on the west-facing coast of the island at the end of a natural rock gully.

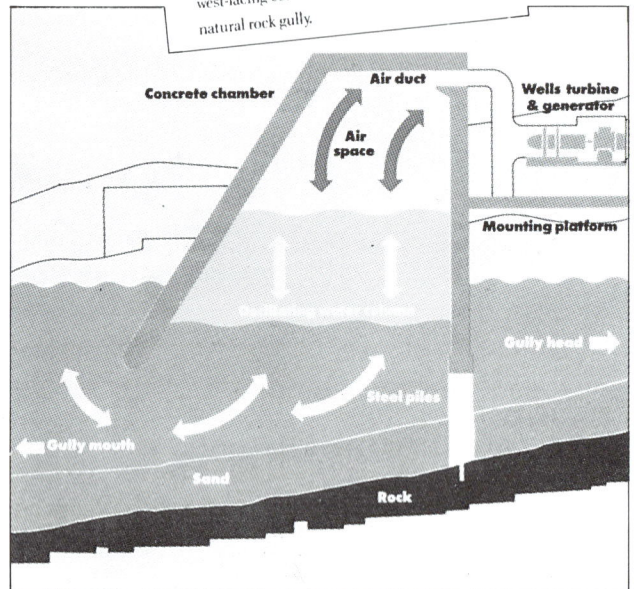

► **Figure 4.26**

What about the natural sources of energy, then – water, wind and sun? Whatever other problems there may be with them, they are never going to run out. The rivers and tides will always be flowing, the winds will blow and the sun will shine. That's why many people see them as the great energy sources of the future.

If only we can harness their boundless energy we can have all the power we could possibly want, for ever. No matter how much we use, these marvellous free sources of energy will always be there to serve us.

There'll be nothing to burn, no pollution of the air, no worries about what we might be doing to the climate. These natural forces must be the perfect answer to all our fuel problems!

So they may be, some time in the future.

The trouble is that we do not yet know how to do these things cheaply or simply enough. We know these things can be done and we know ways of doing them.

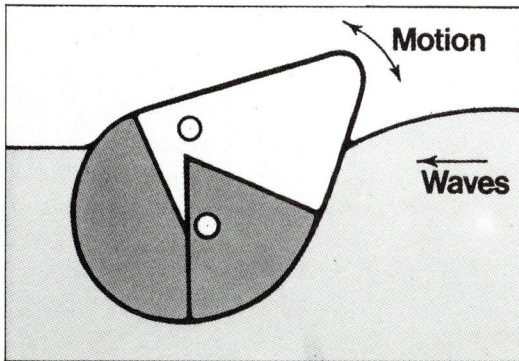

To absorb power efficiently from a wave, a float must have a front surface that moves with the water of the oncoming wave and a back surface that does not disturb the water behind. The cross section shown here is one that meets these requirements well. The float rocks about a central point and has a circular rear section with a front section that is partially circular, but merges into a plane section at about 15 degrees to the vertical in still water.

PROSPECTS FOR UK RENEWABLE ENERGY TECHNOLOGIES

Passive Solar Design	• • • • •	Hydropower:- large scale central generation	• • • • •	**Long shot**
		Hydropower:- small scale (up to 5MW)	• • •	•
Active Solar Heating: - Water	•	Tidal Power	• • •	**Promising but uncertain**
				• • •
Active Solar Heating: - Space	•	Wave Power:- large, open seas (2GW)	•	
Geothermal Aquifers	•			**Economically attractive**
Geothermal Hot Dry Rock	• • •	Wave Power:- small, shore mounted (1MW)	• • •	• • • • •
Wind Power:- on land	• • •			
Wind Power:- offshore	•			

CALL FOR 'WAVE POWER

By Our Parliamentary Staff

THE Government was urged in the Commons yesterday to continue support for research into the use of waves for generating electricity.

Dr DAVID CLARK, from the Opposition Front Bench, said during a debate on alternative sources of energy that it made no sense for an island nation to write off wave power.

MPs on both sides expressed concern after Mr DAVID HUNT, Under-Secretary at the Energy Department, said some technologies, including wave energy, had proved to be uneconomic after fairly extensive research and "field trials."

Pointing out that the department had already spent £17 million on investigating the technical and economic potential of wave energy, Mr HUNT said: "Our policy is to get the best possible value for money from our research and development funds and back the winners."

1 Copy out the table then use the entries listed below to complete its second and third columns.

Type of resource	Description of resource	Examples of resource
Fossil fuels		
Renewable resources		
Inexhaustible resources		

Entries for second column

Can be replaced within a person's lifetime.

Formed millions of years ago; cannot be replaced.

Vast stores of energy, but often difficuilt to obtain.

Entries for third column

Coal
Geothermal heat
Natural gas
Oil
Uranium
Water
Wind
Wood

2 Explain why it is most unlikely that wood will completely replace fossil fuels as the chief source of heat and power.

3 Suggest ways in which inexhaustible resources can be:
   a unpredictable
   b inconvenient
   c dangerous to use.

4 The British government has decided to support wind power, believing it to be the most feasible source of alternative energy in the foreseeable future.
   a State whether you agree with the government's choice or, if not, which alternative source *you* would support.
   b Give detailed reasons for your answer to a. You are expected to make full use of the information in Figure 4.26, not just for the energy source you chose, but also those which you rejected.

5

Using the Hydrosphere

5.1 Introduction: the hydrological cycle

The total amount of 'water' on the Earth's surface never changes. It can however take three different forms:

□ a gas – as water vapour
□ a liquid – as fresh water or 'salty' sea water; also forming mist, fog, clouds and rain
□ a solid – as ice, hail and sleet (snow which has begun to melt).

It can also occupy three different types of location. These are the seas, the land and the atmosphere. All such locations where water is present are known collectively as the **hydrosphere**.

The movement of water between these forms and locations is called the hydrological cycle. Figure 5.1 shows a hydrological cycle which is completely natural, unaffected by human activity.

1 Explain what is meant by the phrase 'water can take three different forms and be in three different types of place.'

2 **a** Draw Figure 5.1.
   b Pair up these key words with their correct meanings. Your copy of Figure 5.1 will help you to do this.

Condensation   Hydrosphere
Evaporation   Precipitation
Infiltration   Run-off
Hydrological cycle   Transpiration

. . . is the changing of water from a gas into a liquid.
. . . is the changing of water from a liquid into a gas.
. . . is the distribution of all forms of water throughout the world.
. . . is the downward movement of water through layers of soil and rock.
. . . is the loss of water from plants.

▼ **Figure 5.1** The hydrological cycle

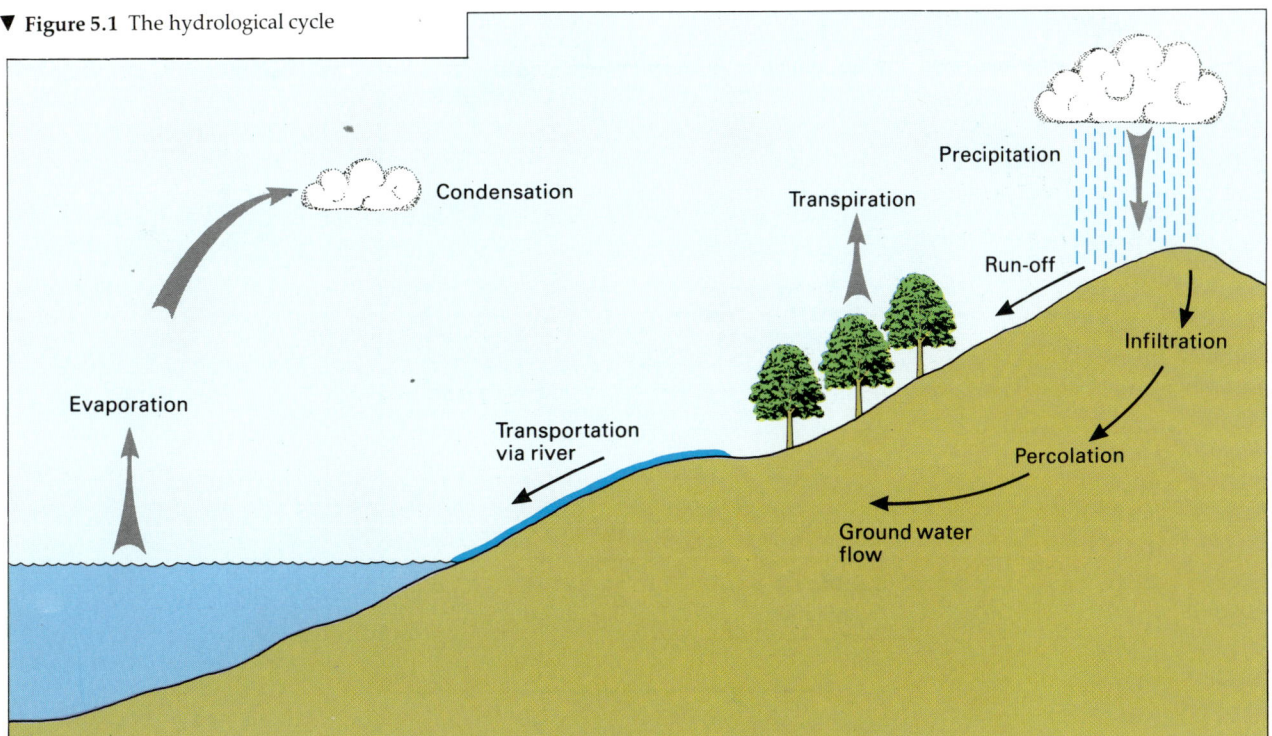

... is the movement of water along a land surface.
... is the movement of water between its different forms and locations.
... is the return of water in its liquid or solid forms from the atmosphere to the Earth's surface.

3 a Draw a simplified flow-diagram which is based on Figure 5.1, colour it, then add a key which identifies the stores and transfers within it.
b Why can this be described as a *closed* system?

4 Explain how *relief* rainfall takes place.

The urban water cycle

Man-made features like roads and buildings can change the natural hydrological cycle in a number of ways. Evaporation, condensation and precipitation still take place; the main differences occur after the rain has fallen on an urban (built-up) area. Much of this rain cannot infiltrate below ground level – the impermeable concrete and tarmac surfaces prevent it from doing so. Figure 5.2 shows that some of this surface water travels through underground pipes instead. These take it to the nearest river, where it rejoins the natural hydrological cycle. Can you suggest why some, but by no means all of the rain follows this route?

Much of the water needed by houses and factories is now taken from local rivers and stored in reservoirs until required. It is then made safe in a water treatment plant. The waste water from the buildings goes underground once again, this time through a network of sewers. They lead to the nearest sewage treatment plant. When cleansed of all harmful bacteria, this water is allowed to rejoin the natural hydrological cycle via rivers or directly into the sea.

5 Draw and complete the skeleton urban hydrological cycle shown below, obtaining suitable entries for it from Figure 5.2 and the text.

6 Suggest how the existence of large built-up areas might affect:
a evaporation rates
b infiltration rates
c transpiration rates.

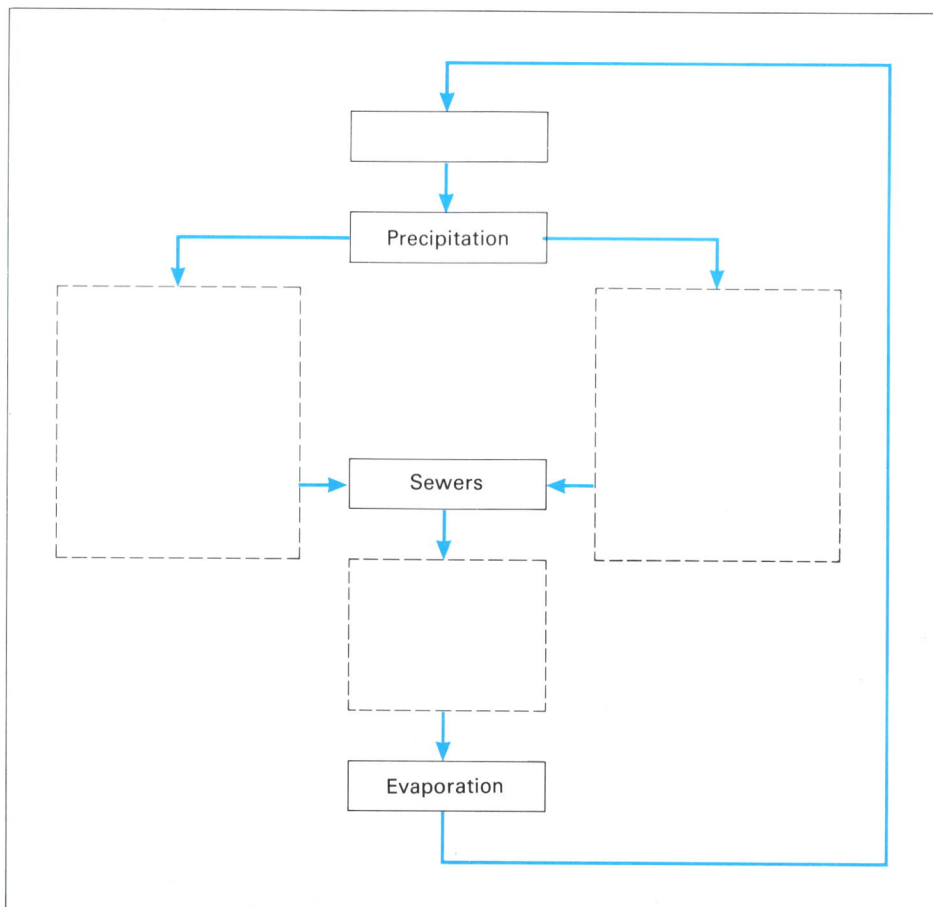

▶ **Figure 5.2** The urban water cycle

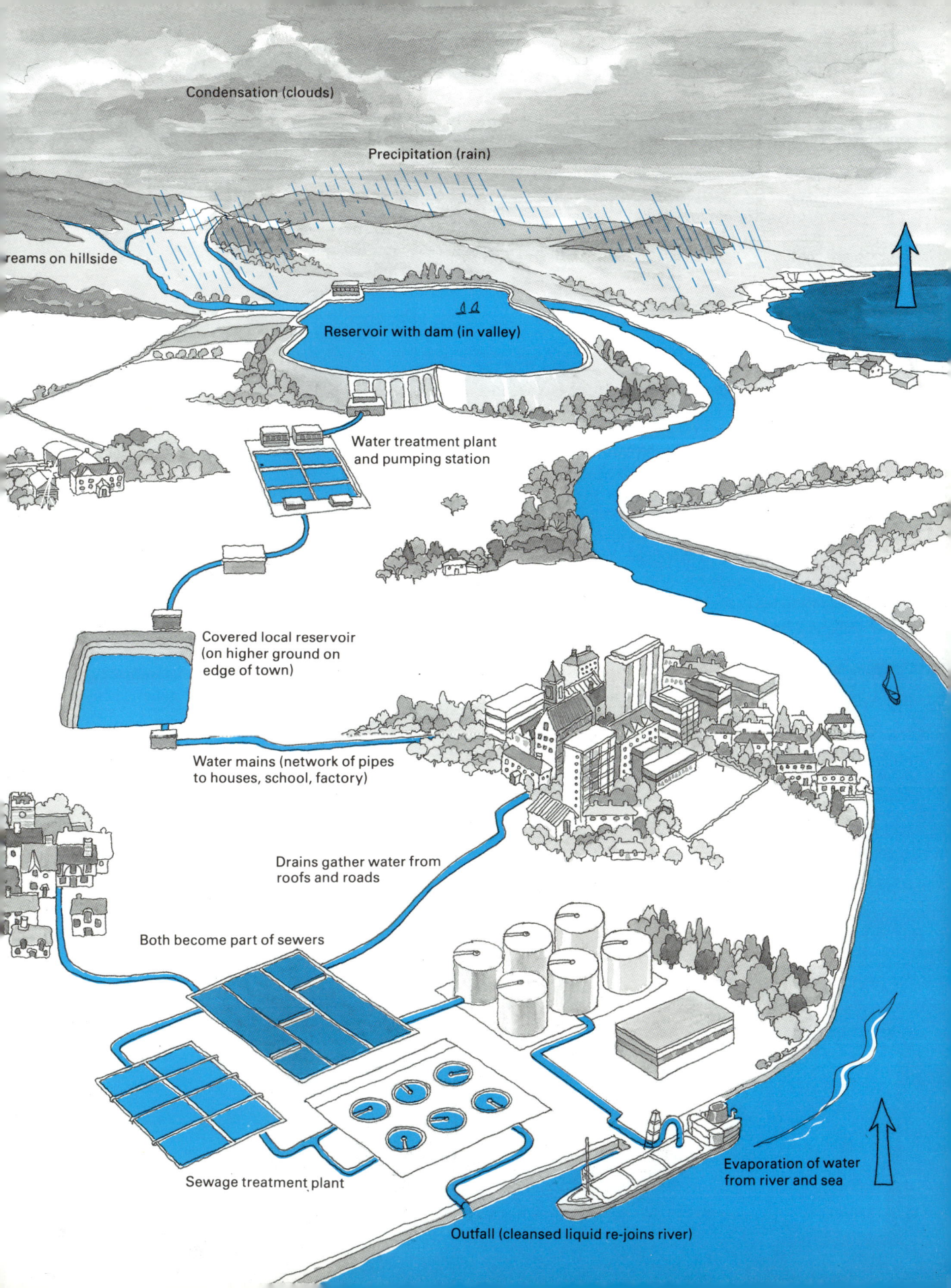

Condensation (clouds)

Precipitation (rain)

reams on hillside

Reservoir with dam (in valley)

Water treatment plant
and pumping station

Covered local reservoir
(on higher ground on
edge of town)

Water mains (network of pipes
to houses, school, factory)

Drains gather water from
roofs and roads

Both become part of sewers

Sewage treatment plant

Outfall (cleansed liquid re-joins river)

Evaporation of water
from river and sea

5.2 Local hydrological study

This study investigates four parts of the hydrological cycle. Your choice of experiments will be decided by the time and equipment available, as well as your particular interests. Each of the experiments should be written up in the usual stages:

Aim or Hypothesis (see page 154 for examples)
Method
Results and Interpretation
Conclusions

Evaporation

This is quite a simple experiment to organise and carry out. All it needs is a large shallow bowl, a ruler, a watch and some water! (See Figure 5.3). The time of day, the duration (e.g. five hours) and the conditions under which the experiment is carried out can be varied as required. You could then investigate the links between evaporation and:

air temperature
wind speed
humidity (the dampness of the air). (A 'wet-and-dry' thermometer is needed to obtain information on humidity.)

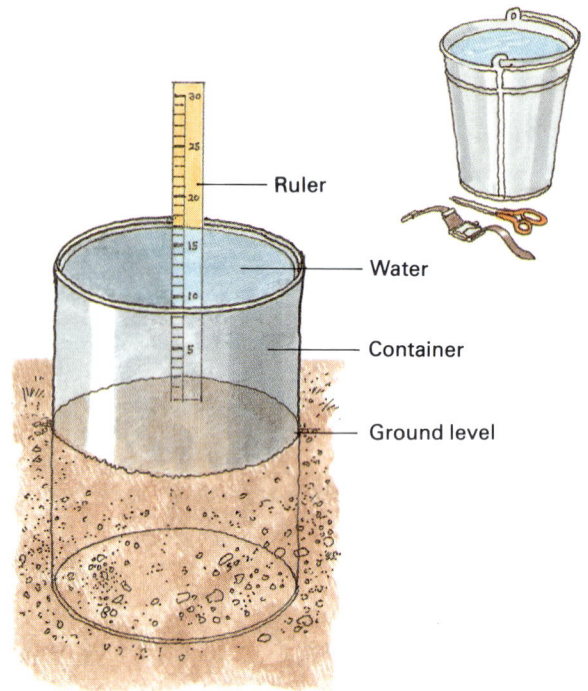

Ruler

Water

Container

Ground level

▲ **Figure 5.4** The equipment used to measure infiltration rates is very basic. A watch, jug and bucket of water are also required

◀ Figure 5.3

Infiltration rate

The speed at which water seeps downwards into the ground is called the infiltration rate. This experiment can also be carried out with very basic equipment (Figure 5.4), but care and patience are needed to produce really useful results. The following hints should prove helpful:

☐ The cylinder should be large and strong (e.g. a metal catering 'tin'), with both ends removed. It's a good idea to beat down any jagged edges!
☐ Select a piece of ground with a type of topsoil you can recognise, then drive the cylinder into it as shown in the diagram.
☐ Place the ruler firmly and vertically inside the cylinder.
☐ Pour water into the cylinder until it reaches a mark on the ruler about 15cm above the soil.
☐ Add extra water at intervals to bring its level back to the same mark, completing a line of the table in Figure 5.5 every time you do this.
☐ Plot the recorded information as a line graph. This will show how the infiltration rate changes before becoming constant. You should work out the 'steady' infiltration rate (in mm per hour), and repeat the whole experiment for different soil types (e.g. sandy, chalk, clay).

▼ **Figure 5.5** Table for recording infiltration experiment results

Time from start of experiment (in mins)	Time taken for water level to fall 5 cm (in seconds)	Infiltration rate (in cm per minute)
0		
1		
2		
3		
4		
5 etc.		

Note 1: *The time intervals in the first column can be increased (e.g. to 5 minutes each) as the entries for the second column become steadier.*
Note 2: *Use this formula to complete the last column:*

$$\text{Infiltration rate (in cm per minute)} = \frac{5 \ (cm)}{\text{Entry in second column}} \times 60 \ (seconds)$$

Transpiration

This is another straightforward experiment! It is designed to measure transpiration (the rate of water loss from a plant's leaves). Place a small branch with plenty of healthy leaves on it inside a large polythene bag. Its opening must be tied firmly so that moisture can-

▲ **Figure 5.6** Measuring the water inside the bag is the most delicate part of the transpiration experiment. The polythene bag can be fitted over the end of a living branch still on its tree if preferred

not enter or leave the bag. After an agreed number of hours (e.g. 24) pour the water which has collected inside the bag into a graduated cylinder (Figure 5.6) and record the amount. The experiment may be repeated to provide more reliable average readings, or to observe how transpiration rates vary with air temperature, wind speed and intensity of sunlight.

Stream volume

Stream levels vary according to the amount of rain falling on their catchment areas (those supplying their tributaries with water). A pole marked off at metre and part-metre intervals is driven firmly into the stream bed or otherwise secured (e.g. tied to a bridge support) and used to record the water level at intervals following a period of rain. As with the other experiments, several 'runs' are needed to get the best results. It would be particularly interesting to link them with measurements of rainfall taken within the catchment area.

5.3 Food for thought

Have you ever been told to 'eat your fish – it will make you brainier'? This sound like an old wives' tale but, like many traditional sayings, it makes a good deal of sense. The reason is that fish are a rich source of protein, which all animals need to keep their brain cells healthy and active.

Some five million people are engaged in fishing throughout the world and produce about 2% of its total food supply. This may not seem very much, especially as 70% of the Earth's surface is covered by the seas and oceans, but there are many reasons for this apparently disappointing performance.

One is the distribution of **plankton**, the tiny animal and plant creatures at the base of the food chain for all larger forms of marine life. Plankton exist in vast numbers, but only where there is a plentiful supply of dissolved minerals such as nitrates and potassium, and these are richest near the sea bottom. They are only accessible to shoals of fish where strong ocean currents carry them up towards the surface (Figures 5.8 and 5.9). Plant plankton also need sunlight to grow and reproduce – just like the larger plants on land – and can only get enough warmth where the sea is fairly shallow.

There are other reasons too. The most sought-after fish belong to two groups. One is the **demersal** fish such as cod which live near the sea bottom and are caught by trawlers (Figure 5.10). The second group (e.g. herring) are **pelagic** fish and are attracted to the surface. They are hunted by drifters (Figure 5.11). The shallowest seas are therefore inhabited by *both* groups.

▼ **Figure 5.7** Natural factors important in deep-sea fishing

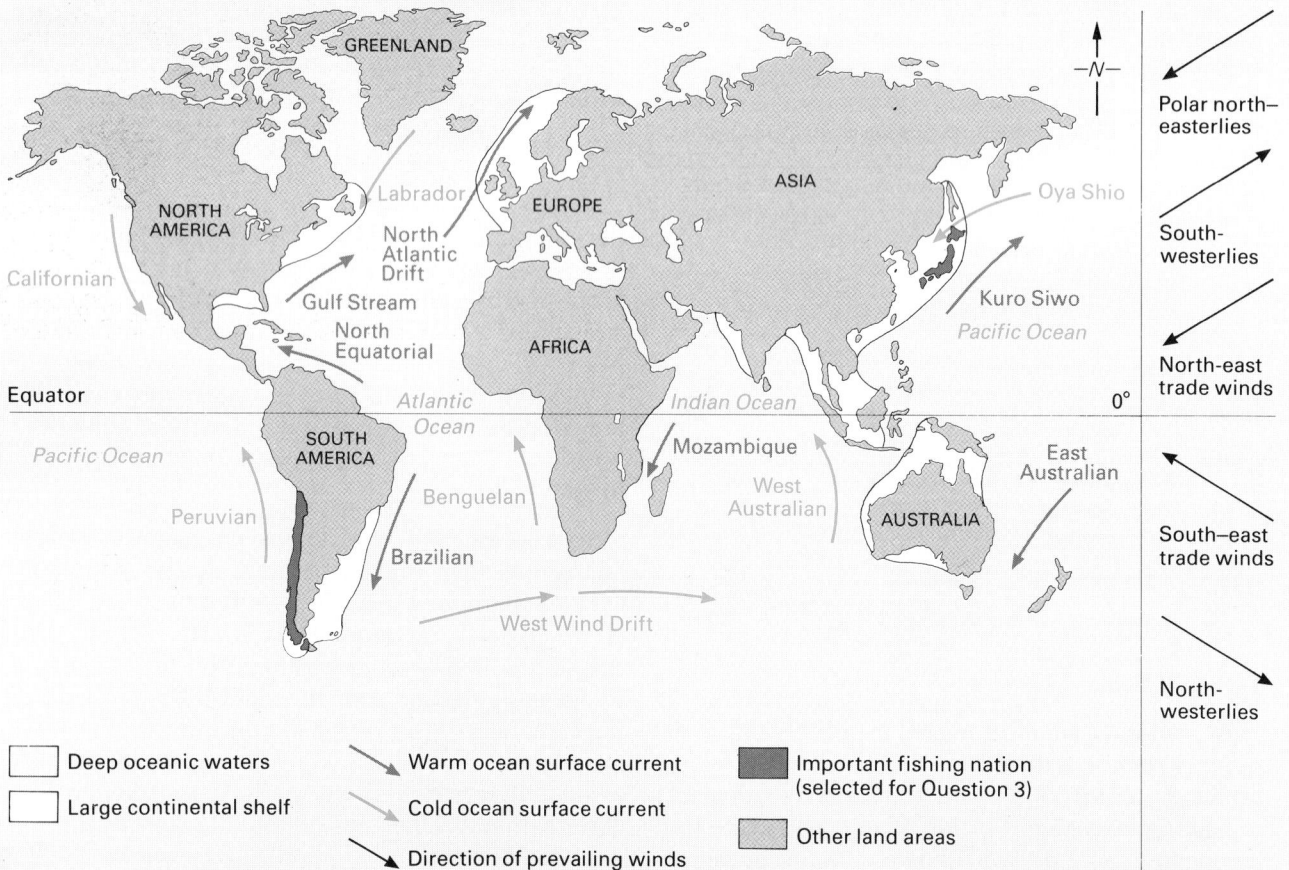

Most of these shallower areas are close inshore, where they are within range of sheltered harbours and the boats operating from them. One such area is the continental shelf off Western Europe, which deepens gradually to about 200 metres before plunging to the depths of the Atlantic Ocean. This was a gentle coastal plain before being submerged at the end of the Ice Age (Figure 5.12).

Apart from the unavoidable 'natural' hazards, today's fishermen now face a problem which is of their own making. The fisherman is basically a hunter-gatherer with little control over the areas he operates in or the activities of other fishermen. This has led to serious over-fishing of the shallowest and richest grounds. Also important is the way modern technology has helped fishermen to locate and trap shoals of fish, then keep their catches in prime condition for much longer before having to return home (see page 85).

► **Figure 5.8** Plankton magnified by 450 per cent

▼ **Figure 5.9** Offshore winds generate ocean currents which ensure a constant supply of plankton near the surface

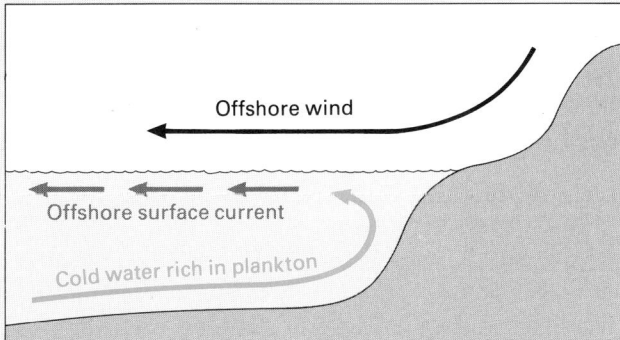

▼ **Figure 5.10** Trawling

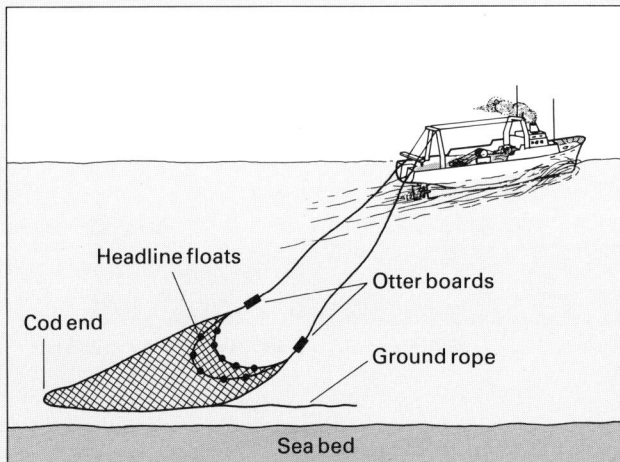

▼ **Figure 5.11** Drifting

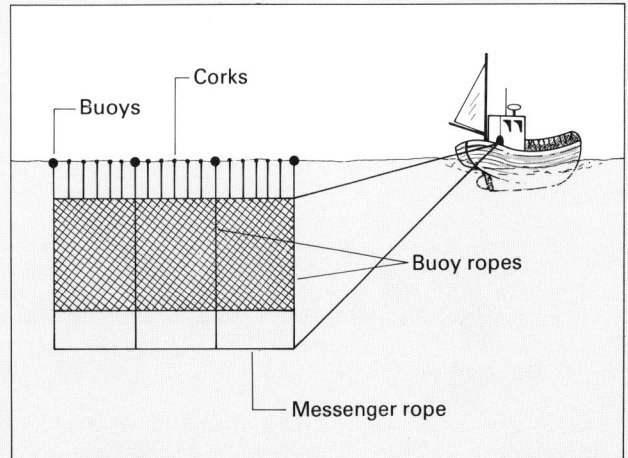

Only recently have the major fishing nations accepted the need to tackle the problem of over-fishing. The EC, for example, now lays down an annual quota for each member country – the maximum tonnage of fish it is permitted to catch in the following year. Individual countries try to enforce these rules inside their own fishing limits, but there are always some skippers who flout them and risk paying heavy fines. Other measures taken in recent years to conserve fish stocks are:

☐ Making it illegal to use small-mesh nets, as they also trap the young fish, thus reducing the numbers available to breed next season.
☐ Inventing new catching methods which keep the fish alive until they can be sorted; at present, the standard nets crush *all* the fish they trap.

1 Write your own notes on:
   a demersal fish/fishing.
   b pelagic fish/fishing.

2 **a** Summarise the main reasons for over-fishing and what action *has* been taken to reduce it.
   b What additional measures do you think it might be worth trying to secure adequate fish stocks for the future? Try to make your proposals as detailed as possible, e.g. by including maps and sketches.

3 **a** Copy the world map in Figure 5.7.
   b Name the countries shaded on this map.
   c Give the main reasons why each of these countries has an important fishing industry. Use named features where appropriate.

▲ **Figure 5.13** A fisheries reconnaisance aircraft flying over a fishery protection vessel

▼ **Figure 5.12** Cross-section of Europe's continental shelf

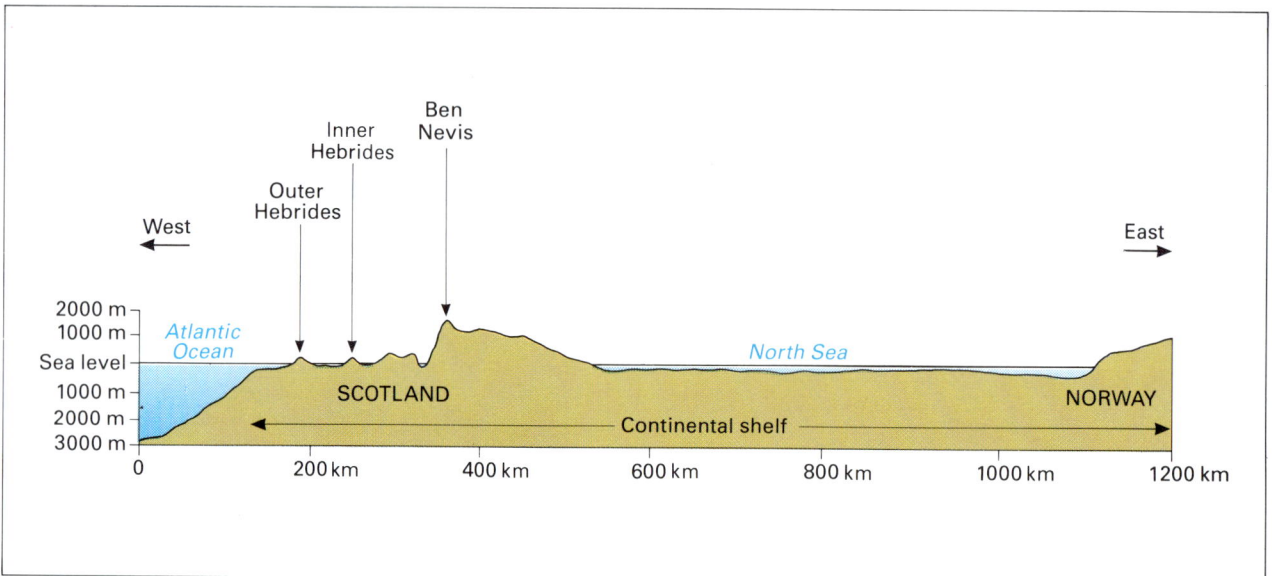

Echo-sounding equipment sends out underwater signals. These rebound off shoals of fish and tell the captain their direction and distance from the trawler.

▼ **Figure 5.14** Many modern devices have made deep-sea fishing more efficient

dar and other navigation help a ship to pin-point osition and so avoid erwater dangers.

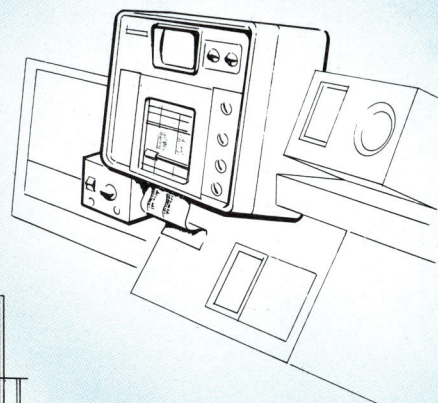

Sloping ramp up which the fishing net is hauled by a powerful winch.

The crew are much safer and drier than in the older, smaller boats which had to stop and haul the net over the side.

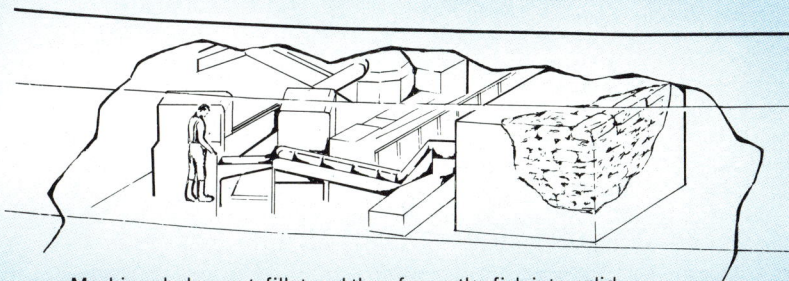

Machines below gut, fillet and then freeze the fish into solid blocks. Doing this keeps the fish in perfect condition and 'freezer-trawlers' can stay at sea for 2–3 months; 2–3 weeks was the operational limit of the older 'fresher-trawlers'.

5.4 Fish farming

Fishing the open sea has always been fraught with danger and increasingly efficient methods of detecting and trapping the shoals has added a further worry: declining fish stocks. One way of overcoming both problems is to follow the example of the land farmer, who operates within a small area on which he can work hard to increase its yield of food. The rearing of fish in a similar 'controlled environment' is called **fish farming**.

Fish farming is not a new idea, for oysters have been cultivated in the warm coastal waters of south-east Asia for centuries; rice-growers in the same region have bred fish in their flooded paddy fields, giving them an extra source of protein-rich food. In Britain, fish farming techniques are now applied to lobsters and salmon. The Highlands and Islands of northern Scotland is our most important fish-farming region (Figure 5.15), and more than 500 full-time jobs have been created there as a result. The key stages are shown in Figure 5.16.

One interesting future development could be the use of large, unwanted oil tankers for fish farming. Initial trials have already been successfully completed in Norwegian fiords, which are very similar to the Scottish lochs. The huge tanks inside the hold would be filled with (salt *or* fresh) water and collected fish droppings pumped out at intervals and disposed of safely.

1 **a** Suggest reasons why 'fish farming' is a suitable description for the activity described in this unit.
b What advantages does fish farming have over traditional sea fishing?

2 With the help of Figure 5.15 and an atlas map of northern Scotland, name any of the following which are important for fish farming:
a 3 *groups* of islands
b 3 *individual* islands
c 3 large *sea* lochs
d 1 large *inland* loch

3 **a** Why is this remote part of Scotland so well suited to fish farming?
b What kinds of seafood are produced there using fish farming methods – and why?
c What benefits is fish farming likely to have brought to the region? (Add to the information given in the text).

4 **a** Account for the surplus of very large tankers at the present time.

b Write down as many advantages and disadvantages of *tanker* fish farming as you can think of.

5 **a** Read the following description of new developments in south-east Asian fish farming techniques, then draw a flow diagram to link the various parts of the food chain mentioned in it. Some parts of your diagram *may* need more than one link.
b What appear to be the main advantages of this particular system of fish farming?

Thailand: Small-Scale Fish Farming

The ODA (Overseas Development Administration) is helping to boost food production in north-east Thailand through the introduction of a simple fish farming technique. Fresh caught fish has always formed a major part of the diet of country people but latterly catches were no longer sufficient due to environmental degradation caused by population pressure and increased use of seasonally flooded fishing areas for rice production. In association with the Asian Institute of Technology the ODA has developed a pilot fish farming project which uses no new technology and builds upon existing farm practices.

▼ **Figure 5.15** Fish farm locations in northern Scotland

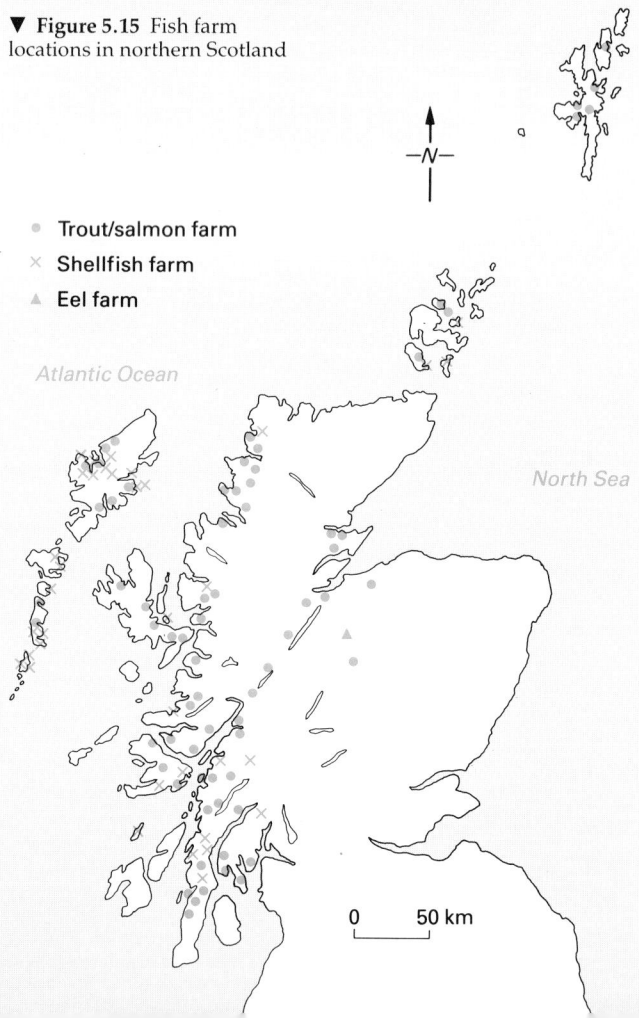

- Trout/salmon farm
- × Shellfish farm
- ▲ Eel farm

Atlantic Ocean

North Sea

0   50 km

Figure 5.16

◀ **a** Salmon ova ▼ **b** Salmon fry

◀ **c** Salmon smolts

▼ **d** Mature salmon ready for sale

Improved strains of an African freshwater tilapia, developed with help from the University of Stirling, have been introduced into village and family ponds. They feed on aquatic weeds whose growth is stimulated by the application of buffalo manure as a fertiliser. The buffaloes are owned by the villagers and used for working the land. The waterweeds may also be grown in separate ponds fertilised by human wastes. The villagers now have a ready supply of fresh fish at very little cost. Latterly ducks have been integrated into the system. Duckhouses are constructed over the ponds and provide a further source of fertilisation for plant growth. The ducks have become another source of food for the villagers who are also able to sell their eggs for cash.

The project has brought significant improvement in the diet of the villagers. No complicated new technology has been introduced. The system is easy to operate. It does not damage the environment and is a natural extension of the villagers' farming practices.

6 a In your opinion, is it likely that fish farming will become the *most* important method of obtaining sea food in the future?

b Give full reasons for your answer to **a**.

5.5 The big ten

1973 was an important year for the water supply industry in England and Wales. The Water Act of that year created the ten water authorities whose areas are shown in Figure 5.17.

It replaced the 200 smaller water undertakings, 1 300 sewerage authorities and 29 river boards which had existed before. They had done much good work but were finding it increasingly difficult to tackle pollution problems. This was because many of the water gathering grounds they relied on were actually outside their 'own' areas. Also, some of the older concerns had very limited financial resources and so were ill-equipped to meet the increasing demand for water. It made one type of authority responsible for all of the following activities:

▼ **Figure 5.17** The ten water authorities

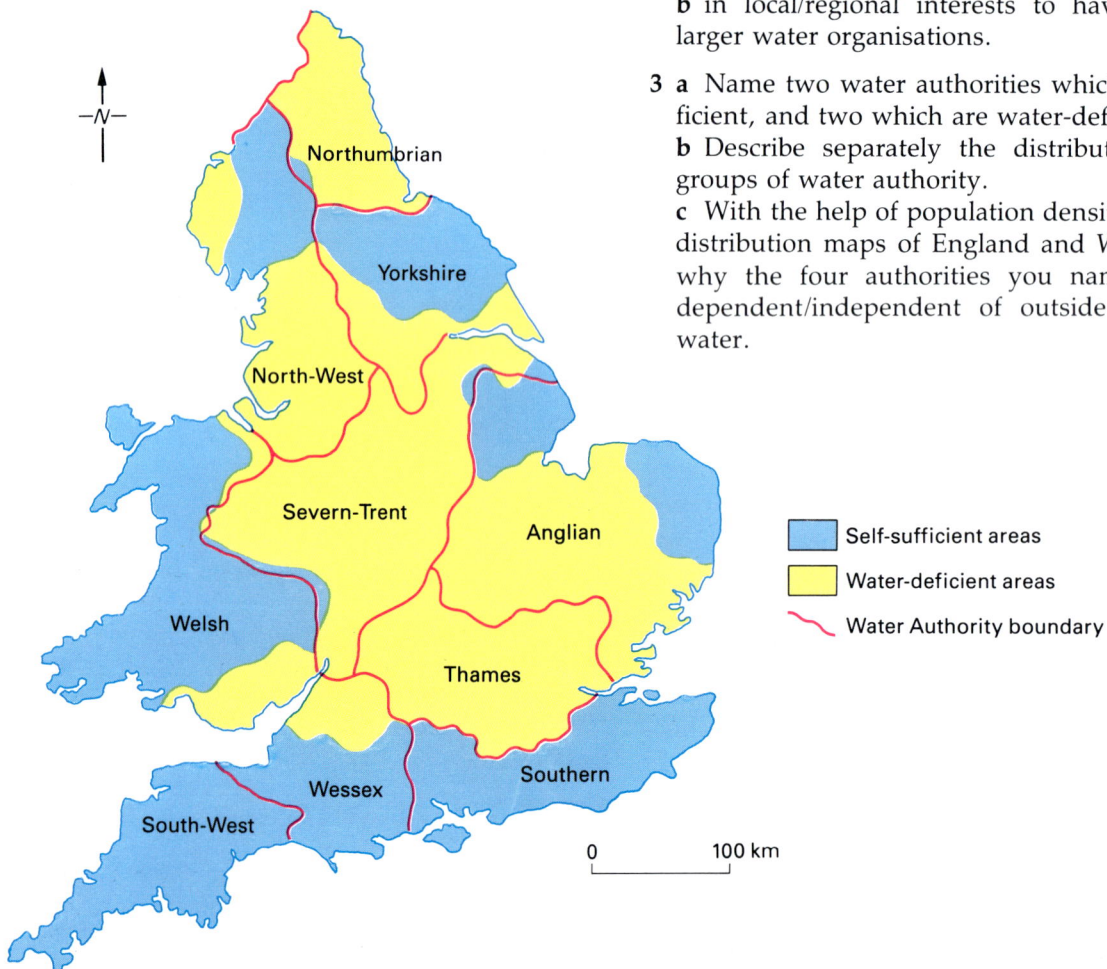

- ☐ Inland fisheries
- ☐ Land drainage
- ☐ Pollution control
- ☐ Recreational use of water
- ☐ River management
- ☐ Sewage processing and disposal.

Figure 5.17 also shows that some of the new water authorities are fortunate in being self-sufficient, while others are said to have a water-deficit because they are forced to 'import' supplies from other areas. The act made it much easier to plan a national water grid by which water might be passed from one part of the country to another in times of shortage.

1 **a** How many water authorities serve England and Wales at the present time?
b How many smaller concerns (of all kinds) did the new authorities replace in 1973?

2 Suggest why it might be
a in the national interest
b in local/regional interests to have fewer and larger water organisations.

3 **a** Name two water authorities which are self-sufficient, and two which are water-deficient.
b Describe separately the distributions of both groups of water authority.
c With the help of population density and rainfall distribution maps of England and Wales, explain why the four authorities you named in **a** are dependent/independent of outside suppliers of water.

Groundwater areas

Major reservoir

— **Pipeline/aqueduct**

● **Major city/built-up area**

▶ **Future barrage location**

Loch Katrine

Glasgow Edinburgh

Kielder

Tyneside

Thirlmere

Solway Firth Teesside

Cow Green

Morecambe Bay

Leeds

Manchester

Dee Estuary Liverpool Derwent Sheffield

The Wash

L. Vyrnwy Nottingham

Leicester

Birmingham

Elan Valley

Tal-y-Bont

London

Cardiff

Southampton

0   100 km

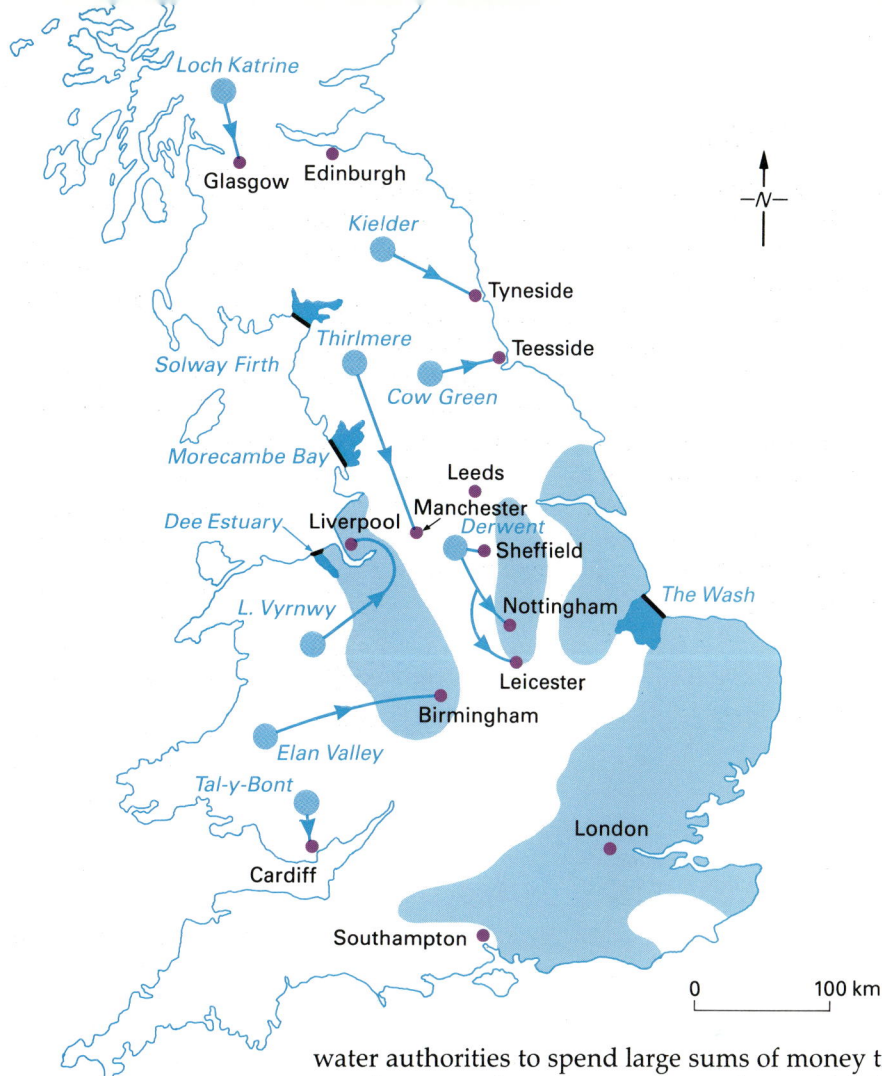

▶ **Figure 5.18** Major water supply arrangements in Britain. This map does not show the many rivers which are also an important source of water

5.6 Britain's water supplies

Water is nature's most precious resource. It keeps us alive, nourishes our crops and helps us to lead healthier and more enjoyable lives; water is vital to quality of life throughout the biosphere. In 1831, when Britain's population was 16.2 millions, an average person in this country used 18 litres of water per day. The equivalent figures for 1981 were 54.8 million people and 180 litres per day. The water demands of industry have also increased over the years. The steel industry, for example, uses 200 000 litres of water for every tonne of metal it produces, and 50 000 000 litres pass through a modern power station every *hour*.

Britain is fortunate in having a generally damp, cool climate as well as the technology and resources to make good use of the rain it receives. However, much of our rain falls in the remote and sparsely-populated mountainous areas. This has forced our water authorities to spend large sums of money transporting water from these areas to others which have a shortage. This unit outlines four ways in which the authorities can obtain the supplies of water they require.

Rivers

Few places in Britain are far from a sizeable river. London can get 73% of all the water it needs from the Thames, and a further 14% from one of its tributaries – the River Lea (Figure 5.19). The problem with river-based supplies is that they are liable to pollution by sewage and industrial waste and so require expensive treatment before being considered safe to use.

Ground water

The main areas where ground water can be obtained are shown in Figure 5.18. One such area is the London Basin, which provides the capital with its third source of water. Underground supplies are especially welcome as they have been filtered while seeping through **porous** rock layers and are beyond

▲ Figure 5.20 Thames Water Authority treatment plant at Farnmoor

▼ Figure 5.19 London's water supply arrangements

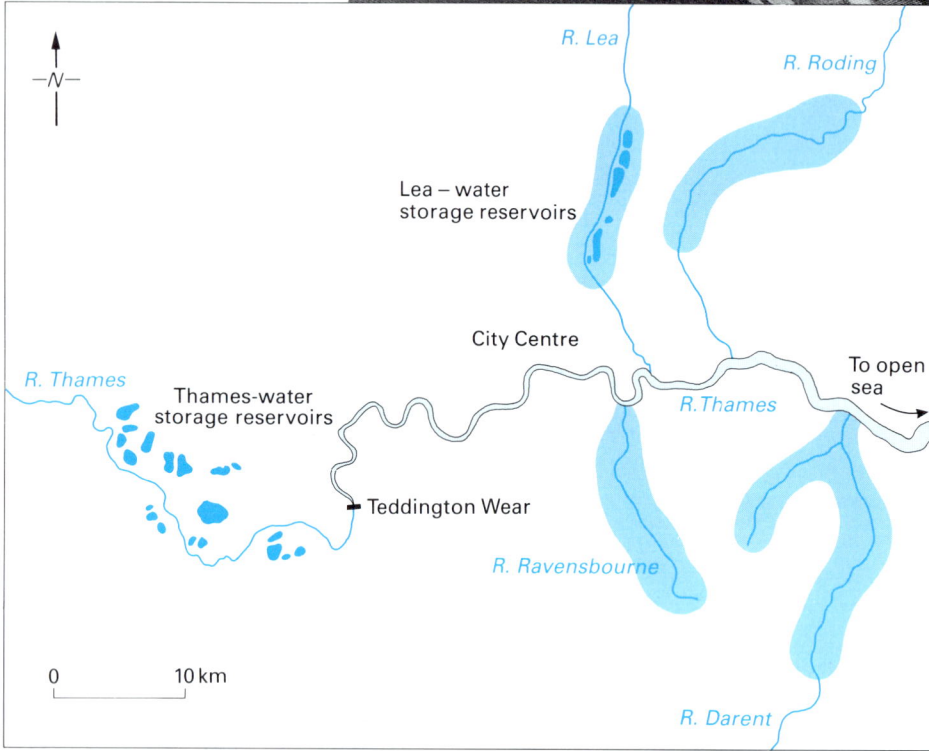

- R. Lea
- R. Roding
- Lea – water storage reservoirs
- City Centre
- R. Thames
- To open sea
- R. Thames
- Thames-water storage reservoirs
- Teddington Wear
- R. Ravensbourne
- R. Darent

0   10 km

Tidal stretch of R. Thames

Tributaries and non-tidal stretch of R. Thames

Ground-water pumping areas

Clusters of reservoirs

Impermeable rock

'Dry' porous rock

'Saturated' porous rock (the aquifer)

Water table

Borehole

Relief rainfall

Percolation of ground water through porous rock

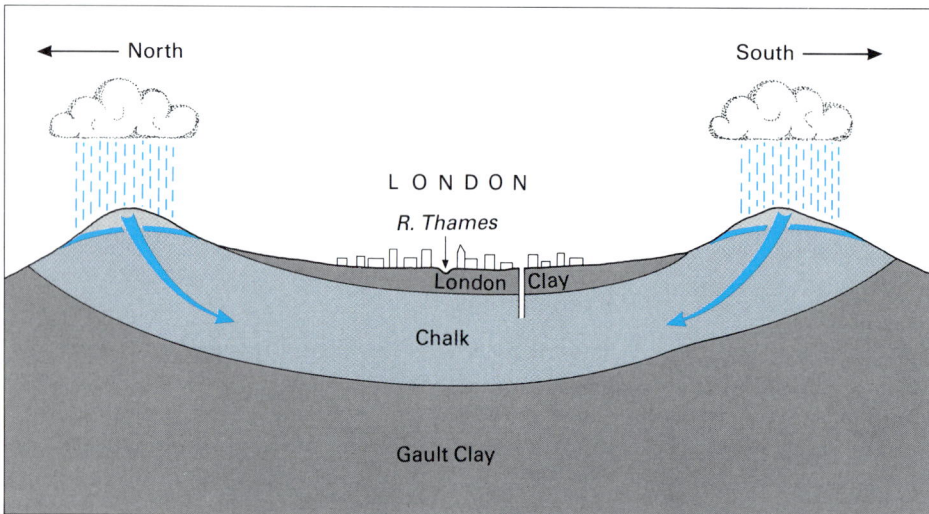

- North
- South
- LONDON
- R. Thames
- London Clay
- Chalk
- Gault Clay

◄ Figure 5.21 Cross-section of the London artesian basin

▶ **Figure 5.22** Birmingham's water is supplied from mid-Wales

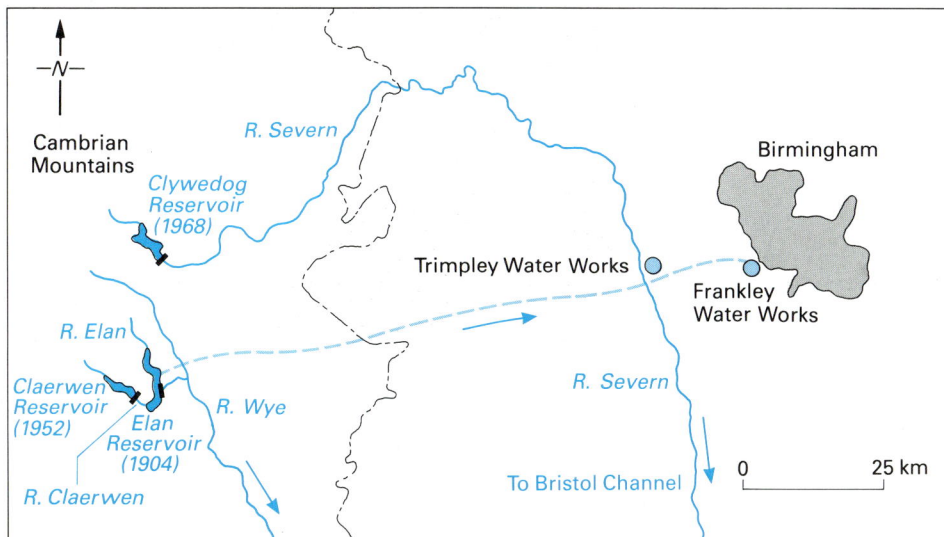

the reach of most forms of pollution. Care must however be taken not to extract water more quickly than the local rainfall can replace it (which is quite a slow process). The water table in the London Basin has dropped considerably for this very reason, which means that deeper bore holes are constantly needed to maintain supplies.

Valley reservoirs

All of Britain's major cities – except London – now rely heavily on valley reservoirs. Birmingham used to take all the water it needed from the River Tame but this had become increasingly polluted during the last century. In 1892, the city obtained government permission to build reservoirs in the Elan Valley in central Wales as well as a 120 km-long aqueduct to transfer the water (Figures 5.22 and 5.23). The total cost was £6 million, a vast sum of money at that time for it could have built five large battleships! The investment proved to be a sound one for the city didn't have to flood any more Welsh valleys for another fifty years. So many other cities have followed Birmingham's example that the Welsh now resist any new proposals to flood their valleys – especially when the water is required by *English* cities!

Coastal barrages

A **barrage** is a long dam built across a wide bay or river estuary. The idea is to allow fresh water streams to replace the sea water behind it and so create a huge reservoir. Figure 5.18 shows that a number of locations around the British coast appear suitable for barrage development, but in 1974 a National Plan for Water

concluded that valley reservoirs should continue to provide most of our water and that coastal barrages do not as yet justify their enormous cost.

1 **a** Devise a table to show this information for 1831 and 1981:
  The population of Britain.
  The average quantity of water used in the home per person per day.
  The total quantity of water used in all the homes of Britain.
  b Write sentences to compare the information in your three sets of figures.

2 **a** Draw a divided bar graph to show London's three main sources of water.
  b How are London's water supply arrangements different to those of most other British cities?
  c Suggest detailed reasons for your answer to **b**.

3 **a** Draw Figure 5.21, adding the names of the two upland areas to your cross-section. (Hint: use your atlas.)
  b Pair up these five key terms used in the Thames Basin cross-section with their best-fit meanings.
  aquifer   Impermeable   water table
  bore hole   Porous
  An ... is porous rock which is saturated (full of water) because it is below the water table.
  The ... is the upper level of the aquifer.
  A ... must reach below the water table if water is to be obtained.
  ... rocks do not let water pass through them.
  ... rocks contain small holes which can store water and allow it to pass through them.

◀ **Figure 5.23** The Elan Valley in mid-Wales has provided much of Birmingham's water over the last 80 years

6 a Make an enlarged copy of this table, then use the following entries to complete it. Note:
  – each entry may be used more than once.
  – each space in the table may have more than one entry.

Type of water resource	Advantages	Disadvantages
Coastal barrage		
Ground-water		
River		
Valley reservoir		

'An unsightly ring of slime may be uncovered when water levels fall.'

'It takes time for the extracted water to be replaced naturally.'

'Low-lying fertile land need not be flooded.'

'Many sites are in remote, rural areas so transport costs are usually very high.'

'May make it difficult for ships to reach ports further along the coast.'

'Nature provides its own water-transport system!'

'Provides additional sites for water sports.'

'Pumping is always needed to raise the water to ready-use header tanks.'

'Replacing salt sea water by fresh water can endanger wildlife.'

'Silting can be a major problem.'

'Some sites are near to densely-populated areas, keeping water transport costs low.'

'Surface water may be lost through evaporation in the warmer summer months.'

'The risk of water pollution is very slight.'

'Turbines can be built into the dams to generate hydro-electric power.'

'Valuable lowland is flooded.'

'Water connot be lost through evaporation.'

'Water is frequently polluted by sewage and industrial waste.'

b Add *at least one* extra entry of your own for *each* type of water resource listed in the table.

4 The following reservoirs are shown in Figure 5.18 Kielder Water, Lake Vyrnwy, Loch Katrine.
For each one:
a Name the range of hills it is in.
b Name the highest peak in this range.
c State the height of this peak (in metres).
d Name the city which this reservoir supplies with water.
e Write down the direct distance (in km) between the reservoir and the city it serves.

5 Describe the *ideal* location for valley reservoirs by writing a sentence about each of these factors:
a Total annual rainfall.
b Seasonal rainfall distribution.
c Altitude and air temperature. (Hint: consider evaporation.)
d Hardness of rock.
e Porosity of rock (i.e. its ability to let water seep through).
f Shape of valley. (Consider depth, width and steepness of valley sides).
g Fertility of land.
h Population density.
i Transport networks.

5.7 The Lancashire Conjunctive Scheme

During the last twenty years, the water authorities have been severely criticised for flooding more and more valleys to meet the increasing demand for water. The Lancashire Conjunctive Scheme was a carefully thought out response to this criticism. It was planned during the 1970s and opened by The Queen in 1980. The word **conjunctive** was included in its name because this means combining different methods of obtaining *and* moving the water. Figure 5.24 shows how the scheme works.

1 Devise a flow–diagram to show the sources, methods of transportation and movements of water in the Lancashire Conjunctive Scheme. You will need to use most of the information given in Figure 5.24.

2 In what ways might this scheme be regarded as:
   a being able to overcome local shortfalls in water supply?
   b environmentally sensitive?
   c very cost-effective in the long-term?

▼ **Figure 5.24** The Lancashire Conjunctive Scheme. **Note**: Stocks Reservoir, Barnacre Reservoir and Broughton Treatment Plant were all in use before 1980

North

South

Stocks Reservoir

Hoghton service reservoirs and pumping station

Service reservoirs

Barnacre Reservoir

Pump house

To Chorley

Hodder aqueduct

Wyresdale tunnel

Outfall

Valve house

Mill Lane cross connection

Settling tanks

Quernmore pipeline

Abbeystead outfall

South aqueduct

Franklaw treatment plant at Catterall

Preston

Lune intake and pumping station

Pumping station

Wyre intake and pumping station at Garstang

Pump house

Filters

R. Ribble

Lancaster

R. Wyre

Coast aqueduct

Boreholes

Bunter sandstone aquifer

Broughton treatment plant

R. Lune

To Fylde Coast

To Fylde coast

5.8 Hydro-electric power

Water is an inexhaustible and increasingly important resource for generating electricity. This unit describes two very different types of HEP system involving rainfall, rivers and reservoirs. Figure 5.25 locates both examples within the Highlands of Scotland, where HEP was first introduced in 1896 for the benefit of the aluminium industry. This demanded large quantities of cheap electricity to smelt (extract) the pure metal from its raw material – bauxite. In 1943 the North of Scotland Hydro-Electric Board was formed. Its main task has been to co-ordinate the work of all the power stations in its area, not just those using water. These range from the nuclear plant at Dounreay to diesel generators on some of the smaller islands.

▲ **Figure 5.25** Locations of the Cruachan and Sloy HEP system

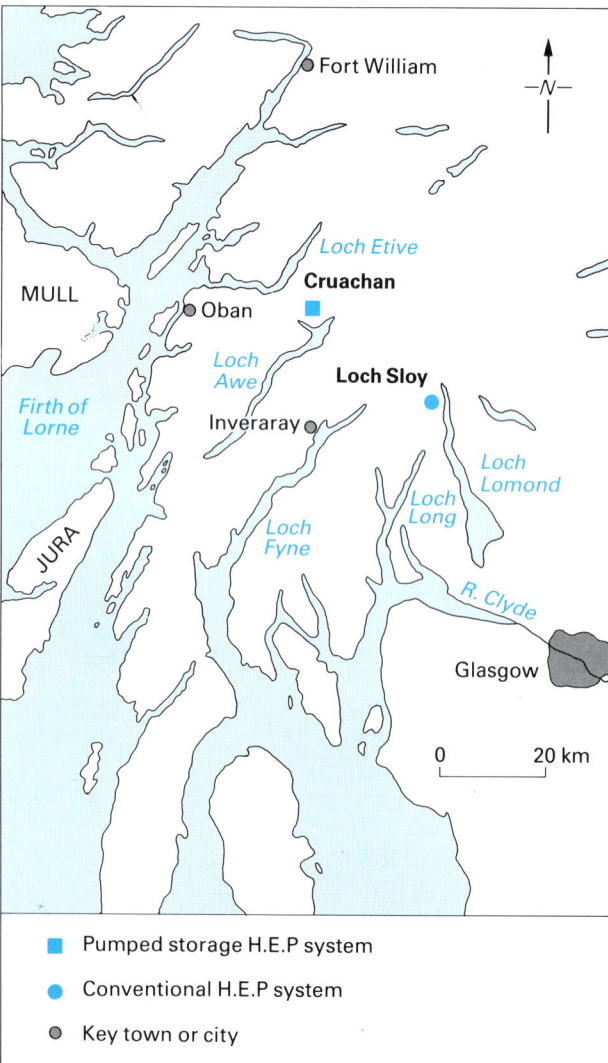

The Loch Sloy **conventional** system.

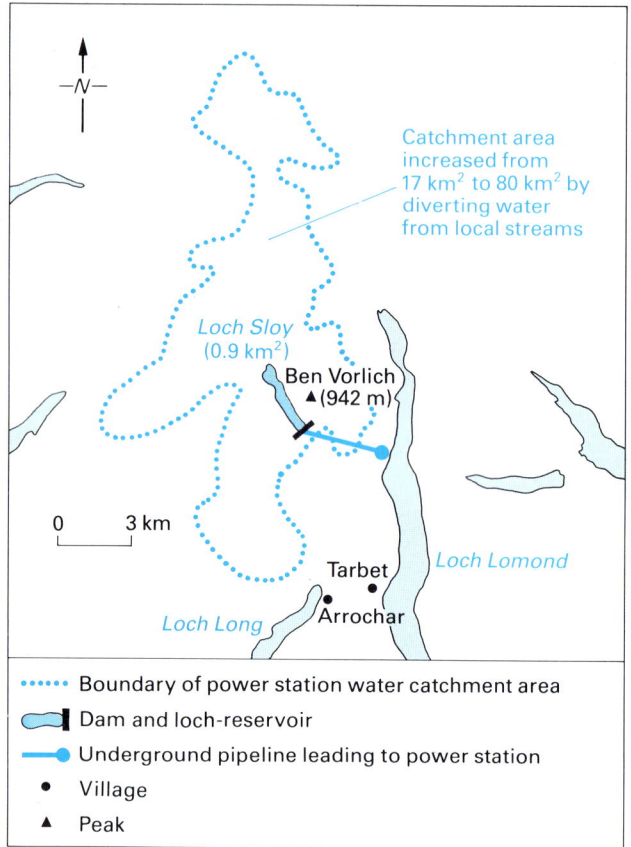

▲ **Figure 5.26** Layout of the Loch Sloy system

▼ **Figure 5.27** Cross-section of the Loch Sloy system, operated by the North of Scotland Hydro-Electric Board

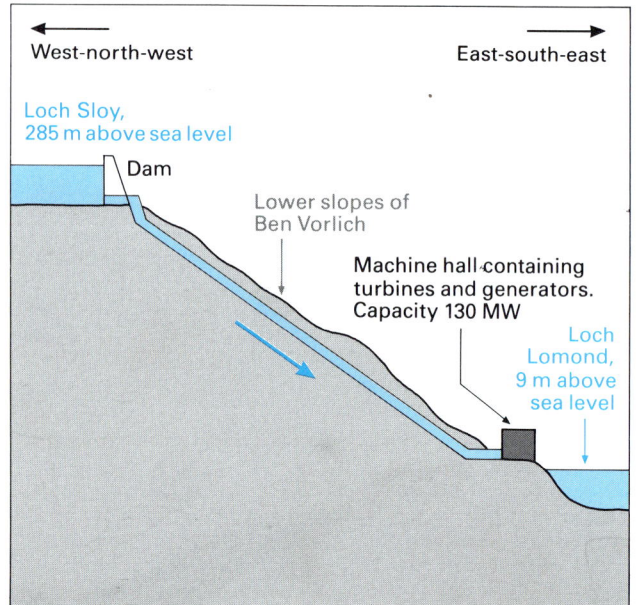

◀ **Figure 5.28** The construction of the Loch Sloy system

The Cruachan **pumped storage** system.

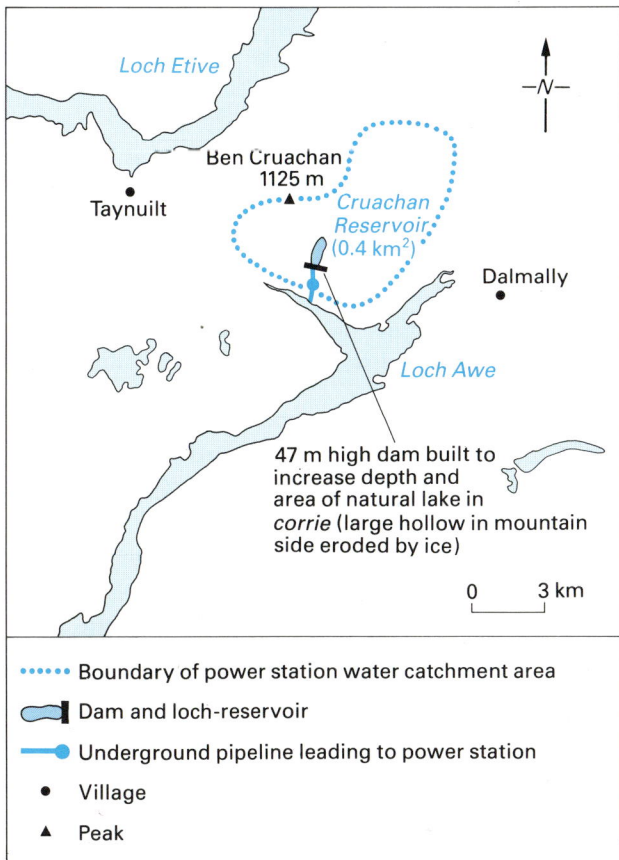

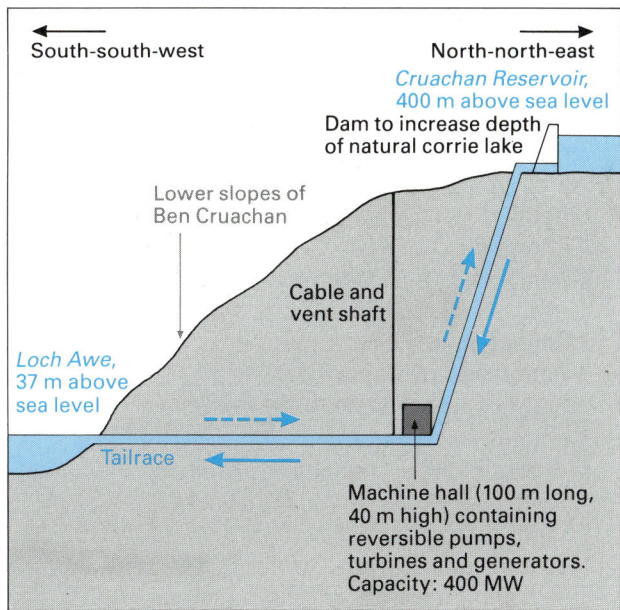

◀ **Figure 5.30** Layout of the Cruachan system

▼ **Figure 5.31** Cross-section of the Cruachan system, operated by the North of Scotland Hydro-Electric Board

⟶ Water flow during peak daytime demand

⇢ Water flow during night time period of power surplus

1 Complete two copies of this data sheet with the help of the illustrations in this unit.

'HEP' SYSTEM DATA SHEET

Type of system: Conventional *or* pumped storage
Name of example: Cruachan *or* Loch Sloy
Operated by:
Generating capacity:
Operational: For long periods *or* only for short periods at peak demand times
Name of upper lake:
Surface area of upper lake:
Height of upper lake above sea level:
Name of lower lake:
Height of lower lake above sea level:
Larger lake is: Lower *or* upper lake
Height difference between upper and lower lakes:
Type of machinery: Turbines and generators *or* reversible pump-turbines and generators

Location of machinery: Inside mountain *or* on surface
Flow of water: Downhill only *or* downhill and uphill, as required
Ways in which the available water supply has been increased:
Additional information: e.g. why it is possible for a power station to use large quantities of electricity in order to generate more at a later time.

2 List as many similarities between the two HEP *systems* and *examples* as you can find.

3 Suggest reasons which help to explain why:
a HEP stations provide only 2% of Britain's total electricity needs.
b This figure is likely to remain fairly steady in future years.
c Diesel generators, *not* HEP systems, are used on most of the Scottish islands.

5.9 Taming the Nile

In Britain, we seem to talk most about the weather, but in Egypt it is the River Nile which occupies peoples' minds. They never grow tired of discussing the levels it has reached, the changing colour of its water, and the way it is affecting their everyday lives. This is hardly surprising, for 19 out of every 20 Egyptians live on its banks or in the **delta** area where it splits up into smaller **distributaries** before entering the Mediterranean Sea (Figure 5.32). This densely populated area includes Egypt's two greatest cities as well as many smaller towns and villages. The basic reason is that Egypt lies in a hot desert region, in which agriculture is possible only in areas having access to water.

There are three ways in which the fellahin (Egyptian farmers) can make good use of the Nile's water:

trapping the flood waters after they have spilled over onto the fields;

lifting the water onto fields which are higher up the valley sides or are further from the river;

saving water which would otherwise flow into the sea.

The four irrigation methods described below have been used in the Nile Valley for thousands of years.

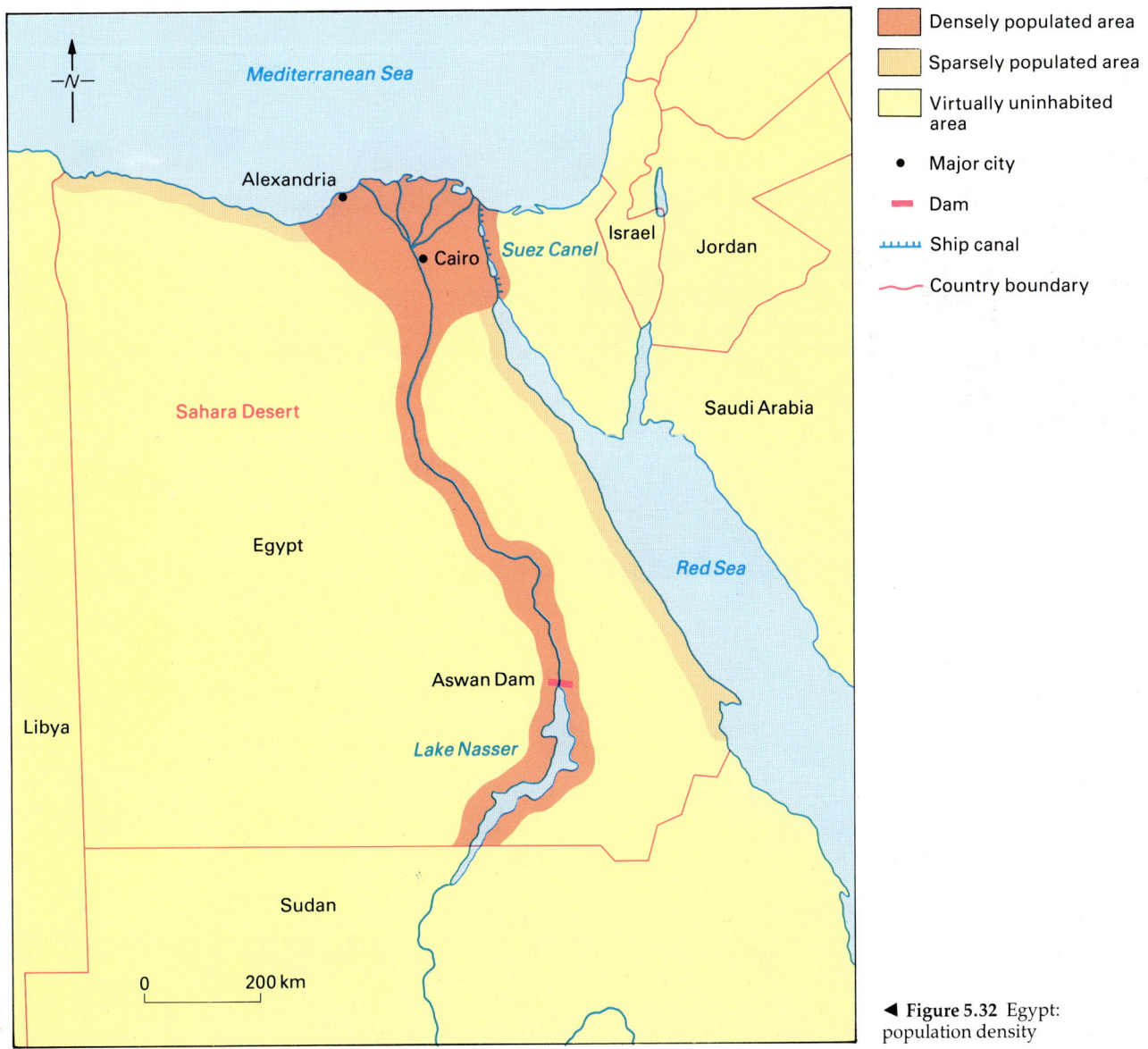

◄ **Figure 5.32** Egypt: population density

Basin irrigation (Figure 5.33)

This is the oldest of all these methods, but can still be seen in areas nearest to the river. It is called basin irrigation because each field (or basin) is surrounded by a low bank of soil and stones. These banks – called bunds – normally have some gaps which allow the flood waters to enter the field. The gaps are then filled in to trap the water, giving it time to soak below the surface and moisten the soil just long enough to grow one crop. Its main disadvantage is that for nine months out of every year the soil is hard and unusable, a great waste of otherwise good farmland. Figure 5.34 demonstrates why the Nile floods regularly and makes basin irrigation possible.

The next three methods are a definite improvement because they allow water to be *lifted* onto the fields, thus keeping them moist for longer. A series of these machines can supply land some distance away from the river which would otherwise remain true desert.

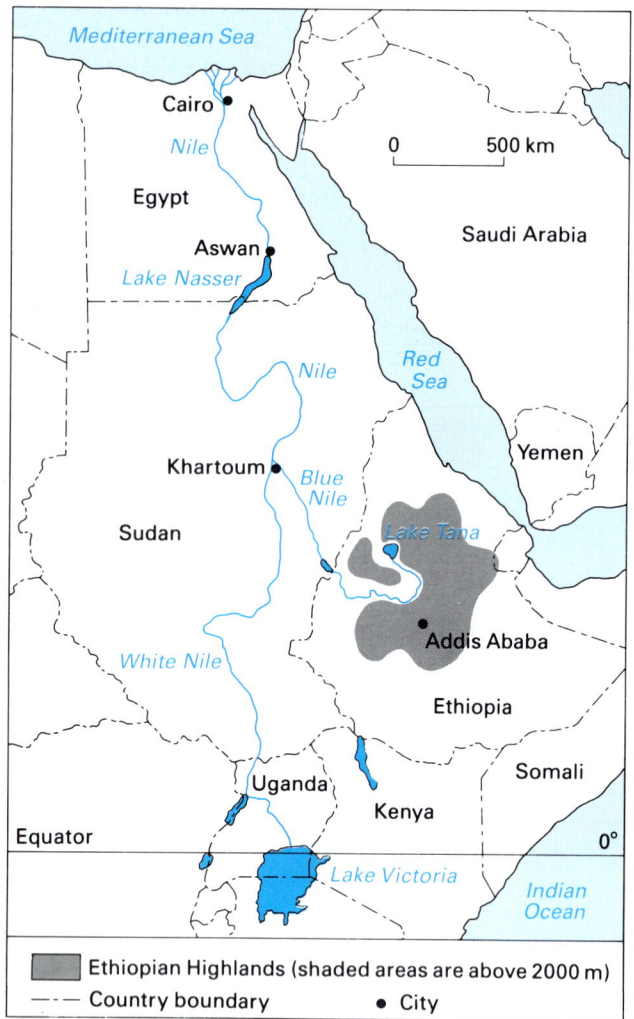

▲ **Figure 5.34a** The Nile Lands

◄ **Figure 5.33** Basin irrigation

▼ **Figure 5.34b**

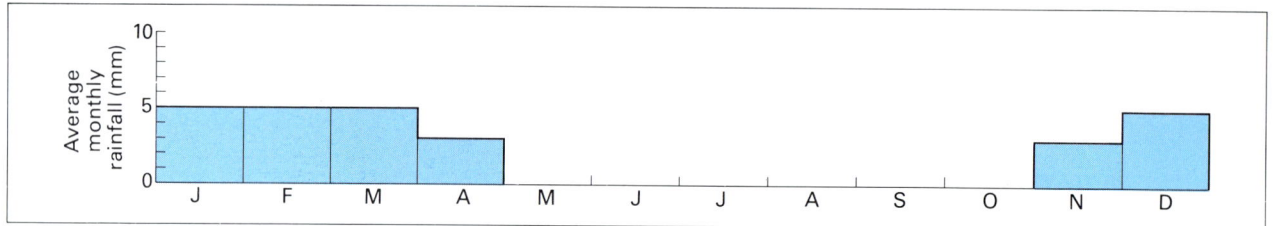

▼ **Figure 5.34c**

Monthly rainfall figures for Addis Ababa

Month	Jan	Feb	Mar	Apr	May	Jun	Jul	Aug	Sep	Oct	Nov	Dec
Average monthly rainfall in mm	15	40	80	90	75	150	275	315	170	30	20	0

▼ **Figure 5.36** Cross-sectional drawing of an Archimede's screw

The shaduf (Figure 5.35)

The shaduf is the simplest of the three lifting devices. It consists of a long pole which is pivoted at the top to a fixed upright post in such a way that it can be moved up and down or swung around. The main disadvantage of this method is that it takes hours of boring, back-breaking work to lift quite small quantities of water.

Archimedes' screw (Figure 5.36)

This device is a little more complicated, but is also operated by hand. Its large wooden cylinder encloses a continuous spiral of blades; these are attached to an axle running down the centre of the machine. The bottom end is staked firmly into the river bed. Operating the screw is hard work in the heat of the day and it is usual for two fellahin to take turns on the handle.

The sakia or Persian wheel (Figure 5.37)

This is the largest and most complex of the three lifting devices, so its main parts have been labelled to help you to do question **4 c**. The sakia takes quite a lot of wood, time and skill to make but is well worth the effort. It can lift much greater quantities of water than either the shaduf or the screw, and one definite advantage is that it can be worked by animals such as camels and bullocks.

The serious disadvantage shared by all three lifting devices is that they are only effective when there is enough water near the river banks. They cannot store water and this is one of the main reasons why a further method has been introduced into the Nile Valley.

▼ **Figure 5.37** The sakia. The letters are for use with question 4c

Perennial irrigation

Here is an amazing fact: for three whole months of every year, *no* water flows from the Nile into the Mediterranean Sea! This is when the river level is at its lowest and evaporation from the hot, desert sun lowers it even further. It is also because so much water has already been taken for irrigation and use in the towns. The level is so low that there is a risk of sea water flowing *upstream*! The salt in this water would ruin the fertile soils of the delta, so long barrages have been built across the mouths of the distributaries to stop this happening.

As we have seen, the greatest problem of all is how to supply the farmers with irrigation water all year round. This is now done by holding back great quantities of water in summer – when there is a surplus. Many dams have been built across the Nile over the last 100 years, the most famous one being completed in 1903 at a place called Aswan (see Figure 5.32 again). This was a good site to choose because a band of hard granite crosses the valley at that point and provides a firm foundation. This dam has since been heightened a number of times to increase the area of the reservoir behind it.

The largest of all the Nile dams was completed in 1953, 6 km south of the original Aswan Dam; called the Aswan *High* Dam, it has enlarged the original reservoir into a vast lake (Figure 5.38), thirty times longer than our own Lake Windermere. Built into the High Dam are a number of sluice gates. These control the flow of water downstream, and hence the supply to the chief farming areas. Turbines also installed in this dam generate enough HEP to supply all the cities and factories in Egypt. This power is now being used by the farmers too, for they are beginning to replace their old irrigation devices with modern electric pumps. These can be switched on at night when it is much cooler and the rate of evaporation lower.

This modern system of storing water in reservoirs is called **perennial irrigation**. Its great advantage is that fertile land in hot climate areas need never lie idle due to a lack of water. This means that two and perhaps three crops can be grown every year where only one was possible before.

There are however some serious problems too. One is the cost. Egypt is a relatively poor country and had to borrow large sums of money to finance the Aswan High Dam project. Another is that the dam traps rich, fine silt as well as water. This deprives the fellahin of their free fertiliser and forces them to buy expensive artificial ones instead. Figure 5.40 shows how another problem caused by the rising waters of Lake Nasser was solved by the Egyptians with the financial and technological support of many foreign countries.

▼ **Figure 5.39** Egypt: 1950 and 1980

Statistic	1950	1980
Population (millions)	15	42
Cultivated area (1 000 km^2)	31	41
Annual production of raw cotton (1 000 tonnes)	390	500
Duration of River Nile flow into Mediterranean Sea (months per year)	12	9
Silt concentration in River Nile downstream of Aswan for month of August (parts per million of water)	2 700	45

▲ **Figure 5.40** Abu Simbel after the Aswan High Dam created Lake Nasser. The giant statues have been raised 70 m and re-sited 200 m back from the original course of the River Nile

1 a Describe which parts of Egypt are:
 i densely populated
 ii sparsely populated
 iii virtually uninhabited.
 b Explain briefly why each of these areas is populated in this way.

2 a Copy the rainfall graph for Cairo shown in Figure 5.34 **b**.
 b Use the information in Figure 5.34 **c** to draw a similar graph for Addis Ababa.
 c In which month is the rainfall heaviest at Addis Ababa?
 d If the river water has to flow about 5 400 km to reach central Egypt, in which month will the level of the Nile be highest in that area? Assume that the river's average speed of flow is 4 km per hour.
 e Write down at least three differences between the rainfall patterns for Cairo and Addis Ababa.

3 State very clearly what these two terms mean:
 a irrigation   **b** perennial irrigation.

4 a Design an information sheet to teach people how to use a shaduf. As the sheet is intended for *illiterate* people (those who cannot read to write) it should consist of a series of simple drawings *but no* labels or written instructions!
 b Now write a 'do it yourself' instruction sheet to tell people how to build an Archimedes' screw. No drawings this time, only clearly-worded sentences!
 c Explain how a sakia works, with the help of the lettered parts in Figure 5.37.

5 Complete an enlarged copy of this table by entering the 'good' and 'bad' points of the four traditional irrigation methods in its boxes.

Irrigation method	Building/ maintenance	Operating	Efficiency
Basin irrigation			
Shaduf			
Archimedes' screw			
Sakia			

6 Describe the effects of the Aswan dams on Egypt – both the country and its people.

7 a Make a (quite large) copy of the *natural* hydrological cycle you drew for Unit 5.1, but without any of its labels.
 b Now add a completely new set of labels which show how each store and transfer within the cycle is affected by building dams and reservoirs such as those in the Nile Valley.

Evaporating irrigation water makes soil salty and infertile

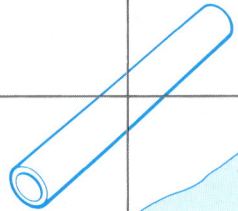

Still water helps breeding of disease-carrying snails and insects

Fish in reservoir provide protein-rich food

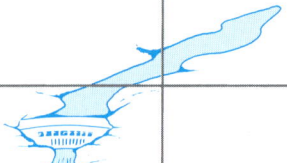

Water lost through evaporation from reservoir surface

HEP improves people's 'quality of life'

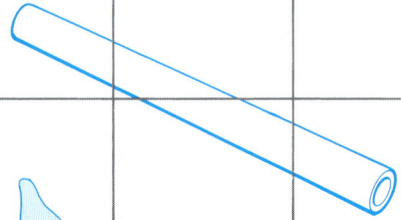

HEP benefits local industry

Dam building creates jobs

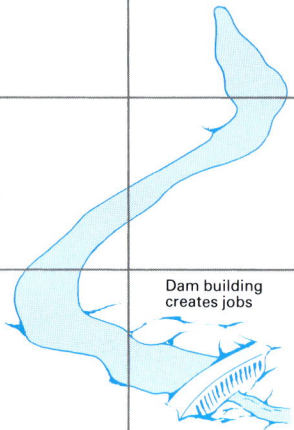

High cost of dam means less investment in houses, factories and roads

HEP powers new irrigation pumps

Lowland flooded; farmers lose land and homes

Fertile silt trapped behind dam; repla with expensive fer

Irrigation means extra crops grown each year

Lower water levels downstream; navigation more difficult

Reservoir improves water supply to homes and factories

Reservoir creates new transport routeway

5.10 Dam the consequences!

Every year, some 700 water storage dams are completed or heightened world-wide. This very high rate of construction suggests that dams and reservoirs can solve many major problems, and of course this is so. Unfortunately they can also create new ones – as the board game in Figure 5.41 is intended to show.

1 a Play 'Dam the Consequences!'. The usual rules of snakes-and ladders apply (e.g. you need to throw the exact score to finish).
b Use the information on the board to complete a table with these headings:

Main advantages of dam-reservoir systems	Possible disadvantages of dam-reservoir systems

The breeding of disease-carrying snails was just one of the problems included in the game you have played. **Bilharzia** – the disease they help to spread – affects at least 250 million people and kills about 10% of its victims every year. It is a 'debilitating' disease. This means it saps the body's strength and makes people appear to be lazy and uninterested in work (Figure 5.42). Bilharzia occurs:

- □ in tropical countries where the water is warm throughout the year;
- □ in *fresh* water;
- □ in still or very slow-moving water;
- □ in water without any traces of copper sulphate;
- □ in areas where there are already some people suffering from the disease;
- □ where toilet facilities are inadequate;
- □ where a certain type of large black snail is present in the water.

2 What appear to be the main effects of bilharzia on:
a individual sufferers?
b countries with many bilharzia victims?

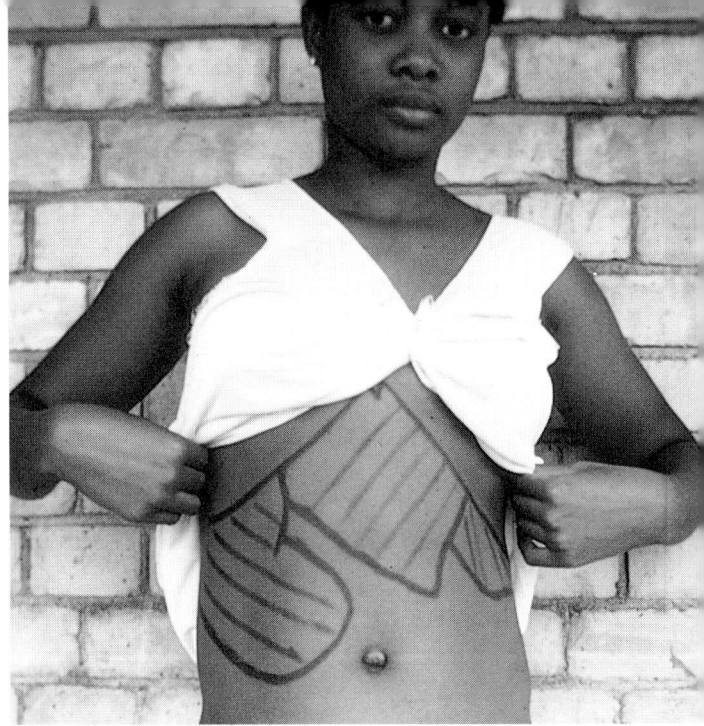

▲ **Figure 5.42** Bilharzia saps people's strength leaving them too weak to work properly. The enlarged liver and spleen are outlined

3 Describe the sequence of events in the bilharzia cycle. Base your answer on Figure 5.43.

4 Suggest ways of controlling the spread of bilharzia.

5 a Try to find out as much as you can about malaria, an even more common tropical disease. This is spread by an insect which also needs stagnant water to breed successfully.
b With the help of the information you have discovered:
i Name the insect which spreads malaria.
ii Name any other diseases spread by this insect.
iii Name at least three countries where malaria its widespread.
iv State how malaria affects its victims.
v Draw a fully labelled malaria cycle.
vi Describe ways of controlling the spread of malaria.

◀ Figure 5.41

▼ **Figure 5.43** Stages in the bilharzia cycle

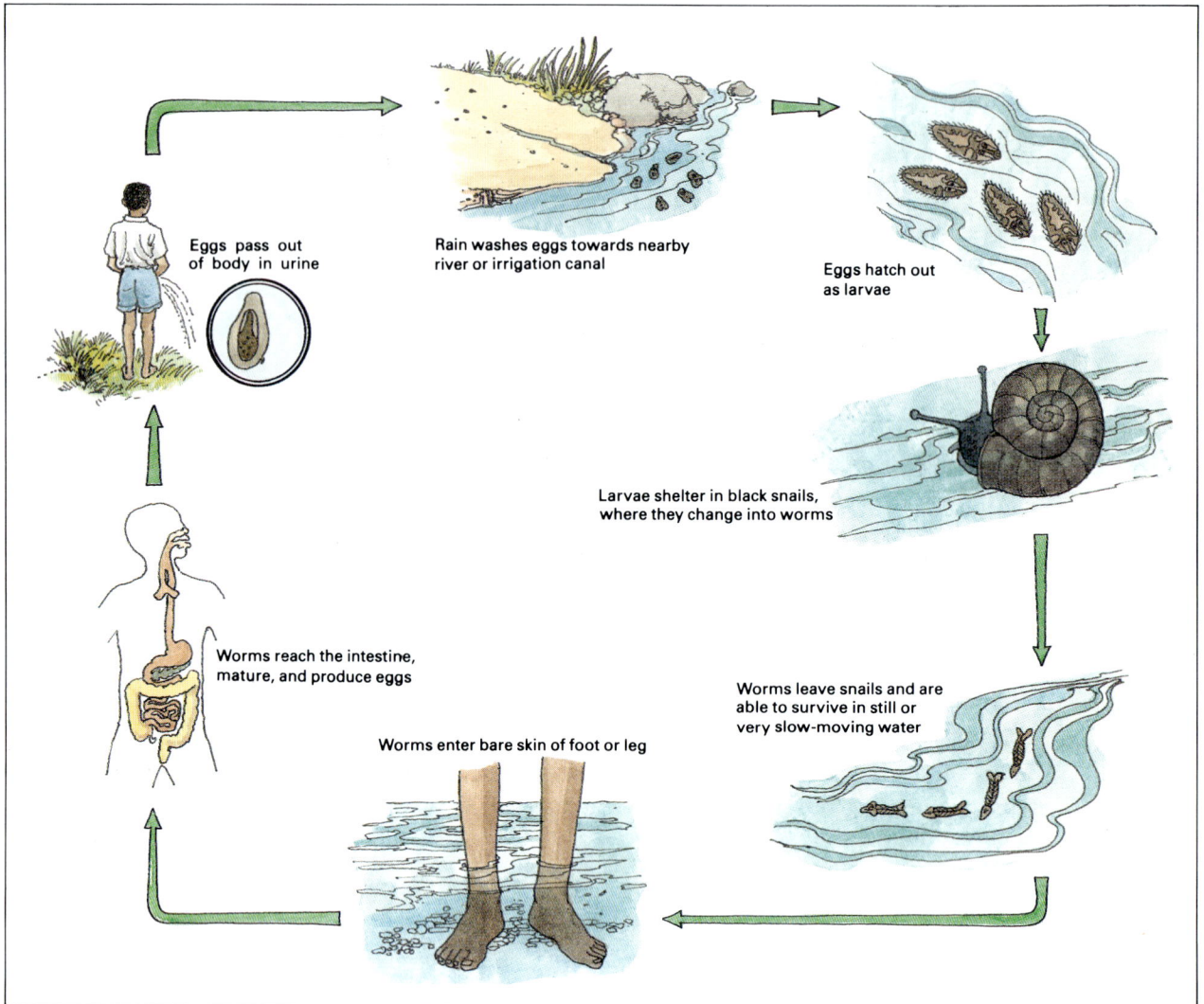

Eggs pass out of body in urine

Rain washes eggs towards nearby river or irrigation canal

Eggs hatch out as larvae

Larvae shelter in black snails, where they change into worms

Worms reach the intestine, mature, and produce eggs

Worms leave snails and are able to survive in still or very slow-moving water

Worms enter bare skin of foot or leg

Fig 5.43

6

Pollution of the Hydrosphere

6.1 Introduction: sewage disposal

Sewage disposal has always been a problem. Figure 6.1 shows one of the main reasons why the problem has increased over the centuries. It also shows what can happen when sewage is not disposed of properly, for the epidemics in medieval times were due entirely to a lack of adequate facilities. The Black Death of 1348–49 killed at least one-third of the total population of Britain and was a form of plague spread by sewer rats. They transmitted it to humans via the fleas which lived on them. It caused large, dark clots of blood to form under the victim' skin – hence its name. However, the Black Death was only one of many similar tragedies, as the next unit will explain.

In earlier times human waste was either left on the streets, dumped in a local stream or taken to nearby farms for use as fertiliser. This unpleasant operation was usually undertaken after dusk, so sewage disposed of in this way was called 'night soil'! Dumping in rivers and streams became more common as the towns expanded, and their densely populated inner areas were increasingly distant from the countryside.

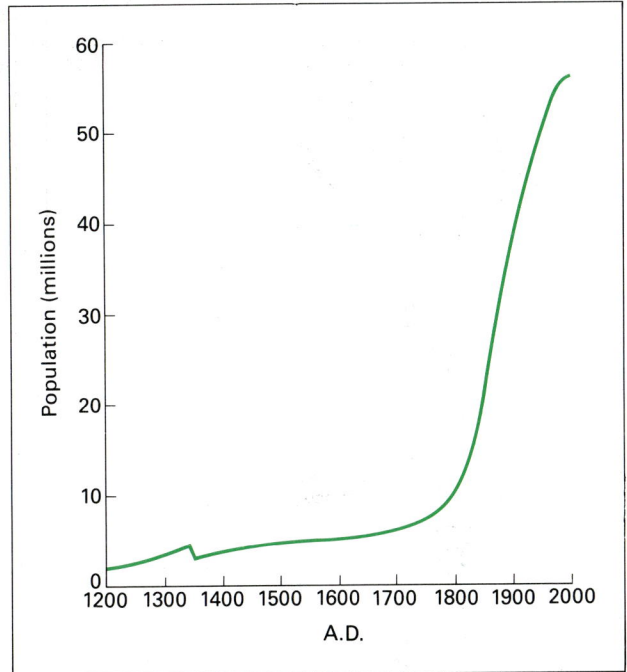

▲ **Figure 6.1** Britain's population change from AD 1200

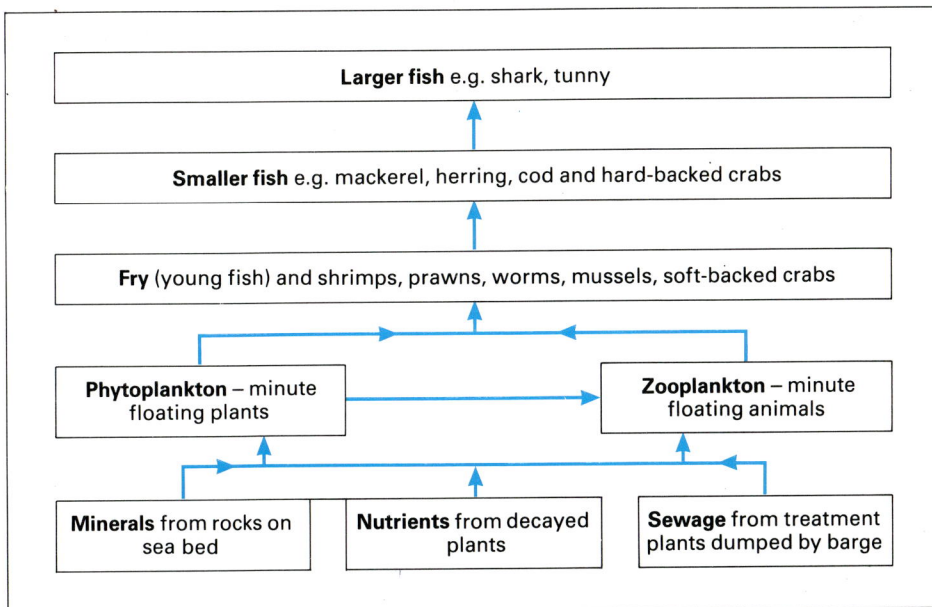

◀ **Figure 6.2** Marine food chain based on three sources of nutrients

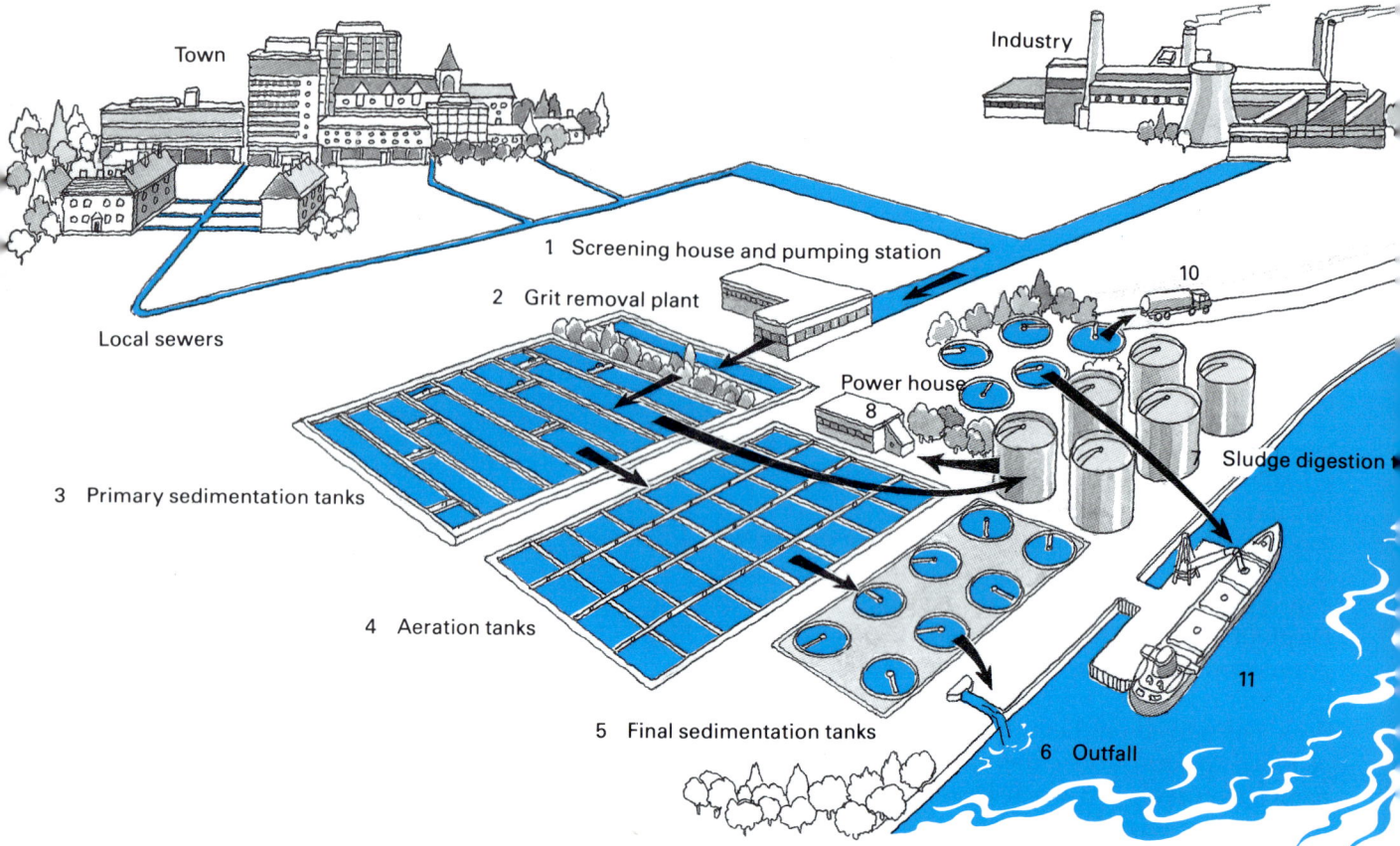

1 Screening house and pumping station
2 Grit removal plant

Power house
8

10

Sludge digestion

3 Primary sedimentation tanks

4 Aeration tanks

5 Final sedimentation tanks

6 Outfall

11

1 Screening house and pumping station Rags, wood, etc. trapped by metal bars then pulped into small pieces, burned or taken to nearby land-fill site.

2 Grit removal plant Sand, grit etc. removed then taken to land-fill site.

3 Primary sedimentation tanks Solid sewage settles on bottom then removed and pumped to 7. Remaining liquid passes to 4.

4 Aeration tanks Microbes feed on sewage and destroy it, leavi only gases and water. Sewage picks up oxygen needed by micro as it is sprayed on to gravel beds in tanks.

5 Final sedimentation tanks Microbes removed and returned to for re-use.

6 Outfall Fully treated water passes into river or sea.

7 Sludge digestion tanks Different types of microbes change sc sewage into 'sludge gas'.

Some untreated sewage is still disposed of in the hydrosphere, but mainly into the sea rather than rivers. Figure 6.2 shows what processes then break down the sewage in a natural and safe way. An increasing proportion of Britain's human waste is treated on sewage farms (Figure 6.3), and this will increase as public funds allow. The EC has also been particularly active in controlling the amount of raw sewage in coastal areas, its main target being holiday beaches. However, some very popular recreational areas (e.g. the Norfolk Broads) remain heavily polluted, in spite of both national and international action.

▲ **Figure 6.3** The layout and operation of a typical sewage treatment plant

1 Copy out only the following statements which are *true*:

'About four million people lived in Britain just before the Black Death.'

'About 1½ million Britons perished during the Black Death.'

'The Black Death probably wouldn't have happened if sewage had been disposed of properly.'

'Raw sewage is dangerous to health because it has not been treated.'

'Night soil wasn't really soil at all, but sewage put on the land to make crops grow better.'

3 Suggest reasons why:

a Modern sewage treatment plants are called 'farms'.

b Sewage disposal is becoming increasingly expensive.

4 Draw a flow diagram to show all the movements of sewage and other materials within the 'farm' pictured in Figure 6.3.

6.2 Cleaning up the Thames

The Thames is Britain's best known river. Until quite recently it was also its most infamous one, which means that it had a very unpleasant reputation. This was due to pollution, which had turned it into little more than a public sewer.

The London area has been a popular place to live in ever since the Romans conquered it about 50 AD built a bridge across the Thames and made Londinium the centre of their new road network. William the Conqueror also recognised the value of London's position and he wasted no time in building The Tower to defend it against attack. London's future was then assured and it quickly grew into one of the largest cities in the world (Figure 6.4). London continued to be a major centre for business, industry and transport and over 7 000 000 people now live and work within 30 km of the city centre.

The early inhabitants of London used the Thames as a convenient dumping ground as well as a natural routeway to the open sea. The condition of the river became so poor that Cardinal Wolsey (Figure 6.5) sited his fine palace at Hampton Court on the south bank of The Thames in open countryside *up-wind* of the capital! He even had a pipeline specially laid to supply the palace with clear water from a local spring.

The saddest phase of the river's history occured during the nineteenth century, when Britain's industrial revolution was at its height and London was growing at an astonishing rate. House and factory building were the chief concerns at that time, and public health was largely ignored. It was inevitable that epidemics would occur and particularly serious outbreaks of cholera in 1849 and 1858 killed more than 25 000 Londoners. Pollution of the Thames reached such a scale that 1858 became known as 'The Year of the Great Stink'. Work began the following year on a new sewage system – but too late to save Prince Albert (Figure 6.6) from dying of typhoid in 1861.

▲ **Figure 6.5 a** Hampton Court Palace

▶ **b** Cardinal Wolsey

▶ **Figure 6.6** Prince Albert – a royal victim of inadequate nineteenth-century sanitation

▼ **Figure 6.4** The site and growth of London

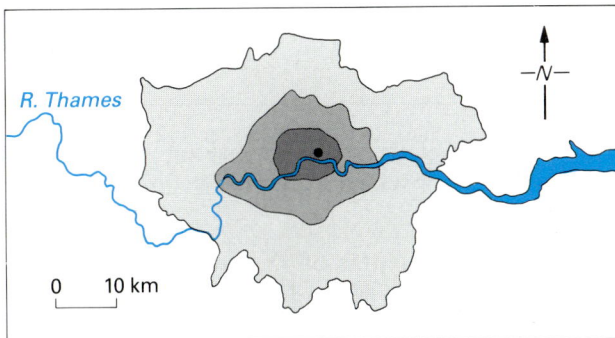

- Site of Roman London (on north bank of the river where slightly higher ground provided a firm foundation for building)

  Built-up area by 1800

  Growth of built-up area 1800–1900

  Growth of built-up area since 1900

R. Thames

0   10 km

► **Figure 6.7** Increasing concern about pollution in the River Thames led to a clean-up. Now salmon can survive in it

▼ **Figure 6.8** BOD sampling

The natural life of the Thames was seriously affected by its increasing levels of pollution. Even eels – which can survive in heavily polluted water – had completely deserted the river by the early 1950s. So too had barnacles – to the great delight of the ship owners, for scraping them off hulls in dry dock is costly and time-consuming. The pollution affected another marine pest, worms which constantly burrow into wooden piers. People unlucky enough to fall into the river at that time were rushed to hospital to have the vile water removed by stomach pump.

In 1979, young salmon were caught in the Thames for the first time since 1860! Many other breeds of fish such as sprats and flounder have since returned to the river – the result of firm action by government and much hard work by the Thames Conservancy

which became responsible for the river's well-being after 1963. One of the chief tasks of the river boards created in that year was to monitor the **biological oxygen demand** of the water in their areas. BOD is the amount of oxygen required to break down sewage and industrial pollutants. It provides a very accurate assessment of pollution levels and allows water authorities to pin-point those stretches which are worst affected. The pollutants are broken down by tiny bacteria which need oxygen to survive and do their good work. In heavily polluted waters, the bacteria may use so much oxygen that very little is left to support fish and plant life.

1 a Draw a table with this title and the two column headings shown below:

A diary of events in the life of the River Thames

Year	Summary of the event

b Complete your table by making an entry for every event for which a date has been given in this unit.

2 a What do the letters BOD stand for?
b Explain why BOD readings are used to monitor water pollution levels.

6.3 The rape of the Rhine

The following article is adapted from an entry in the 16 December 1986 edition of The Daily Telegraph

A wave of anger rises along a poisoned river
It is seven weeks since a chemical spillage devastated the Rhine. Maurice Weaver reports on its legacy.

Dead fish make bad politics. Millions of dead fish, killed by industrial pollution, can be the stuff by which governments are shaken in the conservation-conscious Europe of today. That fact will loom large as environment ministers from the Rhine states meet in Rotterdam today to discuss the outcome of last month's catastrophic chemical spillage into the river's upper reaches.

It was seven weeks ago, at 3 a.m. on a Friday, that the rape of Western Europe's greatest waterway began when 30 tonnes of agricultural chemicals were washed into it during a fire at the giant Sandoz plant at Basle, in Switzerland.

Ten days later the resulting 40 km slick of toxic 'soup' was diluted in the grey waters of the North Sea. Today's gathering of ministers takes place in the shadow of this disaster.

Like the Chernobyl tragedy before it, the Sandoz incident began accidentally but shirked responsibilities and human failings gave it a flying start. No human beings died but untold ecological damage has been done. Fish and eel – 34 varieties of them – lay gasping and dying on the surface in vast numbers. Bird and insect life died as a polluted food chain left them poisoned or starving. The river was declared 'biologic-

▶ **Figure 6.9**

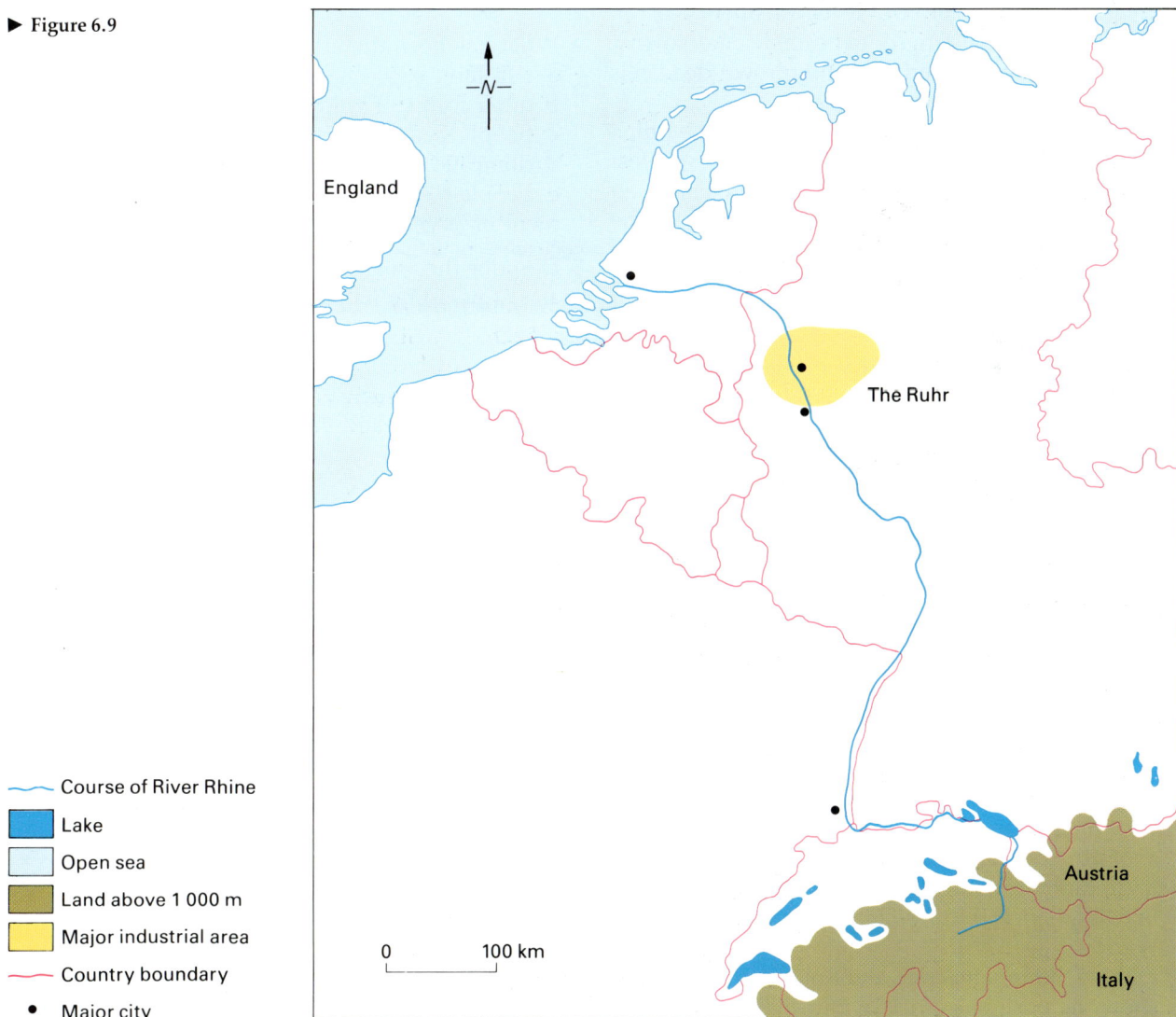

Course of River Rhine / Lake / Open sea / Land above 1 000 m / Major industrial area / Country boundary / Major city

ally dead' from Basle downstream to Karlsruhe in West Germany.

It has focussed attention as never before on an industrial pollution problem that was there anyway, on the poor record of Rhine-bank chemical firms in meeting their responsibilities, and on the will of governments to control them.

The public reaction has been one of outrage. Environmental groups are a strong political force on the Continent, particularly in West Germany where the scourge of acid rain on the forests has made people very sensitive to such incidents. The Sandoz affair will give them lots to talk about and they are determined not to let it be forgotten.

In super-clean, hyper-efficient Switzerland itself, where everything is expected to (and usually does) run like clockwork, the accident has caused national humiliation and anger. Swiss newspapers say an image has been destroyed overnight. The townspeople of Basle have even spat and thrown dead eels at Sandoz company directors.

But it is in West Germany, through which the Rhine flows for 700 km, that the affair is having the greatest political effect. The environmental Green Party, already likely to increase its number of seats in the Bundestag (Parliament) in next month's elections, has staged jointly with Greenpeace a series of highly imaginative protests to highlight the general pollution menace. Rhinesiders hardly need reminding. Hundreds of thousands had their water supplies cut off during November as river water purification plants closed down. Protests from the chemical industry that it has already spent large sums of money on cleaning itself up have received a cool response. Today's meeting in Rotterdam takes place amidst calls for tighter pollution laws, and the Ministers know that the ordinary people will not be easily satisfied this time.

One thing is certain. In the half-timbered guesthouses and elegant restaurants along the Rhine's picturesque valley this Christmas, the merrymakers will be happy to stick to traditional goose and plumpudding. Fish will be off!

1 On a copy of the map Figure 6.9, label these places with their names:
   a North Sea, Lake Constance, The Alps.
   b (In capital letters) BELGIUM, FRANCE, LUXEMBOURG, NETHERLANDS, SWITZERLAND and WEST GERMANY.
   c Basle, Bonn, Duisburg and Rotterdam. (The dots show the positions of these four major cities.)

2 With the help of your completed map:
   a Name all the countries which the River Rhine flows through.
   b Name all the countries for which the Rhine provides a natural boundary line between it and other countries.
   c Explain why there is usually very little pollution in the Rhine *upstream* of Basle.
   d Explain why there might be above-average pollution levels in the Rhine *downstream* of Duisburg.

3 a State when, where and how the pollution incident described in the article took place.
   b According to the writer of the article, was the incident:
   i an accident or caused deliberately?
   ii avoidable or unavoidable?
   iii forgiveable or unforgiveable?

4 What has been the effect of the disaster on:
   a fish life?
   b other forms of wildlife?
   c people's eating habits?
   d domestic water supplies?
   e people's relationships with the senior management of large chemical companies?

5 Describe the most likely *long-term* effects of this disaster (including its political implications).

6.4 The dead seas

The two articles below appeared in the same newspaper – within two days of each other. Read them both very carefully before attempting the questions on the next page.

Britain 'killing all life in North Sea'

By Charles Clover, Environment Correspondent

POLLUTION from Britain is turning the North Sea into the Dead Sea, says the environmental group Greenpeace today in a report based on leaked official studies.

Unless the Government introduces stricter controls on the dumping of industrial wastes and sewage sludge, the North Sea could be damaged irreversibly in the next five years, concludes Greenpeace.

Using confidential status reports compiled by all the North Sea nations and leaked to it, Greenpeace complained about the existence of 'holes' (large areas without oxygen), serious decline in fish stocks, fish disease, and seals, dolphins and porpoises facing extinction.

DAB DISEASED

Greenpeace says that almost 50 per cent of all dab caught in the North Sea in 1984 were diseased and that stocks of cod, haddock, whiting, sprats, sole, sand eels and Norway pout have shown spectacular collapses.

Plankton, the small organisms on which the fish feed, declined by two thirds from 1948 to 1970.

Dolphins and porpoises are mysteriously being driven from the southern part of the North Sea. Scientists are debating whether this is due to pollution, overfishing, accidental catches in fishing nets or increased disturbance from shipping.

Black holes

The Common Seals in the Wadden Sea off the Belgian, Dutch and German coast show the highest levels of PCB (poly-chlorinated biphenol) contamination in the world. Seal population off the Dutch coast fell from 3 000 in the 1950s to 600 in 1984.

Nitrates and phosphates from agriculture have polluted the water, causing three 'back holes' in the North Sea in 1982; the largest of which was roughly the size of Wales.

While other nations are taking a precautionary approach to pollution, says Greenpeace, the British Government is defending its right to use coastal waters as a dumping ground for sewage sludge and industrial waste containing mercury, arsenic and man-made chemicals.

Mr Andrew Booth, Greenpeace's North Sea campaigner, said yesterday: 'The government has licensed industry to damage criminally our rivers.'

(*Daily Telegraph*, 22nd April, 1987)

Article on the 'Greenpeace report'.

Greenpeace claims of a 'dead' North Sea challenged

By Godfrey Brown, Agriculture Correspondent

THE North Sea is not in danger of becoming a dead sea because of pollution from Britain, according to a report by scientists from all the coastal states.

The report, for a ministerial conference in London in November, shows that most of the sea is healthy, say officials at the Ministry of Agriculture and Fisheries.

They have been stung by charges made by the conservation organisation Greenpeace in a report this week, that dumping of industrial wastes and sewage sludge by Britain could cause irreversible damage to the North Sea within the next five years.

'We feel the Greenpeace statements are wildly exaggerated when they are not plainly incorrect,' one official said.

CONTAMINATION LEVELS

The Greenpeace accusations were based on what were said to be confidential reports compiled by all the North Sea coastal states and leaked to the conservation group. But officials insisted the documents were not secret and would be published in due course.

It was true that all scientists and coastal states recognised that in a few definite areas around the North Sea coasts there was evidence of contamination, the most significantly in the Wadden Sea where the Dutch, German and Danish coasts converged, officals said.

'But in our view it is grossly misleading to imply that the status of such areas is representative of the North Sea as a whole, or the responsibility of the UK. It is not,' they added.

It was indisputable that rivers and atmospheric deposition accounted for most of the contaminents reaching the North Sea, and the Rhine was probably the largest single contributor. Sea dumping was a minor factor by comparison, accounting for less than five per cent of heavy metals in the North Sea, officials claimed.

(*Daily Telegraph*, 24th April, 1987)

Article on the 'scientists' report'.

1 Insert the words 'Greenpeace' and 'scientists' in the blanks to complete these statements.
a The . . . report was the first one to be reported on in the newspaper.
b The . . . report states that rivers are the *main* source of pollution in the North Sea.
c The . . . report suggests that most of the pollution in the North Sea is caused by the offshore dumping of waste.
d The . . . report maintains that pollution will cause permanent damage to large parts of the North Sea within the next five years.
e The . . . report argues that *most* of the North Sea is not subject to serious pollution.
f The . . . report blames Britain for much of the North Sea's pollution problem.
g The . . . report lays most blame for North Sea pollution on the countries of mainland Europe.

2 Explain the meanings of these terms:
'hole' (Greenpeace report)
'extinction' (Greenpeace report)
'irreversible damage' (Scientists' report)
'leaked to' (scientists' report).

3 In what ways are the fish in the North Sea said to be affected by pollution?

4 Copy this outline map of northern Europe, then:
a Name the area of the Wadden Sea (see articles).
b With the help of an atlas, name all these countries on the map:

Austria	Netherlands	United Kingdom
Belgium	Norway	West Germany
Denmark	Sweden	
France	Switzerland	

5 What do all the countries named on your map (except Austria and Switzerland) have in common?

Pollution in the Mediterranean Sea

6 Study the illustrations opposite about the Mediterranean Sea area, then account for the high levels of pollution. You are advised to do this under three separate headings:
a physical features (e.g. considering its general shape, the length of its coastline, the existence of islands).
b economic factors, (e.g. GNP, industry, transport and tourism).
c other factors (e.g. population trends).

▶ Figure 6.11

▼ Figure 6.10

The Mediterranean lands

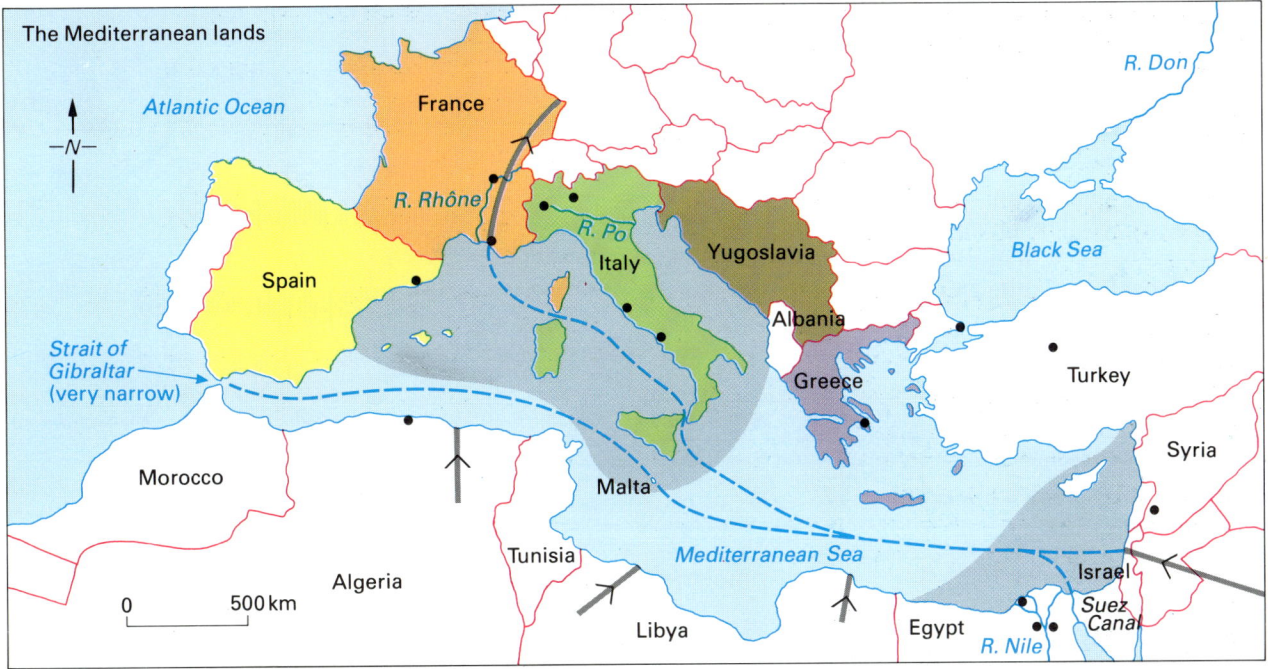

Legend:
- Country boundary
- Millionaire city (i.e. over 1 million people live there)
- Oil pipeline and direction of flow
- Major shipping lanes
- Heavily polluted sea areas
- Major river

Key details for some Mediterranean countries

Country	Population (millions, 1983)	GNP (dollars per person, 1983)
Algeria	20.6	2320
Egypt	45.2	690
France	54.6	10480
Greece	9.8	3910
Israel	4.1	5270
Italy	56.8	6390
Libya	3.4	846
Morocco	20.8	760
Spain	38.2	4770
Tunisia	6.9	1290
Turkey	47.3	1250
Yugoslavia	22.8	2490

Proportions of visitors to the five major Mediterranean tourist countries

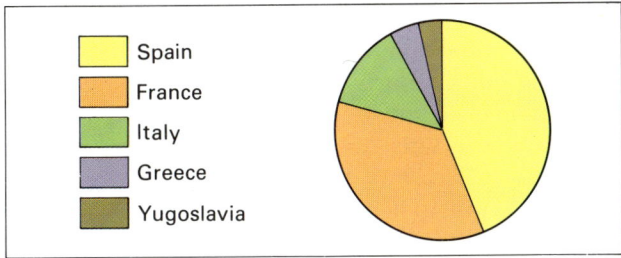

- Spain
- France
- Italy
- Greece
- Yugoslavia

Rome: population change 1910–1980

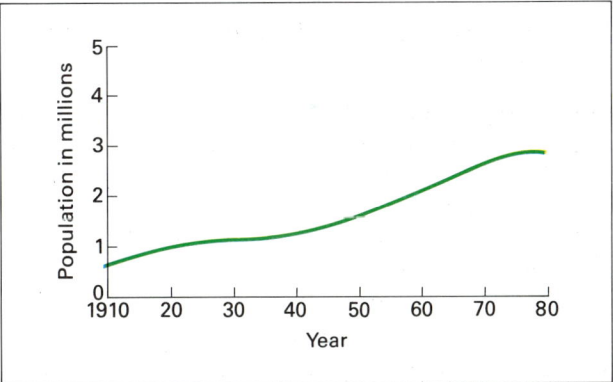

Changing number of Britons taking holidays abroad 1950–1985*

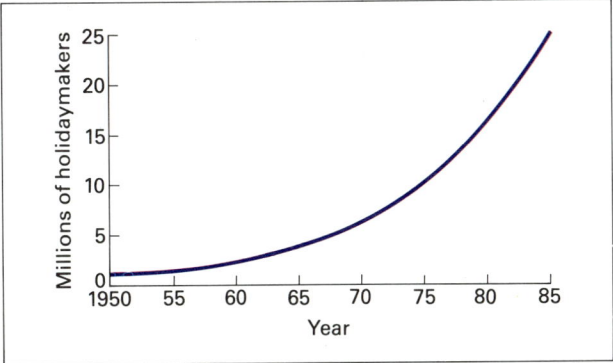

*taking into account the many people who have more than one foreign holiday in a year

6.5 Japan's polluted waters

Japan is one of the world's most fascinating countries. It is also a country of great contrasts, one of which concerns population distribution. Figure 6.12 shows that it has some large, sparsely populated regions as well as far smaller areas where people live much closer together. The Japanese call any of the smaller areas having more than 5 000 people per square kilometre **densely inhabited districts** (DIDs, for short). The table below illustrates three trends in the DIDs taken as a whole.

	1960	1970	1980
Total DID population (in millions)	41	55	70
Total DID population as a % of total Japanese population	44	54	60
Total DID area as a % of total area of Japan	1.0	1.7	2.7

▶ **Figure 6.12** Japan: relief and population density

▼ **Figure 6.13** This person has shrunk – due to Itai-Itai

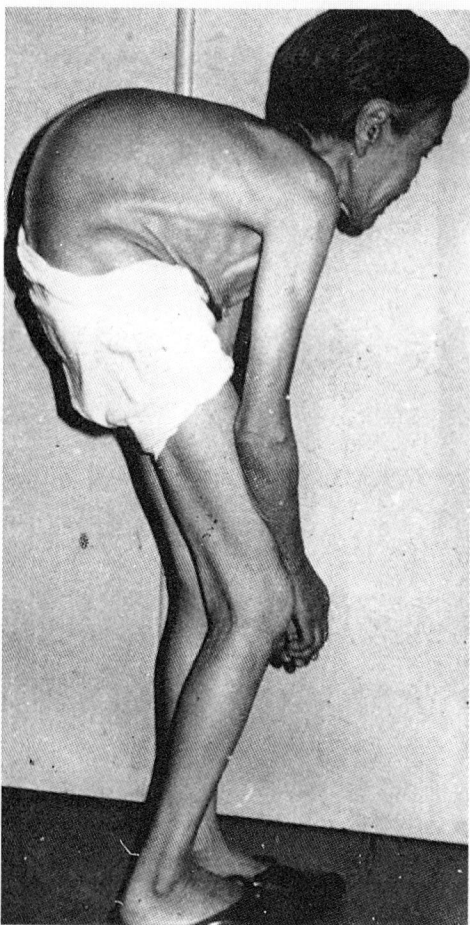

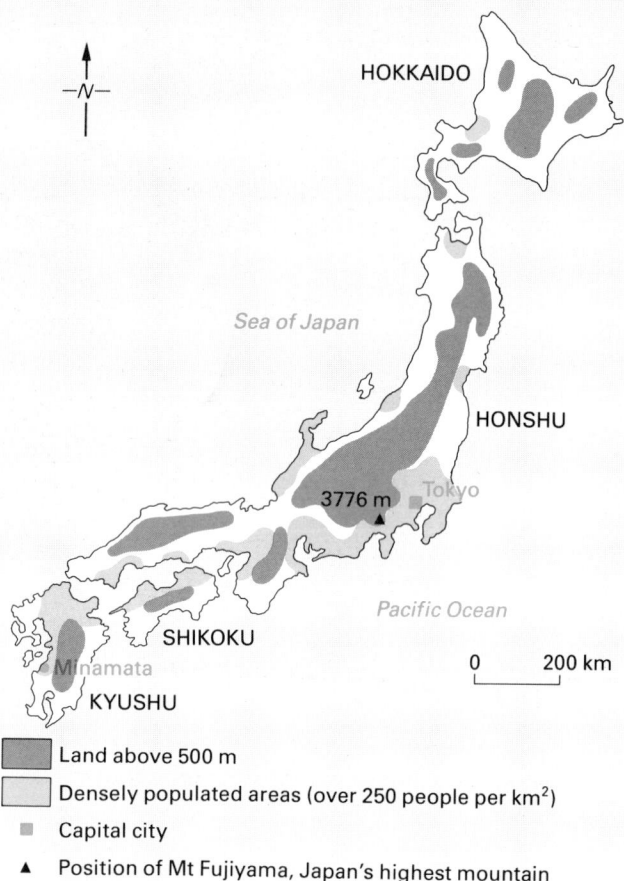

Land above 500 m

Densely populated areas (over 250 people per km²)

■ Capital city

▲ Position of Mt Fujiyama, Japan's highest mountain

Since the Second World War, Japanese industries have been highly successful and exported their products all over the world. During the 1960s, for example, Japan's GNP (overall wealth) increased by about 11% every year – four times the equivalent figure for Britain. Its industrial output also expanded rapidly, at an average rate of 15% per year. The Japanese government encouraged industrial growth but did very little to protect the environment and the people from its worst effects. The Japanese even invented a new word – 'Kogai' – for the environmental hazards created by their country's economic miracle. Unfortunately, it was the 'biologically weak' sections of the population such as the young and pregnant which were most seriously affected by industrial pollution. There have been many cases of human suffering brought about by industrial pollution in Japan. One of them, caused by cadmium poisoning, is the disease Itai-Itai, which is Japanese for 'It hurts – It hurts'. This disease makes the human skeleton so fragile that just shaking hands can break the wrist or fingers. The worst affected suffered a collapse of the spine, and some of them actually shrunk in height by as much as a foot! (Figure 6.13).

Another distressing result of industrial pollution is Minamata Disease, named after the town which experienced it first. Minamata is quite a small industrial centre by Japanese standards. Figure 6.14 shows its position on Kyushu Island. Its traditional occupation was fishing – much of it carried out in the sheltered bay to the west. A factory was opened there by the Chisso Corporation which is engaged in the petrochemical industry. In the 1930s, this factory started to produce Acetaldehyde, a substance needed for making perfumes and medicines. It dumped the waste from this new process into Minamata Bay. As the factory grew, it dumped more and more waste, and after about 20 years of dumping, the people of Minamata began to notice some very curious happenings. Large numbers of fish and birds became very weak, then died; cats started to dance around frantically. By the end of the 1950s, there were very few cats left in the town. Nobody suspected a link between the two happenings. It was only when *people* began to react did doctors and scientists take a close interest. Examination of the victims showed that paralysis and mental illness where the most common symptoms. The cause was then quickly identified as mercury waste and even now, years after all dumping of the lethal waste has ceased, parts of Minamata Bay are still riddled with the poison. The people continue to suffer because mothers who ate the contaminated fish during pregnancy passed the disease on to their babies.

▲ **Figure 6.15** The Chisso Corporation factory at Minamata

▼ **Figure 6.14** The site of Minamata and the Chisso Corporation factory

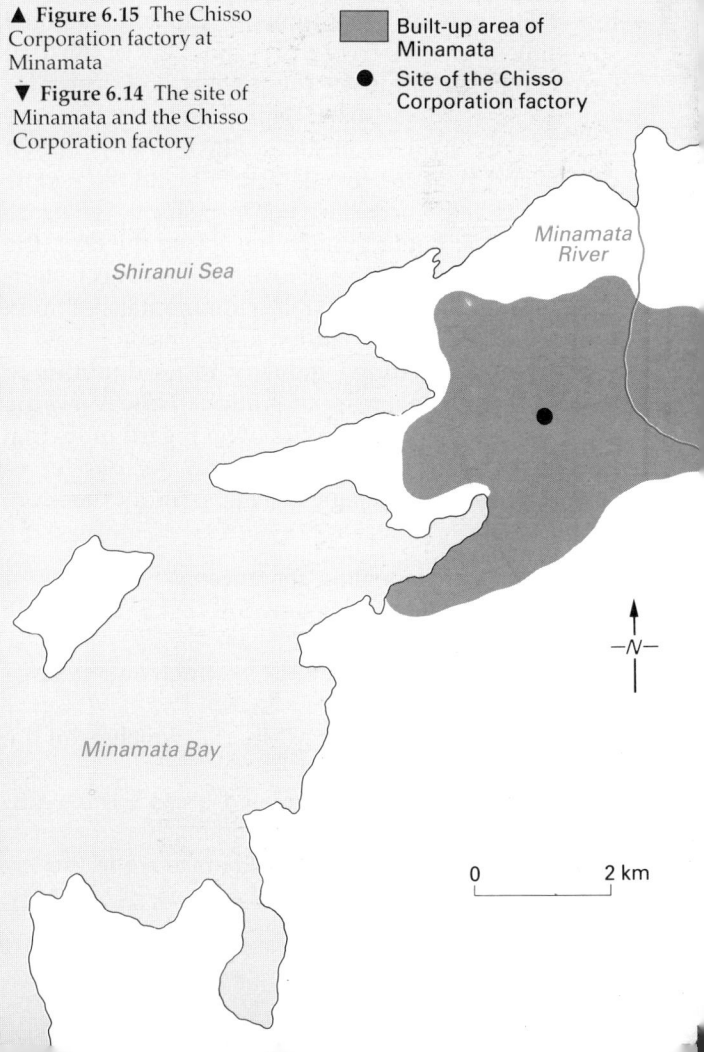

■ Built-up area of Minamata

● Site of the Chisso Corporation factory

Shiranui Sea

Minamata River

–N–

Minamata Bay

0   2 km

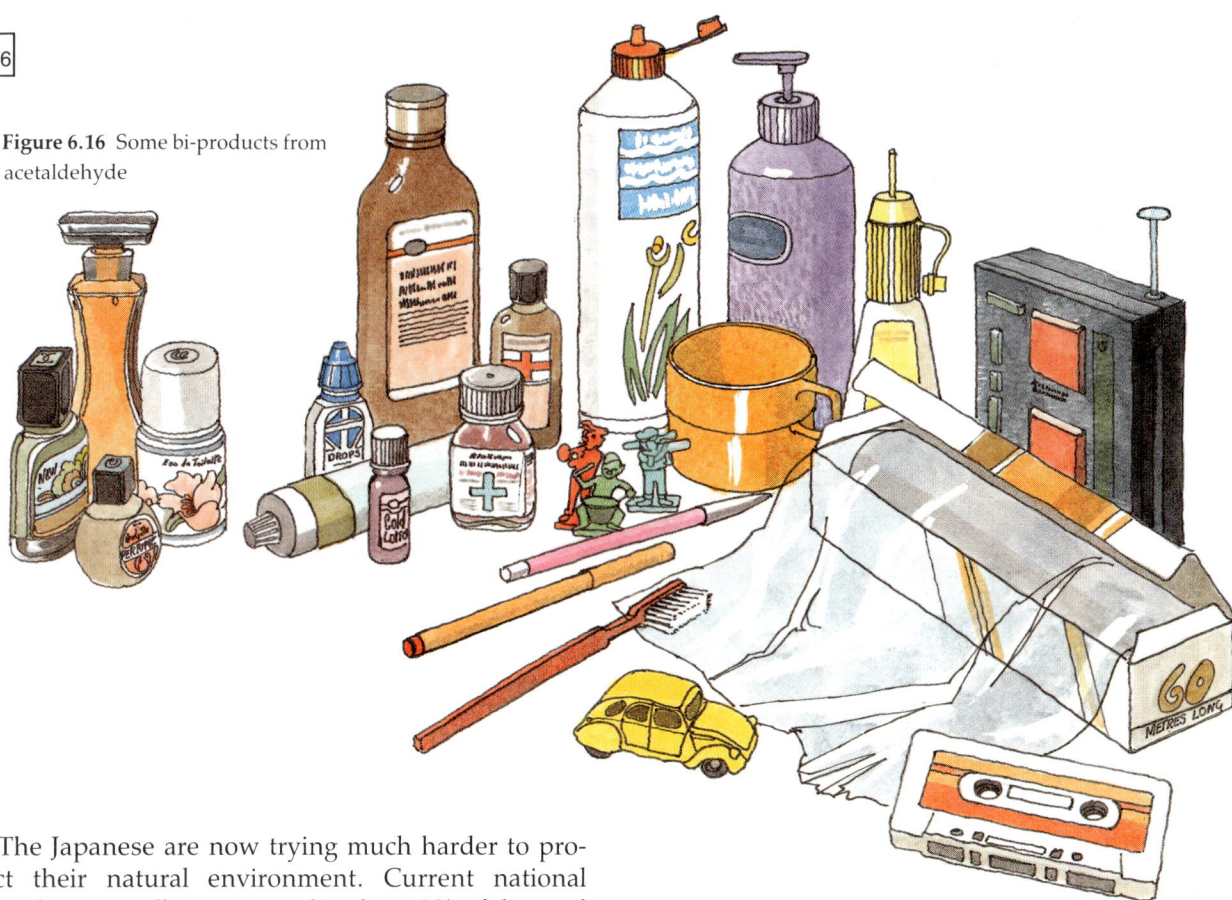

▼ **Figure 6.16** Some bi-products from acetaldehyde

The Japanese are now trying much harder to protect their natural environment. Current national spending on pollution control is about 2% of the total Gross National Product – the highest proportion for any country. Many major Japanese companies are now heavily involved in the production of pollution control and measurement equipment, and the people themselves are increasingly conscious of environmental issues. Public opinion has forced the Diet (the Japanese parliament) to approve a series of acts, starting with the Basic Law for Environmental Pollution Control in 1967. The Pollution Compensation Law of 1974 left manufacturing industry in no doubt as to its environmental responsibilities. However, the Japanese are still 'workaholics' who regard industrial growth as their main priority, and the danger of further pollution in Japanese waters cannot therefore be ruled out.

1 Complete the following sentences:
   a Japan is a country of many SANDILS (un-jumble the last word).
   b Most of Japan's surface is . . . (high and steep *or* low and flat).
   c Japan's highest point is Mt. . . . , which is on the island of . . . .
   d The most densely populated areas are . . . (inland *or* on the coast).
   e The most densely populated areas are in the . . . (north and west *or* south and east).

2 **a** What do the letters DID stand for?
   b What is a Japanese DID?
   c By what *proportion* did the following increase between 1960 and 1980 (e.g. approximately three-quarters' or '. . . times'):
      – Total DID population?
      – Total DID population as a % of total Japanese population?
      – Total DID area as a % of total area of Japan?

3 **a** What does Itai-Itai mean?
   b What caused this disease?
   c How did Itai-Itai affect the human body?

4 **a** Design a flow-diagram which traces the sequence of events in the Minamata pollution tragedy.
   b Imagine that you are witnessing a conversation between the managing director of the Chasso Corporation (who lives in the capital city, Tokyo) and a fisherman of Minamata. The two will be discussing the pollution problem very forcibly because their livelihoods are affected in quite different ways. Write down the kind of conversation you are likely to have heard, remembering that both have families as well as themselves to consider.

▼ **Figure 6.18** The remains of the *Torrey Canyon* after she was bombed by the Navy and the RAF

6.6 Tankers in trouble

Some of the worst cases of pollution at sea have been caused by oil tankers. Oil is sticky, unpleasant and can be very harmful to wildlife. Pollution of the open sea usually happens after a ship has had an accident or her captain deliberately pumps unwanted oil overboard. This is now illegal, and any officers caught doing it can expect to pay heavy fines. This unit describes two very serious cases of pollution involving fully-loaded oil tankers.

On 18 March 1967 the tanker *Torrey Canyon* (Figure 6.17) was nearing the end of her long voyage from Kuwait (in the Middle East) to the British deep-water oil terminal at Milford Haven. She was carrying 150 000 tonnes of crude (unrefined) oil. Her captain decided to take a short cut on the last leg of his journey, but he got his sums wrong and the ship smashed into the Seven Stones Reef at full speed. The hard, jagged rocks ripped open her tanks and 30 000 tonnes quickly escaped into the open sea, forming huge oil slicks on the surface. A stiff onshore breeze drove the slicks eastwards until they reached the popular holiday beaches on the south coast of Cornwall. Seven days later a fierce storm blew up and broke the ship's back, allowing a further 3 000 tonnes to escape. Shortly afterwards, the Royal Air Force was ordered to bomb the wreck and set fire to any oil left inside her tanks (Figure 6.18).

But much damage had already been done. 25 000 sea birds died as a direct result of these oil spillages and countless fish were affected as far away as the Bay of Biscay. So much detergent (washing-up liquid) was sprayed onto the oil to break it up that it too became a hazard to wildlife. Detergents were also used on the beaches, but the worst affected stretches could only be restored by digging up the oily sand with JCBs and taking it away in lorries (Figure 6.19).

► **Figure 6.19** Removing oil–soaked sand from a Cornish beach

▲ **Figure 6.22** Oil pollution causes great distress to wildlife

▲ **Figure 6.20** Oil slick booms in position

▼ **Figure 6.21** A blockship in the Suez Canal

We simply weren't prepared to deal with oil pollution on that scale and it is estimated that the cost of clearing up was over twenty times the value of the *Torrey Canyon*'s cargo of oil! Figure 6.20 shows one modern method of preventing oil slicks from reaching the shore, but this can only be used in reasonably calm weather.

The *Torrey Canyon* disaster was only the first of many. Four years later, a similar incident occured at the most southerly tip of Africa. The tanker *Wafra* was also taking crude oil from the Persian Gulf to Europe. She had to go the long way round Africa because the Suez Canal was closed at that time (Figure 6.21). She too struck some rocks below the surface and great holes in her bottom allowed the oil to flood out. Quite close to where the *Wafra* ran aground is the island of Dassen – an important breeding ground for penguins. Much of the oil drifted onto this small island and its penguins suffered greatly as a result.

The oil stuck to them and made them too heavy to float (Figure 6.22). Those able to reach the shore would try to clean themselves, but this meant swallowing some of it. A 'lucky' few were caught and cleaned by local bird-lovers who gently pressed layers of dry, powdery clay on to the feathers to soak up the oil. We now know that most never lost the scent of their human helpers and would be rejected by other birds because of this.

In 1987, the *Amoco Cadiz* lost 60 000 tonnes of her cargo of crude oil after she ran aground north-west of Brest, off the coast of France.

1 a Make a copy of this map and shade all the land areas on it lightly in green.

──── Oil tanker route (distance in nautical miles)
──── Canal
● Major port
✳ Oil tanker disaster
‑ ‑ ‑ Oil pipeline route

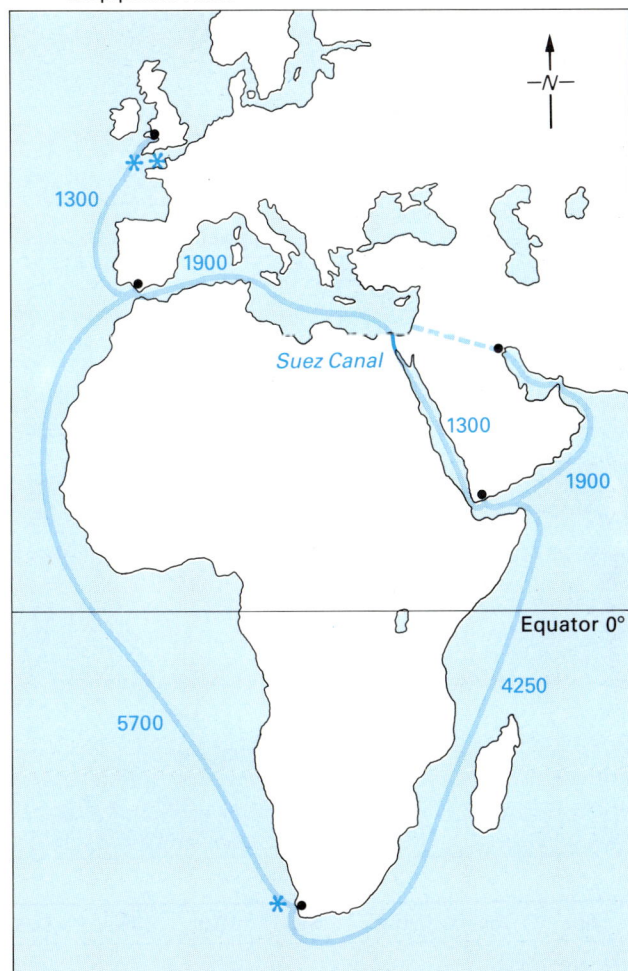

▲ **Figure 6.23** Oil transportation – Kuwait to Milford Haven

b On the map name the three ships which were wrecked in the places marked with a cross.

c With the help of an atlas name these areas of sea on your map:
Atlantic Ocean
Indian Ocean
Mediterranean Sea
Red Sea
Bay of Biscay
English Channel
Red Sea

d Name these places shown by dots on your map:
Aden   Kuwait
Capetown   Milford Haven
Gibraltar

e What are the total distances (in nautical miles) of the voyages from Kuwait to Milford Haven
i via Capetown?
ii via the Suez Canal?

f What is the distance saved by ships using the Suez Canal route?

g Suggest any *disadvantages* of using the Suez Canal.

h Why is it now possible for very large tankers carrying Persian Gulf oil to Europe to sail from the eastern coast of the Mediterranean Sea?

2 Explain why oil tankers pose a great threat to the hydrosphere.

3 Suggest what measures might be taken
a to reduce the risk of tanker accidents, including collision.
b to minimise the environmental damage caused by oil spillages.

4 a Plot this information as a double-line graph.
b Describe the trends shown by your graph.

Year	Length of word's largest oil tanker	Tonnage of world's largest oil tanker
1890	110m	5 000
1930	185m	22 000
1960	247m	70 000
1968	338m	210 000
1985	458m	564 739

c Suggest reasons for any post-1956 trends you have described, under two headings:
i Historical factors
ii Economic factors (including 'economies of scale').
d What factors are likely to *limit* the size of oil tankers?

▼ **Figure 6.25** Antarctica

Deep water	
Ice shelf	
International boundary	
Scientific base	

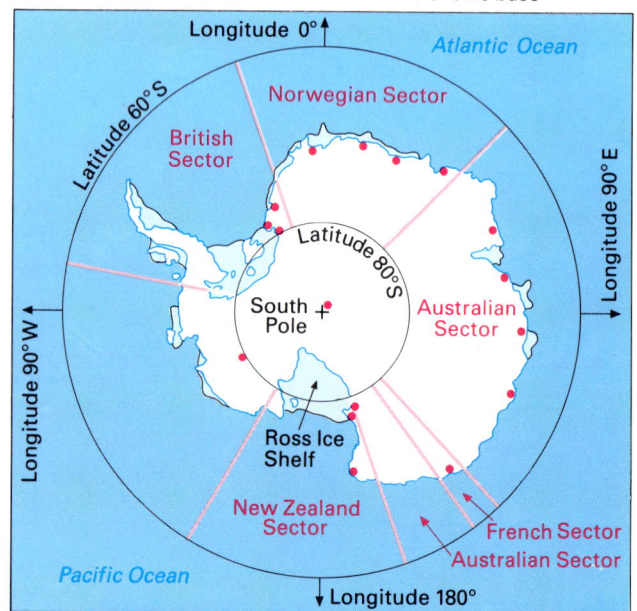

6.7 Frozen assets

We know that the Earth's polar regions are rich in natural resources and that these will become increasingly attractive as the more accessible reserves become exhausted. Large quantities of oil were discovered in northern Alaska in 1969 and question 3 highlights some of the ways in which the developments which followed are already placing its natural environment at risk.

Antarctica's resources have not yet been tapped, due partly to its remoteness and very harsh climate, but also because of an international agreement which prohibits any military activities or new territorial claims in the region. It is to be hoped that the increasing environmental awareness of the 1980s will lead to similar arrangements after this treaty lapses in 1991; also that its valuable reserves of coal and industrial metal ores will be exploited with regard to their long-term effects on this most beautiful wilderness area (Figure 6.24).

1 a Plot this information as a combined temperature-line/rainfall-bar graph.

Month	Jan	Feb	Mar	Apr	May	Jun	Jul	Aug	Sep	Oct	Nov	Dec
Average monthly temperature in °C	−30	−36	−54	−59	−58	−57	−60	−60	−59	−53	−40	−29

b Describe the main features of the Antarctic climate shown by your graph.

c What problems might developers face due to the gale-force winds which are a feature of the region?

d Give at least four other reasons why industrial development has not yet taken place in Antarctica.

2 a Describe the present territorial arrangements on the Antarctic continent.

b Suggest reasons for the pattern you have just described.

Question 3 appeared in a recent geography examination. When answering this question, you should not merely quote facts from the passage and the map, but try to identify *links* which are likely to exist between them. The best way to do this is write full sentences (e.g. '... because ...') which can include reasons as well as facts.

(NEA geography – Joint Examination Question 2(c) paper 2)

The region shown on the map below (Alaska and part of Northern Canada) has been described as a 'beautiful wilderness environment'. It is the home of various species of rare Arctic wildlife such as the Arctic hare, as well as the home of the ~~Eskimo~~ Inuit, whose traditional economy is based on hunting and fishing. The ~~Eskimos~~ Inuis depend for food, clothing, shelter and transport on such creatures as seals, whales, fish, caribou and other Arctic wildlife. The Arctic Ocean and Bering Sea are frozen for nine months of the year, but the Pacific remains ice-free due to a warm ocean current. As a result, the vast reserve of crude oil at Prudhoe Bay is brought overland by pipeline, cutting across the annual migration routes of the caribou (a type of deer) as they move northwards, grazing on the tundra vegetation. The southern coastline is rugged and spectacular, but lies along an earthquake belt and experiences many earth tremors. Several towns have increased greatly in size as people move into this region from elsewhere in the USA, from Canada, and from the local ~~Eskimo~~ Inuis population; all are searching for jobs in the oil industry and related services.

3 Using specific information from the map and data above, suggest the possible consequences for the ecosystem of parts of this region resulting from the exploitation of crude oil at Prudhoe Bay.

▶ **Figure 6.26**

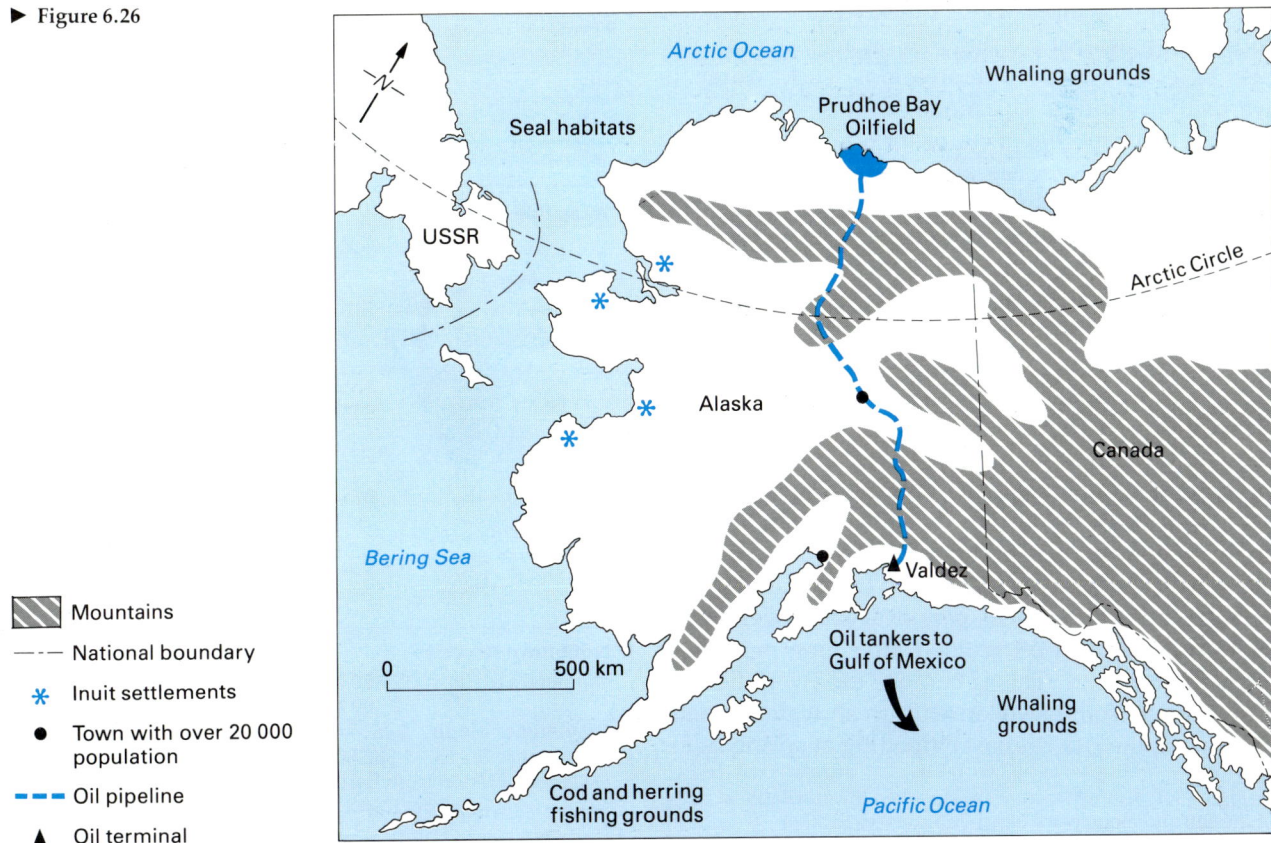

7

The Hostile Hydrosphere

7.1 Introduction: why Canute failed

King Canute, who ruled England from 1016 to 1035, is best known for something he tried to do – and couldn't! He faced the oncoming waves and ordered the tide to turn back, but succeeded only in making himself look extremely foolish. We now know why he failed, for recorded changes in sea level have been closely linked to the positions of the moon and the sun relative to the Earth. This knowledge is of great value to people living on the coast as it helps them to predict when the highest **spring tides** will occur.

In fact most spring tides don't pose a serious threat. They are at their highest twice a month and all sea defences should be high enough to cope with them. Such tides can however become very dangerous when other, far less predictable events occur at the same time. Strong onshore winds quickly cause sea water to build up against a coast. Falling air pressure may also be crucial as deep **depressions** 'suck' water towards their centres. This alone can raise the sea level by a metre or more in a couple of hours. This is why radio shipping forecasts always state whether local air pressures are falling, steady or rising.

Some stretches of coastline are more prone to flooding by the sea than others. Large river estuaries are particularly at risk because of their funnel-shape. The height of an incoming tide constantly rises as the estuary containing it narrows. The Bristol Channel is probably Britain's finest example of this. Very wide at its entrance to the west, it leads into the Severn Estuary and then the River Severn itself.

The end result is the Severn Bore (Figure 7.2) which surges upstream and may reach one metre higher than the general level of the river. On a much smaller scale, you may have noticed how the wake of a boat gets steeper as its ripples pass over shallower water. Estuary shorelines often flood after long periods of heavy rain inland. This is because the rivers flowing into them become swollen with fresh water, greatly increasing the risk of coastal flooding at spring tides.

▶ **Figure 7.1** Spring/neap tides occur when the gravitational pulls of the sun and moon work together/against each other

1 Complete these tidal definitions by inserting 'high', 'low', 'moderately' and 'very' in the blank spaces as suggested by Figure 7.3:
'Neap high tides are ... ... high tides.'
'Neap low tides are ... ... low tides.'
'Spring high tides are ... ... high tides.'
'Spring low tides are ... ... low tides.'

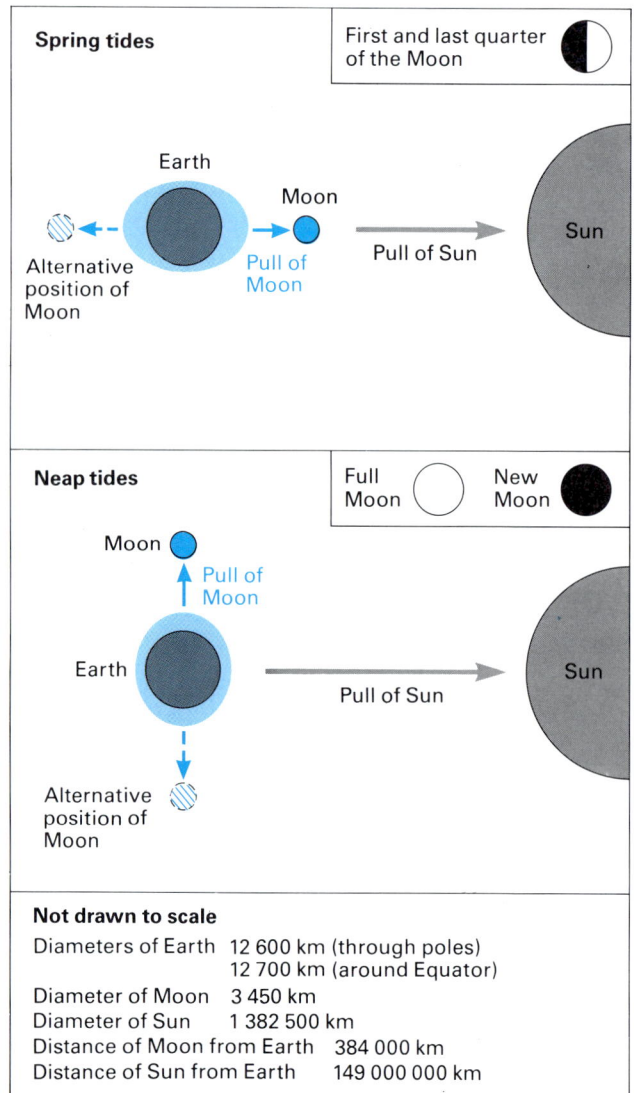

Spring tides — First and last quarter of the Moon

Earth — Moon — Pull of Moon — Pull of Sun — Sun
Alternative position of Moon

Neap tides — Full Moon — New Moon

Moon — Pull of Moon — Pull of Sun — Sun
Earth
Alternative position of Moon

Not drawn to scale

Diameters of Earth	12 600 km (through poles)
	12 700 km (around Equator)
Diameter of Moon	3 450 km
Diameter of Sun	1 382 500 km
Distance of Moon from Earth	384 000 km
Distance of Sun from Earth	149 000 000 km

◀ **Figure 7.2** The Severn Bore

▼ **Figure 7.3** Spring and neap tides on a stretch of coastline

Spring high tide

Spring low tide

Neap high tide

Neap low tide

2 Copy out this summary of the information in Figure 7.1, using you own words to fill the blanks.

'High and low tides depend upon the movements of the . . . and the . . . around the Earth. Both 'pull' the waters of our oceans and seas, creating high tides which occur once every . . . hours. The . . . has the stronger pull; although it is . . . ~~smaller~~ bigger than the . . ., it is much . . . away from us. When the sun and the moon are in . . . with the Earth, they pull together to create . . . tides. . . . tides occur when the Sun and the Moon are at . . . angles to the Earth's position.'

3 Using your own words as far as possible, explain how each of the following may increase the risk of coastal flooding:

a air pressure
b rainfall
c wind speed and direction
d the shape of the coastline
e the gradient of the sea bottom offshore.

4 Name one large British river estuary (apart from that of the River Severn), and explain why it is likely to experience flooding at certain times. Use detailed atlas map information as well as the basic ideas contained in the text.

▼ **Figure 7.5** The Thames Barrier

7.2 The Thames barrier

In late January 1953, eastern Britain suffered its worst flooding within living memory (Figure 7.4).

Thousands of square kilometres of lowland were overwhelmed by the floods and about 300 people drowned. A number of circumstances combined to produce the exceptionally high sea level at that time:

☐ The sun and the moon were exactly in line with the Earth, thus creating peak spring tides.
☐ Very low air pressure drew additional water into the southern part of the North Sea.
☐ An intense depression generated onshore winds which gusted up to 160 kmph from a north-westerly direction. These added a **storm surge** to the already abnormally high sea levels.
☐ South-eastern England is gradually sinking at a rate of about one metre every 150 years, making its coastline increasingly prone to flooding by the sea.
☐ Sea levels throughout the world appear to be rising constantly, even if very slowly.

Fortunately for London, some of the existing protective sea defence walls along the lower reaches of the Thames were breached (broken through) quite early on. This meant that the low-lying and sparsely populated areas bore the brunt of the flooding instead of the heavily built-up areas further upstream.

It was not until the early 1970s that engineers were able to design a **barrier** across the Thames which could cope with the strongest surge tides yet still allow large ships to reach inner London's docks. Parliament approved their plans in 1972 and the Thames Barrier (Figure 7.5) was completed 11 years later. It cost almost £500 million, and a further £200 million was spent raising the banks downstream to contain the water held back by the structure. One-quarter of the total cost was met by the Greater London Council, the balance from central government funds. Both authorities believed it was money well spent as it protected 1 000 sq km of lowland and the homes of 1½ million Londoners (Figure 7.6).

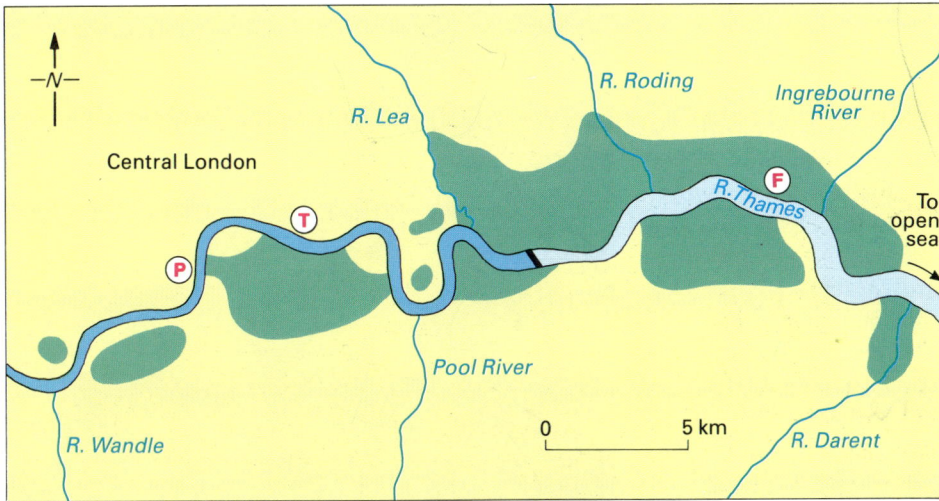

◄ **Figure 7.6** Location of the Thames Barrier

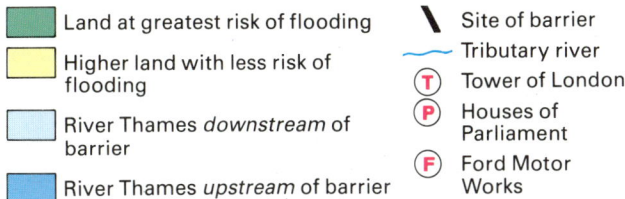

▼ **Figure 7.7** Operation of the Thames Barrier gates

Key

- Land at greatest risk of flooding
- Higher land with less risk of flooding
- River Thames *downstream* of barrier
- River Thames *upstream* of barrier
- Site of barrier
- Tributary river
- T Tower of London
- P Houses of Parliament
- F Ford Motor Works

Gate in normal position

Upstream (west) — River flow — Downstream (east)

Gate in process of closing

Gate fully closed and in protective position — Surge tide from open sea

The barrier consists of ten huge gates 20m high which can be quickly moved into position to close the river. Gauges showing tidal levels at strategic points within the Thames Estuary are constantly monitored and linked to computers programmed to estimate the most likely effects of not activating the barrage. There are four 200m-wide openings to allow shipping to reach the Pool of London 8km further upstream. Most local people like their new barrage and are relieved that it does not have the tall concrete towers which featured in some of the rejected designs.

1 a What happened to convince people that it was worth building such a costly barrier across the River Thames?
b What was the total cost of the flood prevention scheme, and how was this money obtained?
c What reasons might the British government have had for subsidising the Thames barrage scheme?

2 a What did the engineers have to bear in mind when designing the barrage?
b With the help of the drawings opposite, explain how the barrage is able to meet these requirements.

3 In what respects has the Thames barrier
a failed to protect some areas from flooding?
b created new problems for the area immediately around it?

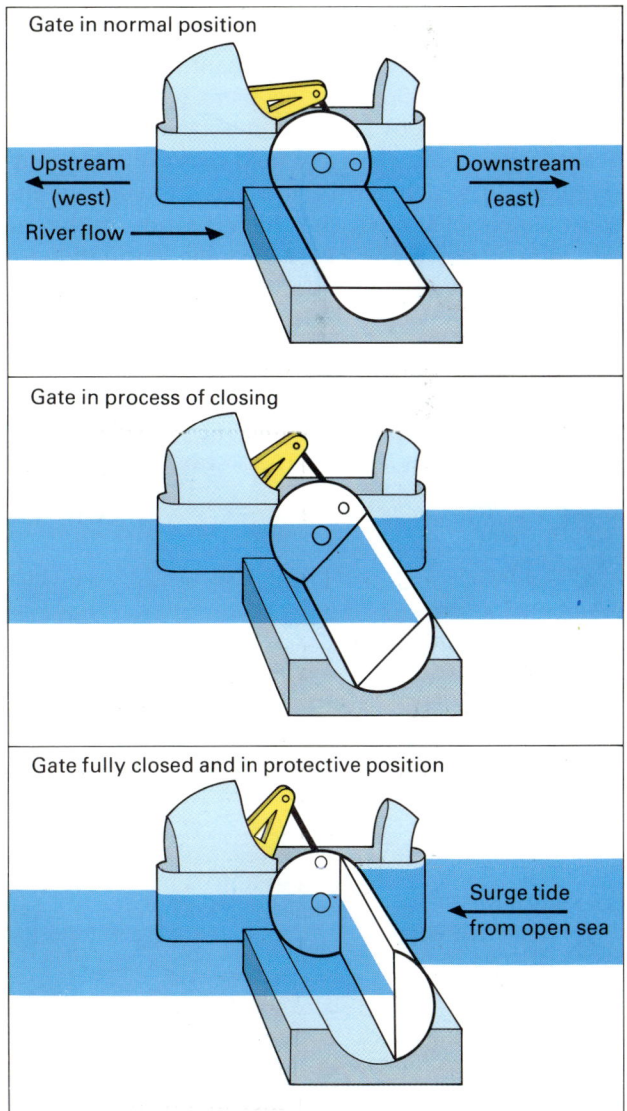

7.3 The Dutch Delta Plan

The fierce storms of 1953 described in the last unit hit the Netherlands particularly hard. Hurricane force winds devastated the low-lying areas on its North Sea coasts, claimed 1 800 lives and drove over 70 000 people from their homes. The Dutch reacted swiftly. The following year they launched the Delta Plan and work on it continued until 1986, when Queen Beatrix officially opened the final – and largest – phase. This involved building two artificial islands and a series of barrages to cut the East Scheldt estuary off from the open sea. The Dutch opted for a barrier (which allows water to pass through it) rather than a barrage. A barrage would have been much simpler to design and construct, but a change to fresh water habitats would have endangered the delta's rich plant and birdlife.

Figure 7.8 gives you some idea of the scale of this remarkable engineering feat. The channels between the islands are up to 40m deep. 65 'piers' built of concrete and weighing about 18 000 tonnes each form a spine across these channels. They hold massive steel gates (Figure 7.9) which can be lowered to keep out the most violent of storms. The shifting sands on the sea bed would have made a very unstable foundation for the piers, and so it was decided to lay a 'mattress' filled with rubble and gravel under each one. The mattresses are heavy enough to withstand the swift currents which are a feature of this delta.

▲ **Figure 7.9** The East Scheldt Barrier

1 List any three facts about the storm which led to the Delta Plan.

2 **a** Describe the problems which faced the engineers working on the Delta Plan.
b Explain how the Plan's engineers responded to these problems.

3 Apart from the East Scheldt barrier, what changes have been made to this area as a result of the Delta Plan? (See Figure 7.8.)

▶ **Figure 7.8** The Dutch Delta Scheme. The Lek and Waal are distributaries (outlets) of the River Rhine

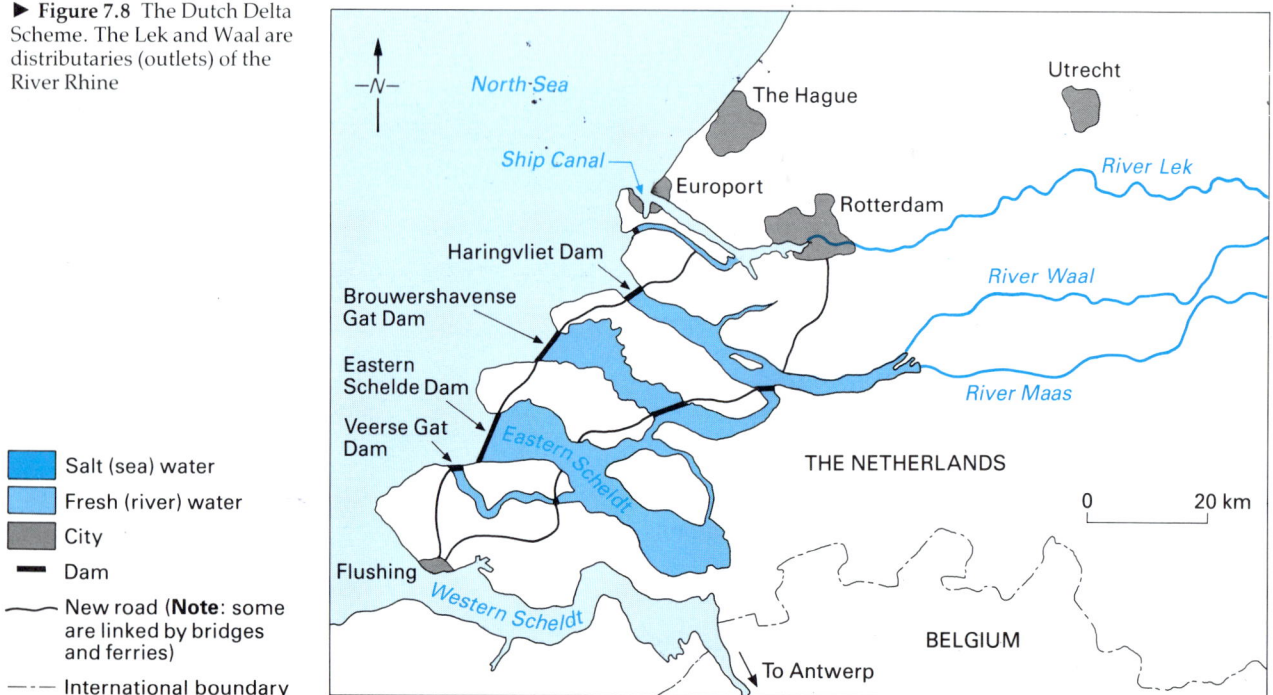

7.4 Storm surges in Bangladesh

Listed below are six sets of facts about flooding in the south-east Asian country of Bangladesh:

Set 1 In 1962, 25 000 inhabitants of Bangladesh were drowned in floods.

Set 2 On one Thursday in 1970 – the local people still call it 'Black Thursday' – well over 100 000 people lost their lives in the same part of Bangladesh, where the Rivers Ganges and Brahamaputra flow into the Bay of Bengal. At least half a million farm animals were also drowned and about 10 000 fishing boats dashed to pieces. Seawater salt ruined large vital rice-growing areas. Whole villages were devastated and countless farm tools such as hoes were swept away by the flood waters.

Set 3 In May 1985, over 5 000 people were killed in the same way – by tidal waves 12 metres high. These people also perished on the fertile plain and islands of the Ganges Delta.

Set 4 All three disasters were the result of typhoons sweeping across the southern part of the Bay of Bengal. These areas of extremely low air pressure produce winds of up to 240km per hour and very high storm surges.

Set 5 Bangladesh received a great deal of international help after each disaster. Foreign aid included food, clothing, tents and blankets, as well as some money to help rebuild the Delta's shattered economy.

Set 6 The rivers flowing into the Bay of Bengal behave in a similar way to the River Nile (see Unit 5.9). The Ganges and the Brahamaputra also have their sources in high mountain ranges, and produce flooding much further downstream when swollen with additional water. This seasonal increase in river levels has been greatly affected by widespread deforestation on the lower slopes of the Himalayas. Each flooding adds an extra layer of fine silt which has accumulated over many thousands of years to produce a broad and extremely fertile flood plain. Near the coast, some of this deposited 'alluvium' has created low-lying islands and the rivers divide up into smaller distributaries which flow between them. The Ganges Delta therefore experiences regular and highly beneficial river flooding as well as the kind of storm surge flooding which took place in 1962, 1970 and 1985. Many of the villages are built on the islands and have stilts which help them to cope with the seasonal changes in river level.

1 Copy the map in Figure 7.10, then replace the question-mark labels with their correct place names (e.g. write 'Bay of Bengal' instead of '?Bay').

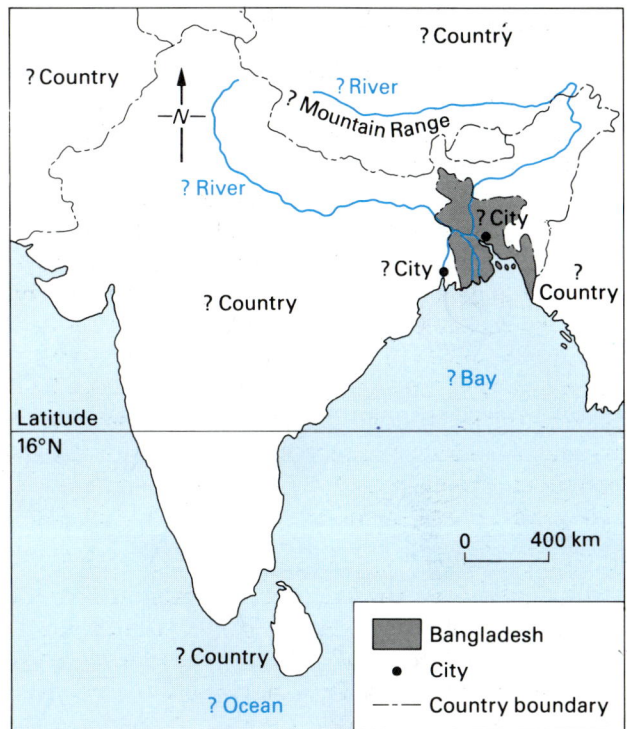

▲ **Figure 7.10** The Indian sub-continent

2 **a** In which ways is the shape of the Bay of Bengal similar to that of the Bristol Channel/Severn Estuary? (See Unit 7.1.)

b How wide is the mouth of the Bristol Channel from St Govan's Head to Hartland Point?

c How wide is the mouth of the Bay of Bengal along line of latitude 16°N?

d How many times wider is the Bay of Bengal in **c** then that of the Bristol Channel in **b**?

e What is the normal maximum height of the Severn Bore?

f How high was the Bay of Bengal storm surge of May, 1985?

g How do your answers to **d** and **f** compare?

h What factors have helped to make the storm surge in the Bay of Bengal so much higher?

3 Copy out only the following statements about tropical cyclones which are *true*:

'Tropical cyclones occur in areas of very low air pressure.'

'They may create tidal waves (storm surges) up to 12m high.'

'They may produce wind speeds of up to 240km per hour.'

'They never blow away from the Equator – always towards it.'

▲ Figure 7.11

▼ Figure 7.12 Tropical cyclone formation and movement

4 a Explain why delta areas are prone to serious flooding.
  b Describe the benefits and advantages of flooding (for whatever reason) in such areas.
  c State how the local people have adapted to the threat of flooding.

5 Imagine that you are a member of a team of experts flown out to Bangladesh to advise on flood control. Your appointment requires you to meet in small groups to discuss and then produce a brief written report on how the Ganges Delta should respond to the threat of serious flooding. The Bangladeshi government wishes your report to concentrate on three themes:

1 The ways in which the harmful effects of any kind of flooding may be reduced **without any regard to cost**.

2 The measures which a *poor* country such as Bangladesh might be able to afford.

3 The measures which are likely to be most effective against *storm surges*.

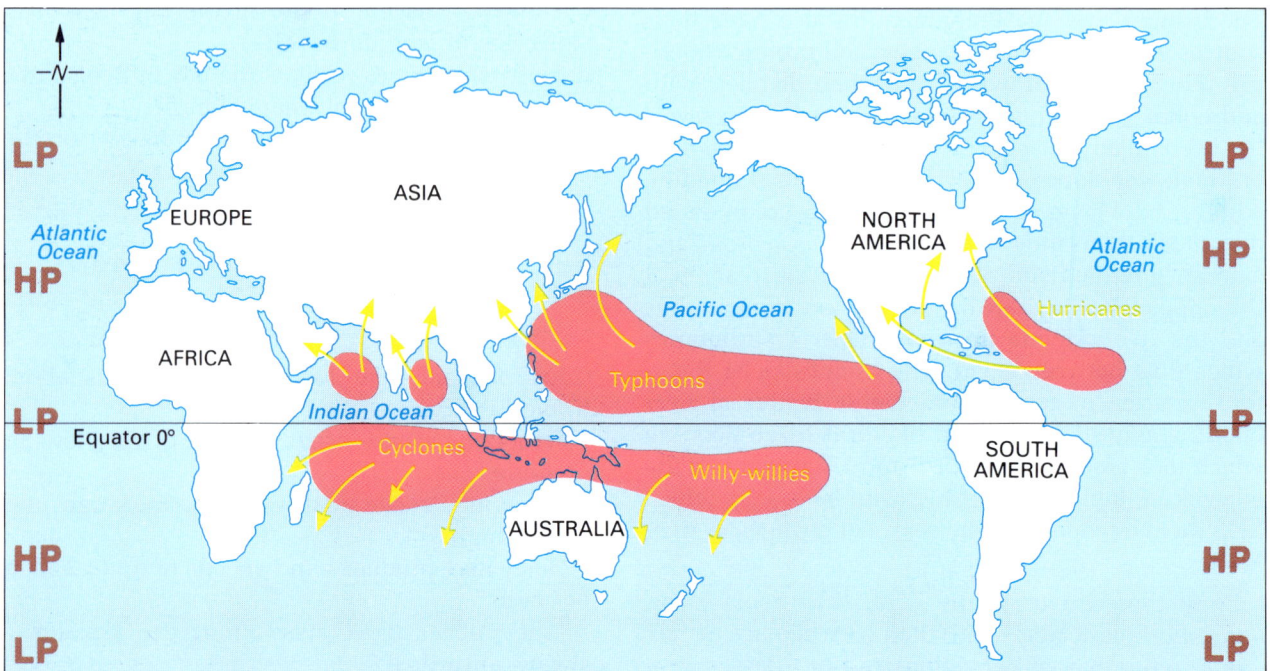

	Cyclone formation zones
	Cyclone tracks
HP	Belt of high air pressure
LP	Belt of low air pressure

7.5 TVA to the rescue

The North American river, the Tennessee, is a tributary of the River Ohio which in turn flows into the Mississippi (Figure 7.13). The Tennessee itself is quite a sizeable river for it carries about 25 times as much water as our own River Thames. Its large catchment area is on the western slopes of the Appalachian Mountains, which attract a good deal of relief rainfall. The river caused such serious flooding in 1926, 27 and 28 that the American government formed the Tennessee Valley Authority (TVA for short) in 1933 – a special organisation to investigate the problem and suggest measures to reduce it in the future.

The TVA discovered that much of the flooding was due to soil washed off the bare hillsides. This choked the river, causing it to break its banks. It also discovered that this soil erosion was the result of farming methods used in the area ever since the 'White Man' first settled in the late 1700s. The poor farming families – nicknamed 'hill-billies' – seemed largely unaware of the damage they were doing to the land around them. Figures 7.14–7.17 show four of their unhelpful farming methods and the TVA's responses to them. The Authority also financed the building of many dams. These helped to reduce water levels in the rivers, especially just before the heavy winter rainfall.

But the TVA was much more than just a flood-control authority. It also wanted to create jobs and attract people into this remote and somewhat **inaccessible** region. Its dams generated hydro-electric power and its reservoirs provided homes, farms and new factories with a reliable water supply. It sponsored greatly improved leisure facilities for sailing, fishing and camping. It even built a new canal to make it easier to move goods both into and out of the area.

The Tennessee Valley Authority was remarkable in being the first organisation to tackle all the problems in an area dominated by one river. Most local people think it has done an excellent job. Of course, it did make some mistakes because much of what it was doing was pioneer work. For example, the reservoirs tended to silt up very quickly. The dams trapped the early winter run-off from the hills and the mass of silt carried by it was therefore able to settle on the bottom.

▼ **Figure 7.13** The TVA area

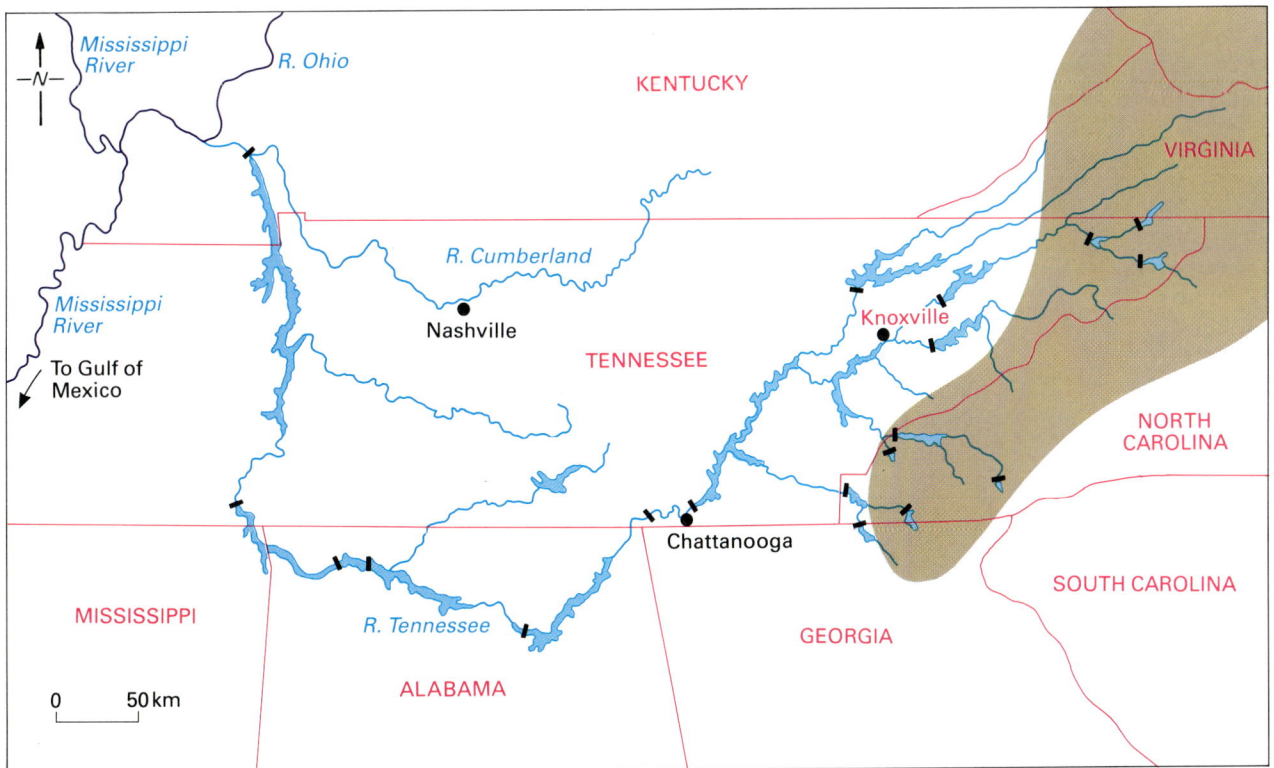

Figure 7.14 Erosion linked to the grazing of animals

Figure 7.15 Erosion linked to the direction of ploughing arable land. The correct term for the right hand method is contour ploughing

Figure 7.16 Erosion linked to tree cover

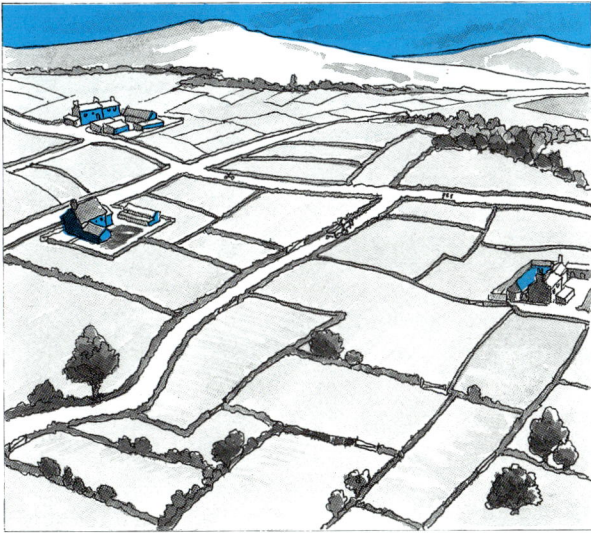

Figure 7.17 Erosion linked to cropping patterns. The scene on the right is the result of crop rotation (see unit 3.3)

1 **a** Re-arrange the following in the sequence in which they occur:

Relief rain falls on the Appalachian Mountains.
Water flows into Atlantic Ocean.
Water flows into the Gulf of Mexico.
Water flows into the Mississippi River.
Water flows into the Ohio River.
Water flows into the Tennessee River.

b Describe the general position of the TVA within the United States (see the world map on page 157).
c Describe the nature (e.g. the relief) of the TVA area as shown by Figure 7.13.

2 **a** What do the letters TVA stand for?
b When and why was the TVA created?
c How has the TVA helped to:
i create jobs?
ii improve the accessibility of the area?
iii increase recreational provision?

3 Answer **a–d** for *each pair* of illustrations in Figures 7.14–7.17.
a Describe what is taking place in the left-hand picture.
b Explain how this activity encourages soil erosion.
c Describe the alternative activity shown in the right-hand picture.
d Explain how this activity can help to reduce soil erosion.

4 What are the main benefits of the comprehensive regional planning concept pioneered by the TVA?

7.6 The British climate

British weather is notoriously changeable, due largely to variations in wind direction and air pressure. Temperature and rainfall readings taken over many years do however suggest that there are certain basic patterns even to our own rather bewildering climate.

Each of the boxes in Figure 7.18 contains three pieces of climate information, all of them based on the annual readings for over 100 years. (Note: the temperatures are correct for sea level, as no allowance has been made for the cooling effect of high land.) The area on the map has been divided up in this way because we can identify certain climate differences between the north and the south, as well as between east and west. The two lines on the map which separate these areas are called **isotherms** – lines which join places having the same temperature.

1 **a** Draw Figure 7.18 on an outline map of the British Isles.
b Label each isotherm on your map with its most likely temperature (choose from: 0°C, 5°C, 10°C, 15°C and 20°C).
c Enter the 'temperature range' in each box. This is the *difference* between the high summer and lower winter temperatures.

2 Copy out and complete each of these statements about the climate of the British Isles.
a The eastern parts of the British Isles are generally much ... (cooler *or* warmer) than those in the west.
b The northern parts are slightly ... (cooler *or* warmer) than those in the south.
c The temperature range is ... (greater *or* smaller) in the north than the south; it is also smaller in the ... (east *or* west) than the ... (east *or* west). This means that the ... (north-east *or* north-west *or* south-east *or* south-west) has the most extreme climate of all because it has the greatest temperature range.
d The wettest areas are generally in the ... (east *or* west) and ... (north *or* south) of the British Isles. The wettest area of all is the ... (north-east, north-west, south-east *or* south-west); the driest is the ... .

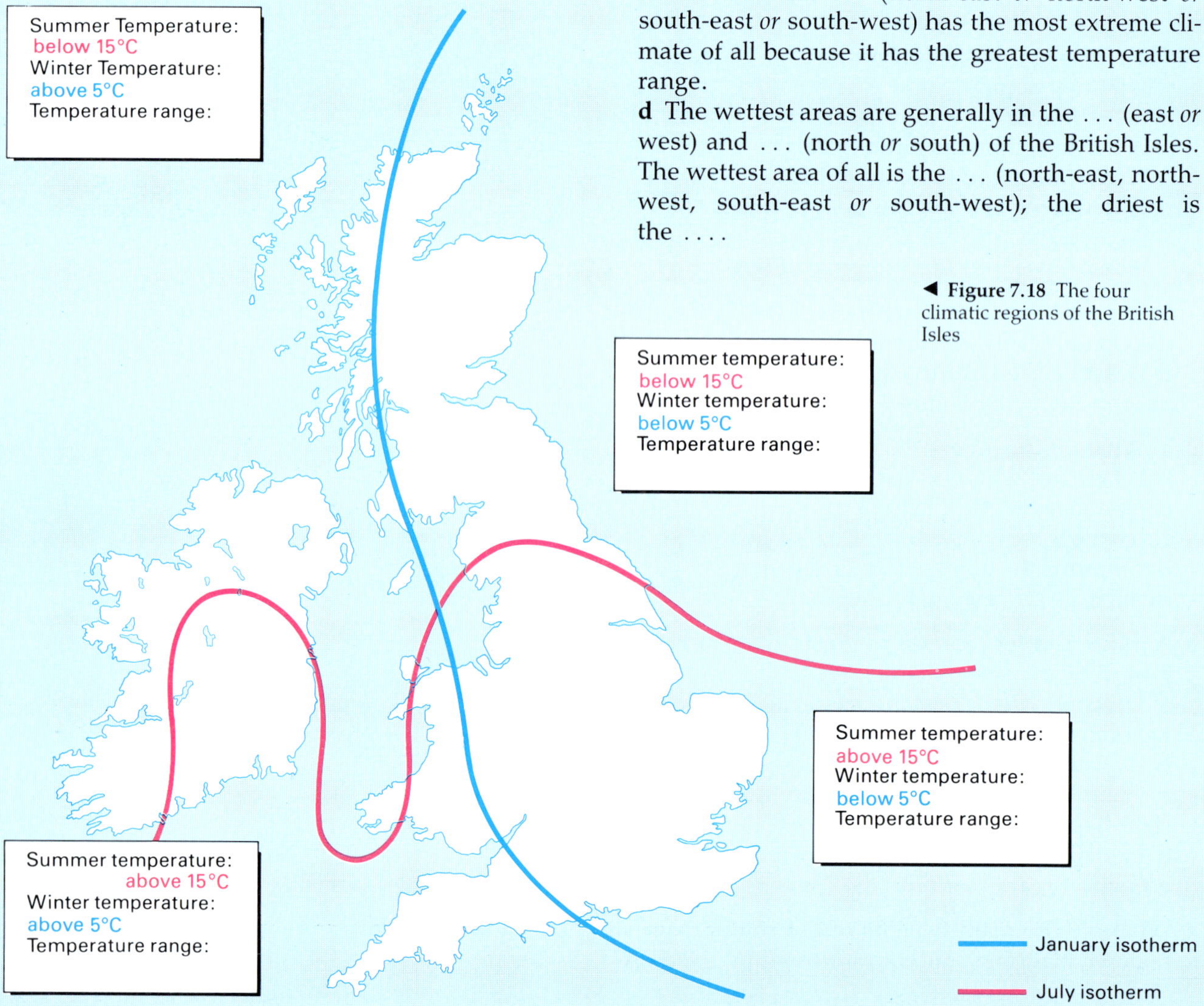

◀ **Figure 7.18** The four climatic regions of the British Isles

Summer Temperature:
below 15°C
Winter Temperature:
above 5°C
Temperature range:

Summer temperature:
below 15°C
Winter temperature:
below 5°C
Temperature range:

Summer temperature:
above 15°C
Winter temperature:
below 5°C
Temperature range:

Summer temperature:
above 15°C
Winter temperature:
above 5°C
Temperature range:

January isotherm
July isotherm

Figure 7.19 (left map)

Depressions sweep in from the west, bringing periods of heavy rain

Land over 400 m
Land 100–400 m
Land below 100 m

Ben Nevis 1343 m

Sca Fell ▲ 978 m

▲ Snowdon 1040 m

0   200 km

—N—

North Atlantic Drift

Warm sea current generated by tropical maritime winds

—The sun is the most important source of heat in summer, but not in winter (due to its changing position in the sky)

Europe's continental climate is much warmer in summer and colder in winter than that of the British Isles

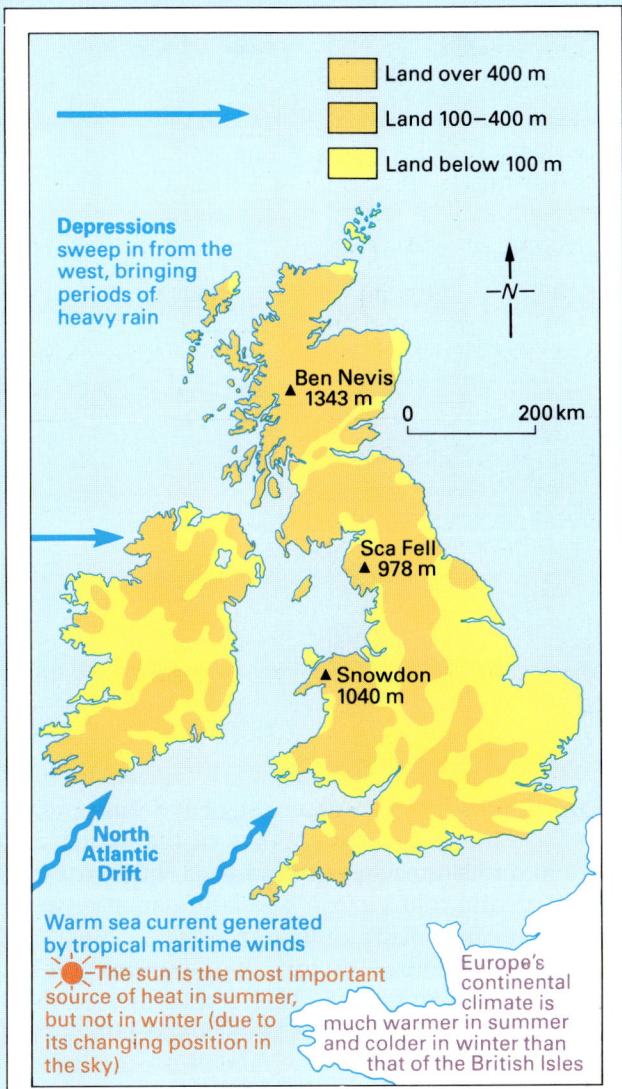

Rainfall pattern due to the tropical maritime (prevailing south-westerly) winds

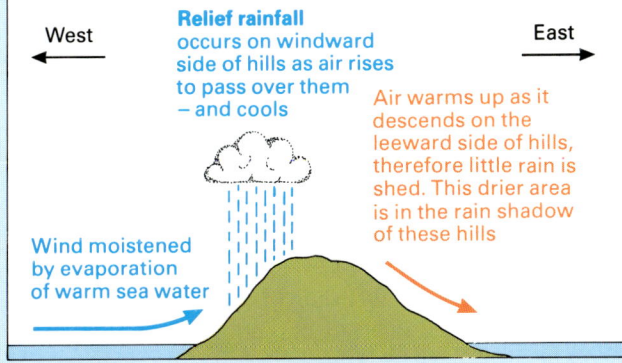

West ← → East

Relief rainfall occurs on windward side of hills as air rises to pass over them – and cools

Air warms up as it descends on the leeward side of hills, therefore little rain is shed. This drier area is in the rain shadow of these hills

Wind moistened by evaporation of warm sea water

▲ Figure 7.19

Figure 7.20 (right map)

Polar maritime winds
Cool in summer
Cold in winter

—N—

Polar contintental winds
Rarely blow in summer
Very cold in winter

Mainly convection rainfall in summer

Tropical maritime winds
Warm in summer
Mild in winter

0   200 km

Tropical contintental winds
Very warm in summer
Rarely blow in winter

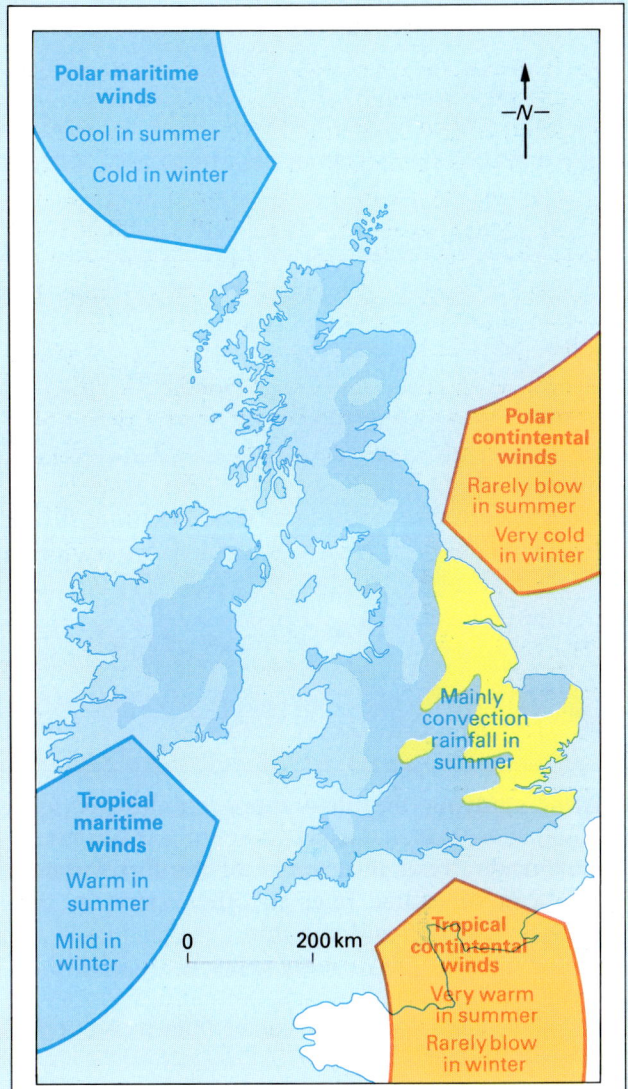

Total annual rainfall over 1500 mm
Total annual rainfall 1000–600 mm
Total annual rainfall below 600 mm
Moist winds
Drier winds

Typical wind rose for north-west Scotland

—N—

Typical wind rose for south-east England

▲ Figure 7.20

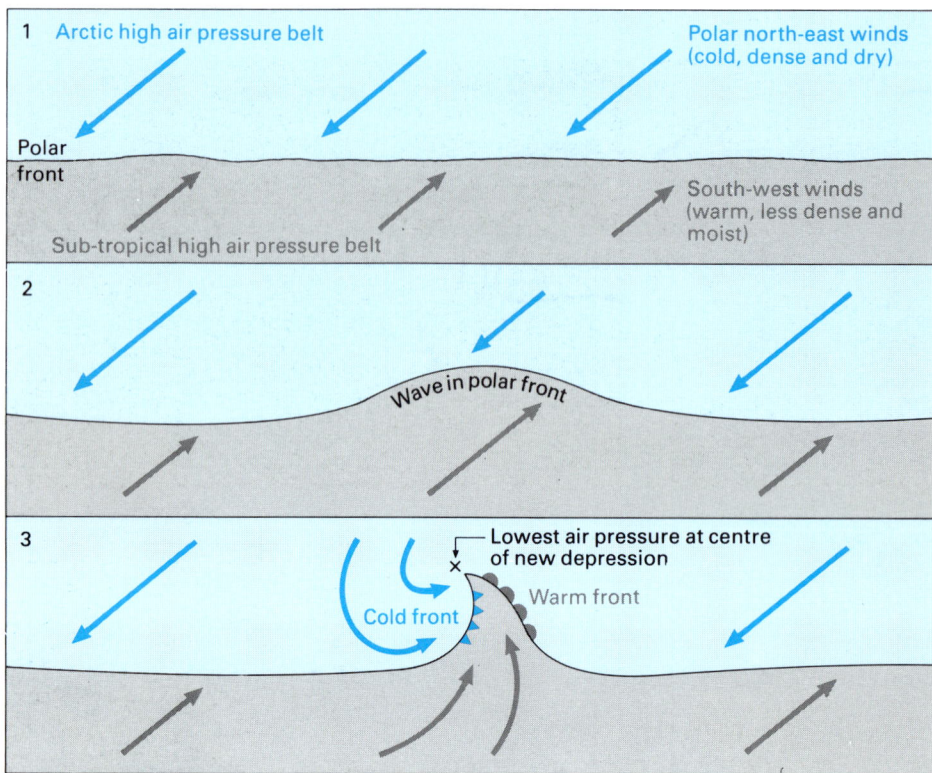

3 After studying the illustrations on the previous page, give reasons which help to explain these statements about the climate of the British Isles. You can of course refer to other maps in this book/an atlas when doing this.

a In *summer*, the western areas are cooler than those in the east.

b The northern areas are cooler than those in the south – *throughout the year*.

c The temperature range is greatest in the south-east.

d The wettest areas are in the north and west.

e No part of the British Isles is *permanently* in a rain shadow.

The basic climate patterns you have just described often vary a good deal in the short-term, depending on whether the British Isles are experiencing depressions or anticyclones.

Depressions

Much rainfall is associated with depressions. These are areas of low air pressure created when two quite different wind belts meet (Figure 7.21). The two moving air masses do not mix together, but 'battle' with each other and eventually produce a series of depressions. The colder, heavier air within them occupies most of the space just above the ground; these are the cold sectors. Some of the lighter and warmer air also reaches ground level, but most of it lies above the cold sectors. The boundaries between the sectors are called fronts.

The cold air constantly tries to undermine (get beneath) the warm sector. This forces the warmer, damp air to rise. It cools as it rises and rain is produced in the usual way. The rainfall is concentrated around the two fronts (Figure 7:22). Depressions move slowly eastwards, pushed along by the warm south-westerly winds which helped to create them. As their different sectors and fronts pass overhead, places can expect to have the changeable weather usually associated with low air pressure systems.

4 a Explain briefly how depressions are formed. Figure 7.21 will help you to describe the direction, temperature, density and dampness of each wind belt.

5 When the two cold sectors have completely undermined the warm sector, an occluded front is produced (see Figure 7.22). After class discussion, describe how the weather in an occluded part of a depression is likely to be different to that in its other areas.

▼ **Figure 7.22** Changing weather conditions produced by a typical depression

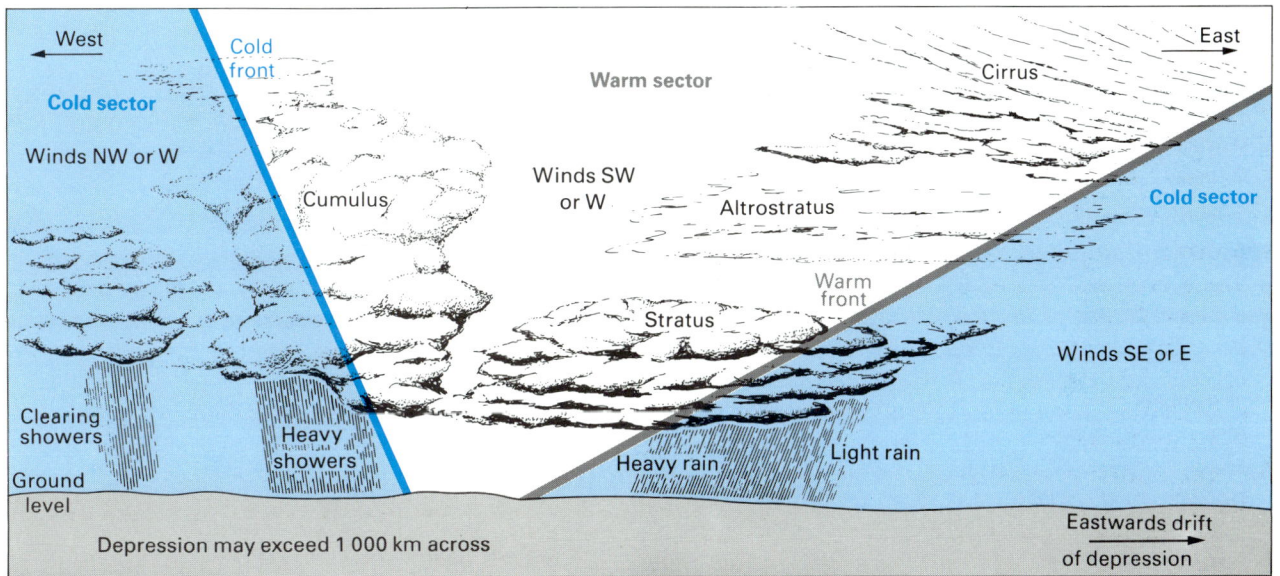

West ← | East →

Cold front

Cold sector

Warm sector

Cirrus

Winds NW or W

Cumulus

Winds SW or W

Altrostratus

Cold sector

Warm front

Stratus

Winds SE or E

Clearing showers

Heavy showers

Heavy rain

Light rain

Ground level

Eastwards drift of depression

Depression may exceed 1 000 km across

Anticyclones

Anticyclones are areas of high air pressure, and so produce weather which is very different to that associated with depressions.

6 The following questions are based on the synoptic chart in Figure 7.23.

a Describe the basic features of an anticyclone, under these headings:

Air pressure
Wind speed
Speed of movement over the Earth's surface

b According to the information in Figure 7.23, what kind of weather is usually associated with anticyclones on a typical summer's day?

c (Possibly after class discussion) state how this pattern is likely to change:

i at night.

ii in mid-winter.

▼ **Figure 7.23** Synoptic chart of a typical anticyclone in mid-July. What is the link between wind speed and distance between isobars?

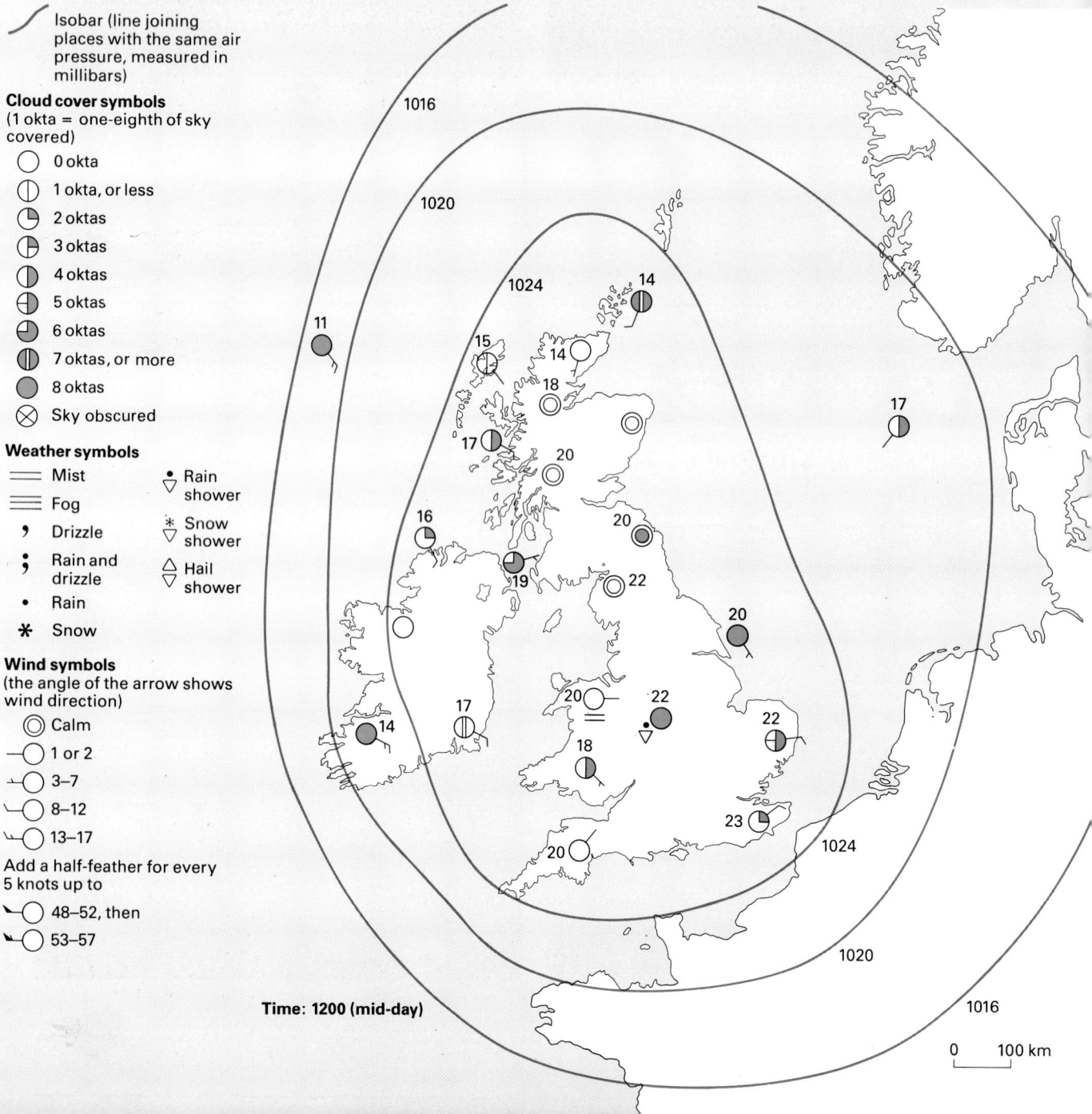

Isobar (line joining places with the same air pressure, measured in millibars)

Cloud cover symbols
(1 okta = one-eighth of sky covered)

○	0 okta
	1 okta, or less
	2 oktas
	3 oktas
	4 oktas
	5 oktas
	6 oktas
	7 oktas, or more
●	8 oktas
⊗	Sky obscured

Weather symbols

═	Mist		Rain shower
≡	Fog		Snow shower
,	Drizzle		Hail shower
;	Rain and drizzle		
•	Rain		
✳	Snow		

Wind symbols
(the angle of the arrow shows wind direction)

◎	Calm
	1 or 2
	3–7
	8–12
	13–17

Add a half-feather for every 5 knots up to

	48–52, then
	53–57

Time: 1200 (mid-day)

0   100 km

7.7 The drought of '76

The British Isles rarely experience extremes of climate. Few of our summers are really 'hot' (many people would say that *none* of them are!), and heavy falls of snow in lowland areas are so infrequent that they soon cause widespread disruption. We are therefore quick to dramatise weather conditions which are out of the ordinary. For example Autumns which are much milder and drier than usual are nick-named 'Indian summers', and cold spells below −5°C described as 'Siberian' even though that part of northern Asia experiences many months below −30°C every year! Our climate rarely justifies this kind of exaggeration, but the drought of 1976 was one of the exceptions.

Both the summer and the winter of the previous year had been much drier than usual (Figure 7.24) and the low levels in many of our reservoirs were beginning to cause concern by the spring of '76. A state of crisis was not however officially declared until the middle of July – after months of clear skies and very little rain, much of which had been evaporated by the above-average temperatures. Some reservoirs dried up completely during July and August (Figure 7.26).

Unfortunately, we did not have a National Water Grid which could have piped water to the regions in greatest need. Instead, fleets of road tankers were rushed into service to take emergency supplies to remote farms and villages. Standpipes (Figure 7.27) became a common sight, even in cities which had previously spent hundreds of millions of pounds to secure 'reliable' water supplies!

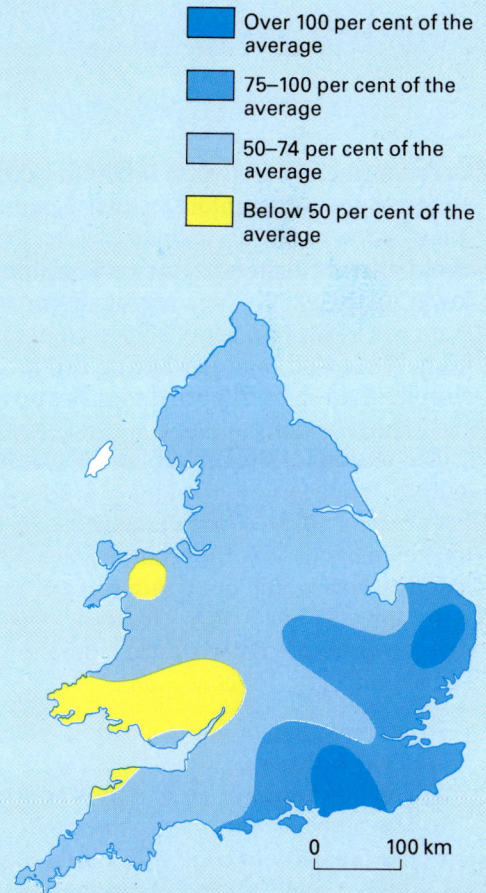

▼ **Figure 7.24** Rainfall distribution in the British Isles in an average year

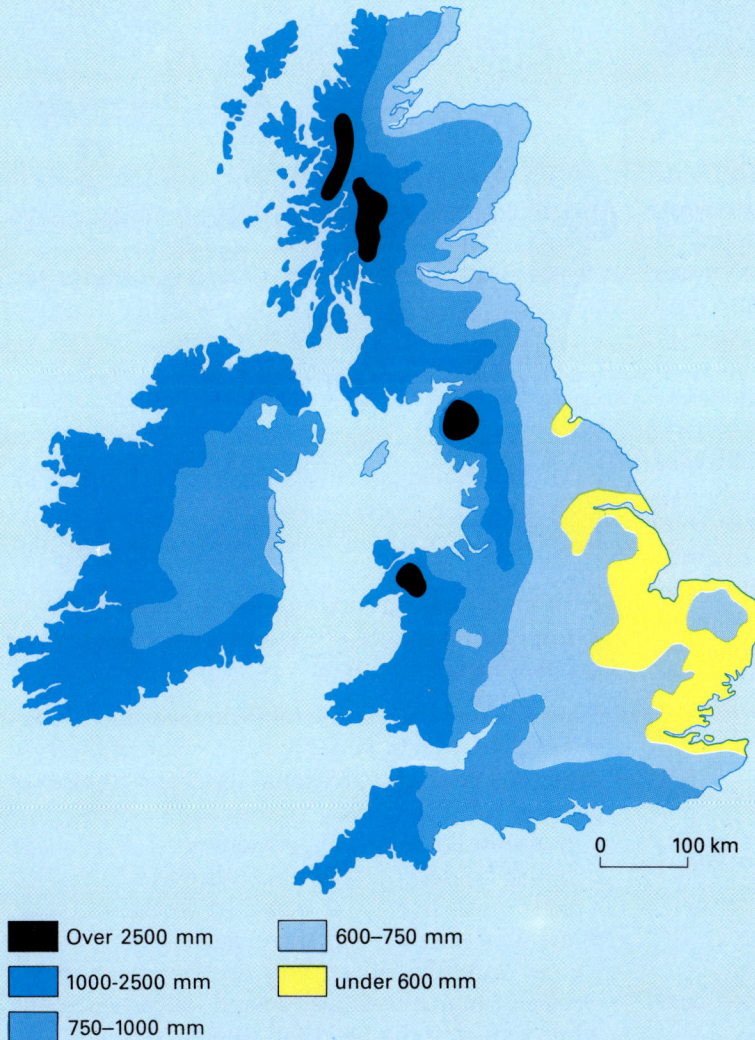

Legend:
- Over 100 per cent of the average
- 75–100 per cent of the average
- 50–74 per cent of the average
- Below 50 per cent of the average

Legend:
- Over 2500 mm
- 1000-2500 mm
- 750–1000 mm
- 600–750 mm
- under 600 mm

0 100 km

0 100 km

▲ **Figure 7.25** Rainfall in England and Wales during February-July 1976, as a percentage of the usual total for these months

▲ Figure 7.26

▲ **Figure 7.27** Stand-pipes were a common sight during the summer of 1976

▼ **Figure 7.28** Food prices in 1976 were much higher than usual!

The farmers were worst hit by the drought. Cattle suffered great discomfort as their pastures dried out; many thousands of animals were slaughtered to avoid further distress, and milk yields were much lower than usual. The output of cereal crops and vegetables was also seriously affected. Shop prices of home-produced food reached record levels and extra supplies had to be imported to make up any deficiencies (Figure 7.28).

The reason for the drought of '76 was basically very simple. Far fewer depressions passed over the British Isles during 1975–76 than is normal. As the previous unit explained, it is the fronts of these low air pressure systems which bring much of our rain and generally unsettled weather. Instead, we experienced high air pressure anticyclones – the bringers of calm, stable and very dry conditions.

1 How did each of the following help to create a water shortage in 1976:
   a The occurence of depressions and anticyclones?
   b The above-average temperatures?
   c Our inability to cope with a prolonged drought?

2 With the help of Figures 7.24 and 7.25, describe:
   a The pattern of water shortfall in 1976.
   b The normal pattern of rainfall distribution.
   c The significance of linking the information contained in these two maps.

3 Suggest reasons why:
   a The milk yield per cow was generally low during 1976.
   b The country's total milk production was also much lower than usual.
   c Home-produced food was more costly to buy.
   d Imported supplies of food helped to keep shop prices unusually high.

4 State whether each of the following was most likely to have suffered or benefited as a result of the 1976 drought, and give reasons for your choice of answer.
   a house builders   **e** pensioners
   b house holders   **f** school teachers
   c prison warders   **g** transport workers
   d manufacturers*   **i** travel agents
   * think carefully about you answer, as hot dry weather can increase the demand for certain goods while reducing the need for others.

7.8 Desertification

Desertification is the spread of true desert areas due to human activities and changes in climate. These facts, and the scene in Figure 7.30, speak for themselves:

- In 1980, about 10% of the world's land surface was classified as true desert.
- In 1986, at least 20% of its land surface was classified in this way.
- 30 million km² of agricultural land has already been lost due to desertification; this is equal to the total land area of Africa!
- About 600 million people now live in true desert or semi-desert areas; the present population of the whole world is about 4 500 million.

▲ **Figure 7.30** Severe gullying in a part of Australia affected by prolonged drought

1 a What is the process called 'desertification'?
b By what percentage did the world's desert area *increase* between 1980 and 1986?
c What *fraction* of the world's population now lives in desert-type areas?

2 a Is desertification a problem:
- only between the Tropics of Cancer and Capricorn?
- only outside these tropics?
- in many parts of the world both between the Tropics of Cancer and Capricorn and in cooler regions nearer the poles?

b Which continent has the largest area of true desert? (See Figure 7.29).
c In which continent is the greatest area at risk from desertification?

▼ **Figure 7.29** Areas prone to desertification

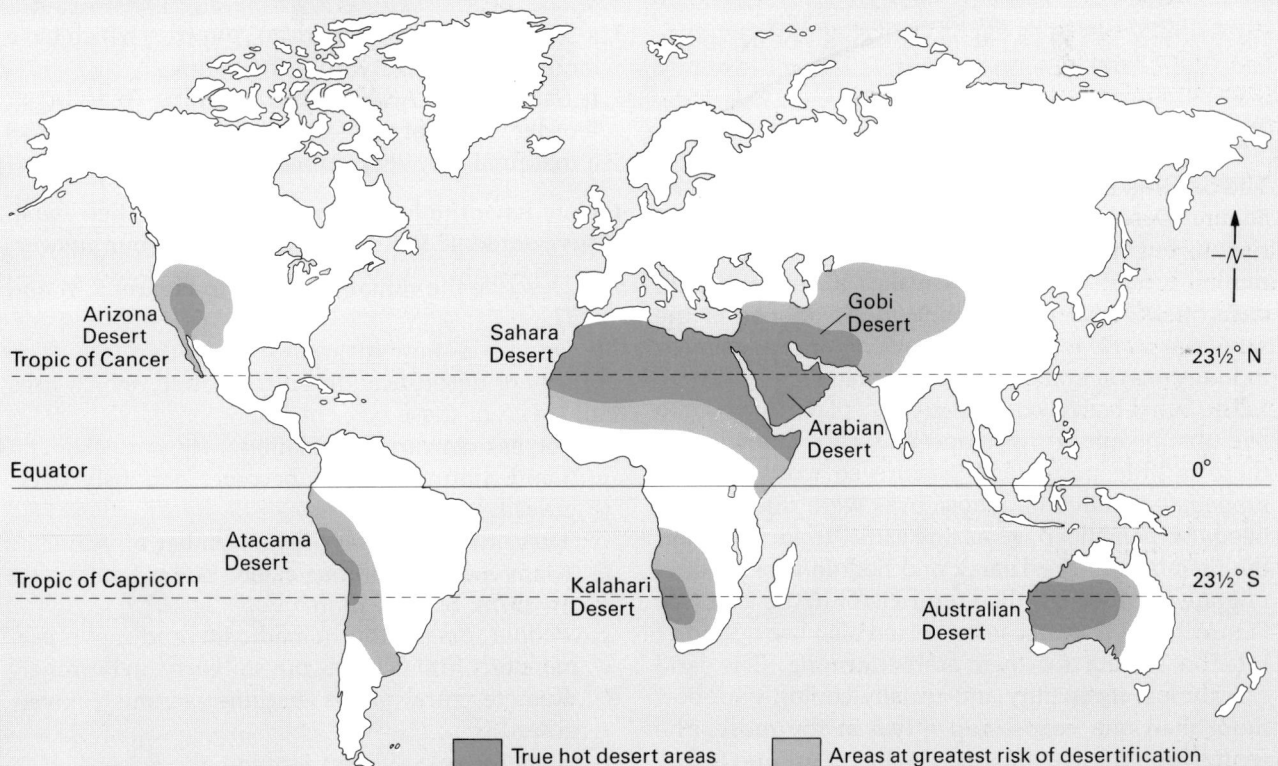

True hot desert areas Areas at greatest risk of desertification

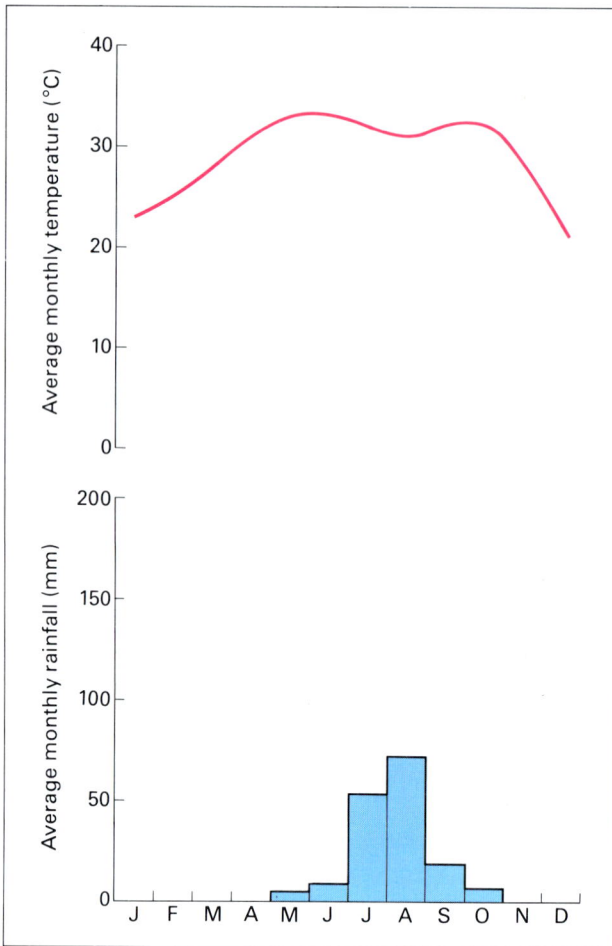

▼ **Figure 7.32** Variations in the Sahel's total annual rainfall for 1960–85 compared with the region's average since 1900

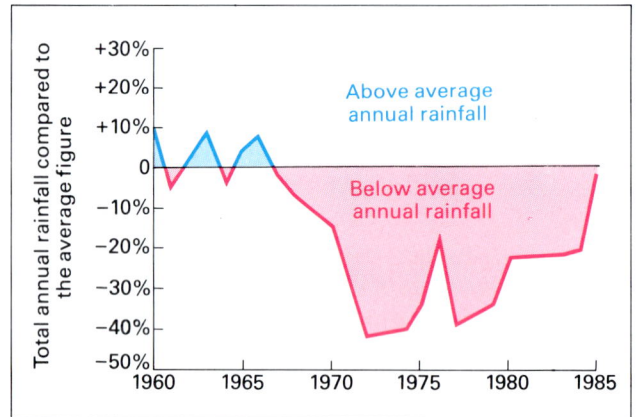

Desertification in the Sahel

The Sahel is the large area immediately south of the Sahara Desert. It is part of the savanna natural region, but has well below the average total annual rainfall for this region; this makes it very prone to desertification. It hasn't made the headlines in the same way as Ethiopia but its problems are very similar in many ways, and are getting worse ...

The Sahel has never been an easy place in which to live. Its people grow crops and rear animals but there is little permanent pasture so many became nomads – wanderers, whose lives were ruled by the needs of their sheep, goats and cattle. In the summer, the members of the Tuareg and Beduin tribes would migrate northwards, then return later in the year (see Figure 7.31). The tribesmen would also use a kind of rotation system for their arable farming. The land quickly lost its fertility and usually couldn't support more than one year's crop – two at the most. The farmer would leave the tired patches of ground fallow

for a few years to give their soil time to recover. Dry wood was gathered and burned to provide fertiliser ash. Water supplies were limited but every tribe had its own wells and these were respected by visiting nomads. This whole system worked, but only because the area was sparsely populated. It was a finely balanced affair which became upset during and since the 1960s (Figure 7.32).

3 **a** Name any six West African countries which have large areas of land within the Sahel.
b Sahel is an Arabic word meaning 'margin' or 'border'. In what ways can the Sahel be regarded as a marginal (i.e. very difficult) farming area?

4 How have the local people adapted to their harsh environment? Refer to Figure 7.31 in your answer.

5 **a** Describe the climate patterns in Figures 7.31 and 7.32.
b Design a flow-diagram under the title 'The effects of desertification on the Sahel', which uses all seven of these box-entries:
'Increase in rural population.'
'Land around villages becomes seriously over-grazed.'
'Less annual rainfall over a number of years.'
'Many people without a job. Some families on the brink of starvation.'
'People forsake the nomadic life and move permanently into villages, but still carry on farming.'
'Remote rural areas become seriously over-grazed.'
'Some people give up farming altogether.'

7.9 The greenhouse effect

Most of us know that oxygen is essential to life on Earth. It is only in recent years, however, that scientists have begun to fully appreciate the importance of *carbon dioxide* – the gas which all animals constantly produce, and then expel by breathing out. Although carbon dioxide comprises only 0.3% of the total volume of air in the atmosphere, it filters out some of the sun's most harmful rays and helps to keep temperatures within the biosphere reasonably constant. Even small changes in the proportion of carbon dioxide within the atmosphere can have very serious, long-term consequences.

1 a Draw the double-line graph in Figure 7.33.
 b Describe both trends shown by this graph.
 c How do these trends appear to be linked?
 d Extend both lines on the graph up to the year 2050, assuming that the patterns of change up to the present continue well into the next century.
 e Make predictions for the year 2025 with the help of your extended lines.

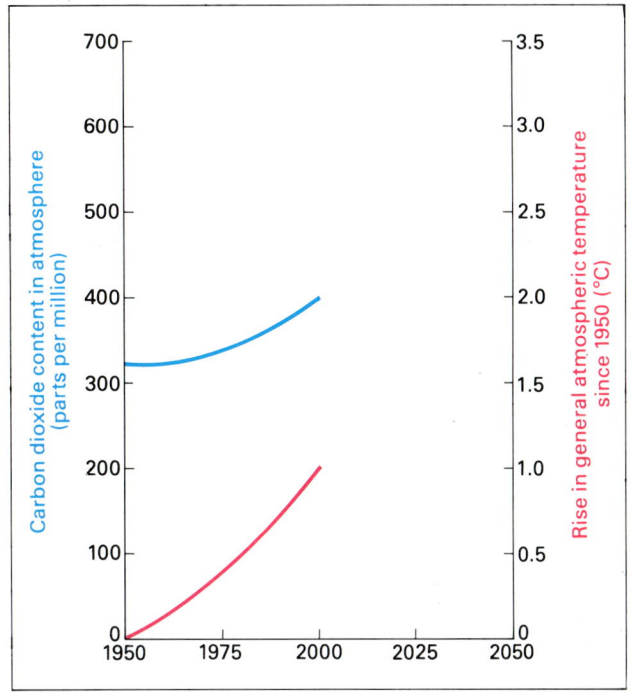

▲ **Figure 7.33** Trends in atmospheric temperature and carbon dioxide content since 1950

▼ **Figure 7.34** The carbon/carbon dioxide cycle. Note that exchanges of carbon dioxide also take place between soil, air, water and marine life

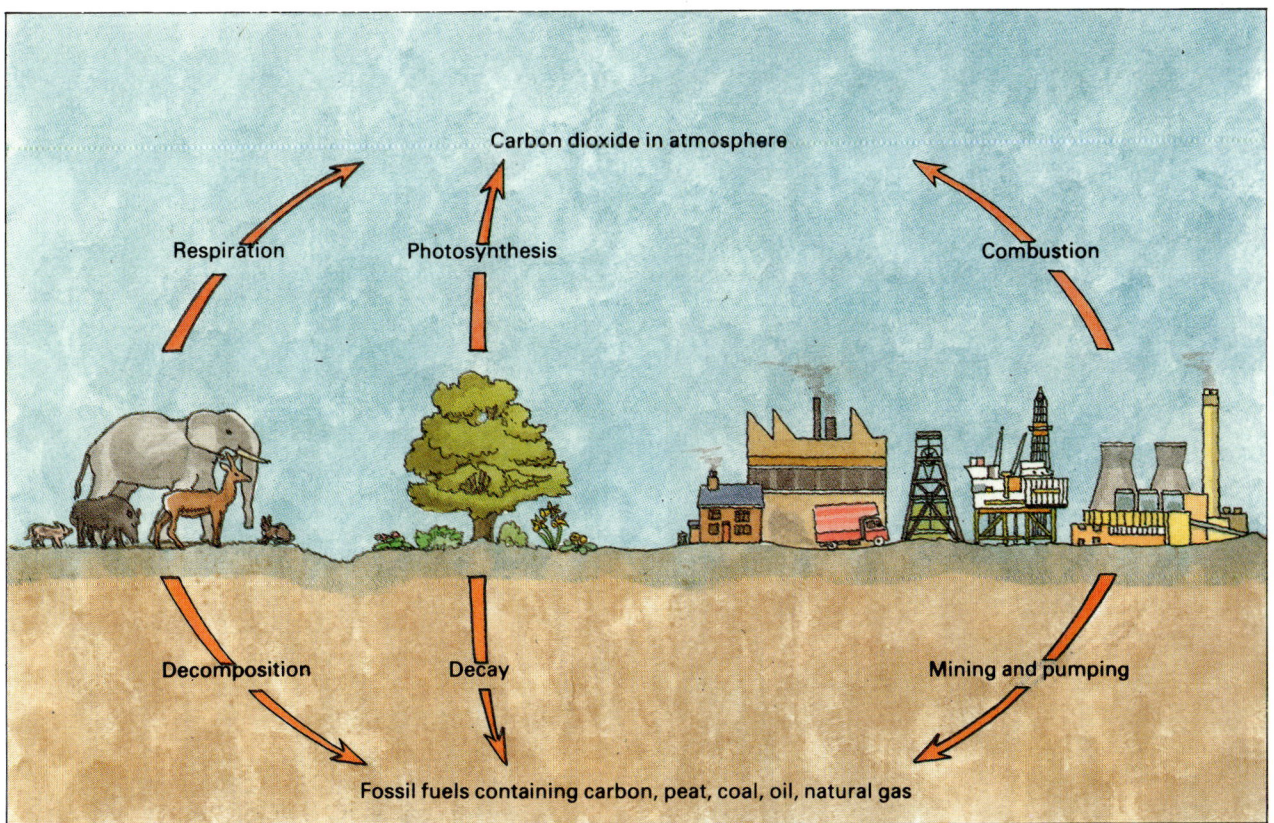

◄ and ▲ **Figure 7.35** Causes of recent imbalance in the gases which make up the atmosphere. Can you explain *why* each activity is disturbing the atmosphere?

2 **a** How is *solid carbon* stored in the biosphere?
b How does *carbon dioxide* 'flow' between plant and animal life?
c Why have carbon dioxide levels in the atmosphere increased considerably since the first (British) Industrial Revolution?
d Why have average world air temperatures also increased during the same period?
e Why has the term 'The Greenhouse Effect' been coined to describe recent atmospheric trends? (Hint: think of conditions inside an ordinary greenhouse.)

3 Explain how increasing carbon dioxide levels in the atmosphere are linked to likely changes in each of the following. In **c** – **e**, you will first have to state what these changes are likely to be!
a Higher soil erosion rates in countries bordering the Mediterranean Sea (Unit 1.3 should be consulted for ideas).
b An increasing need for protective measures such as the Thames Barrier (Unit 7.2) and the Dutch Delta Plan (Unit 7.3).
c Desertification immediately south of the Sahara Desert (Units 1.3 and 7.8).
d Oil-related operations in Alaska (Unit 6.7).
e Agribusiness in Britain (Unit 3.4).

8

Role Play Exercises

8.1 Factory location planning exercise

A paper manufacturing company has decided to build a medium-sized plant (requiring 0.25 km^2 of land) in the area shown by the Ordnance Survey map extract on page 144. Figure 8.1 shows the type of factory which the company has in mind for Nottingham, part of which can be seen in the upper half of the extract. It has chosen this general location because Nottingham is believed to have certain advantages:

☐ a reasonably central location within Britain;
☐ excellent road and rail links which can be used to transport both raw materials and finished products;
☐ a modern regional airport nearby which can be used by company directors and specialist workers who have to travel a good deal between sister plants in other parts of the British Isles;
☐ a plentiful water supply – essential for the manufacturing processes, and useful for the disposal of 'safe' waste materials;
☐ a large workforce within easy travelling distance. The city has a good labour-relations record;
☐ attractive countryside, and a wide range of recreational and other amenities within the city itself. These should prove helpful when encouraging employees to move from other regions.

Nottingham City Council welcomes the prospect of new factories able to create jobs and bring increased prosperity to the area. However there is a widespread feeling amongst local residents that a chemical factory would pose unacceptable threats of air and water pollution. Some have already expressed concern about air pollution caused by the large coal-fired power station at Ratcliffe-on-Sour, to the south of the River Trent.

▼ **Figure 8.1** The Bowater-Scott paper mill at Barrow-in-Furness, Cumbria

▼ Figure 8.3

Inputs	Processes	Outputs

Inputs

Electricity from paper mill's own generating station burning coal or oil plus power obtained from National Grid

Wood pulp imported from Scandinavia. Most transported from east coast port by lorry, but trains and barges could also be used

China clay from south Cornwall to produce a high-quality paper with a smooth finish. Can be transported by rail, road (or coaster to east coast)

Water in very large quantities. Obtained from nearby river or stream

Processes

Mixing of wood pulp, china clay and water to produce a slurry

↓

Spreading of slurry into a thin film

↓

Evaporation of most of water content from the slurry

↓

Drying on heated cylinders to remove remaining water

Outputs

Emissions of grit, ash, carbon dioxide and sulphur dioxide from generating station

Paper which is delivered to London and other large markets by lorry

Warm water returned to nearby river or stream. This can cause thermal pollution which is harmful to fish. Waste products contained in water discharged from the mill may also pose a threat to wildlife

▲ **Figure 8.2** Systems diagram based on the manufacture of high quality paper

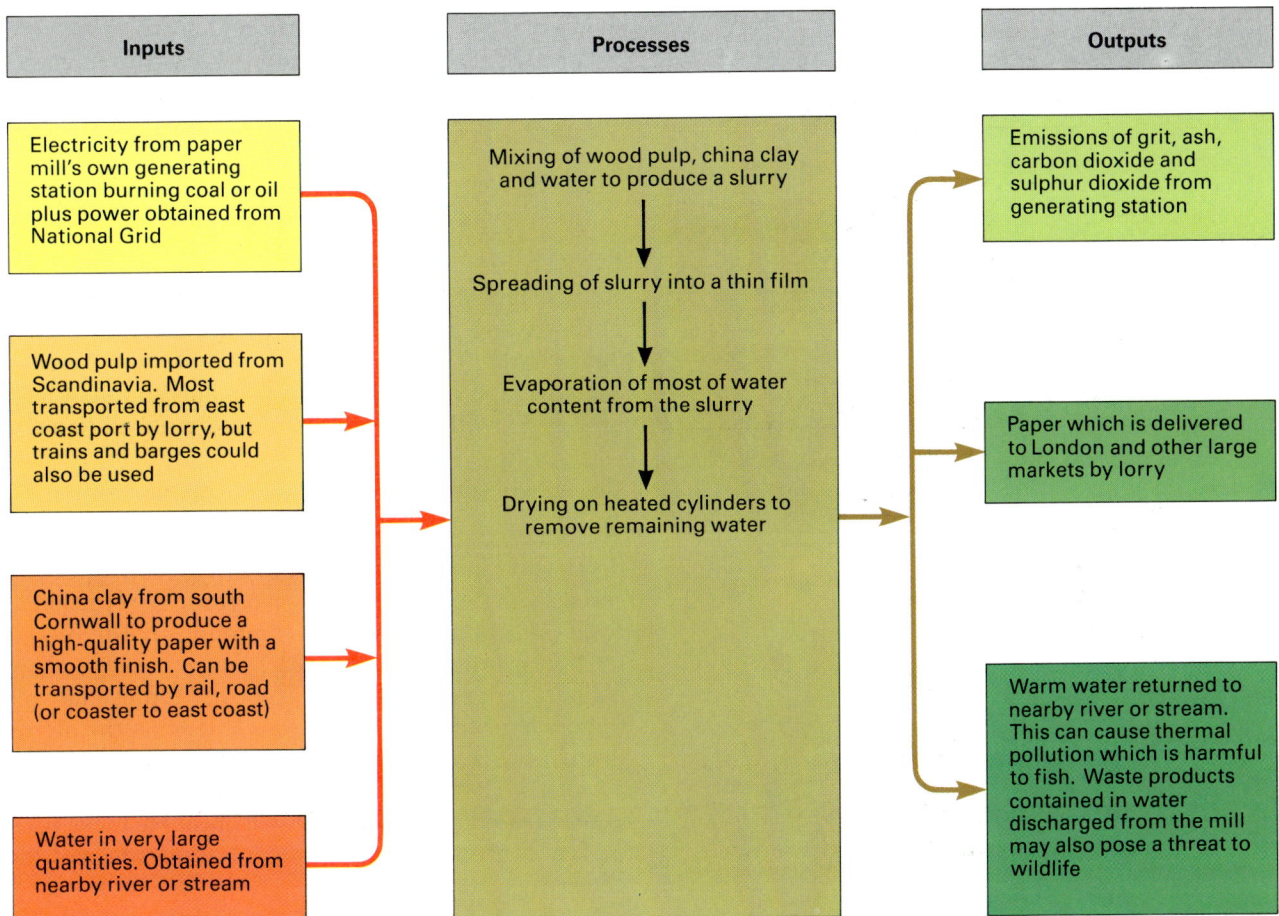

The company has proposed three alternatives sites for the new plant, and is keen to obtain the view of the local community on the merits and drawbacks of them all. They are:

Site A at GR 505335
Site B at GR 462312
Site C at GR 492275

The purpose of this planning exercise is for both the company and the local community to assess the suitability of each site before making their own recommendations. They then take into account all possible opinions before coming to a 'democratic' decision based on a free vote. The three phases in the exercise are described below.

Phase one: completion of reports

For this first phase, every member of the class will:
a act as a representative of either the company or the local community
b investigate one of the three alternative sites
c be given a particular theme to investigate. There is a set of themes for each group of representatives.

For company representatives

1 Suitability of the site for building the proposed factory. (Consider: area, relief, whether the land is well or poorly drained.)

2 Factors determining the value of the land (e.g. present use of land and how attractive it might be to other possible land users).

3 Adequacy of existing communications (i.e. railways, motorways and main roads) for the movement of materials and products.

4 Availability of large quantities of water for processing and waste disposal.

For local community representatives

1 Likelihood of pollution (to air, water, etc).

2 Scale and nature of disruption to the local area (e.g. traffic noise, vibration).

▲ **Figure 8.4** The three alternative sites

3 The ease with which workers can travel between the site and nearby housing areas (this involves minor roads as well).

4 Likely effects on the present landscape.

5 Likelihood of loss of amenities (e.g. footpaths, 'open space', possibly coarse fishing).

Every representative agrees to prepare a detailed written report which highlights the advantages and/ or disadvantages of his/her own site *with regard to the chosen theme*. These reports may include fully-labelled sketch maps and other kinds of illustration. Phase One ends with a display of all the completed reports.

Phase two: company/local community meetings

You will have been given enough time to study the displayed reports, and been advised to look especially carefully at those from your own group of representatives (i.e. company or local community). The reason for this will now become clear!

Phase two requires all the company representatives to hold a meeting. Its purpose is to discuss the merits of each site in turn, then decide which one should be adopted. The local community representatives will attend a similar meeting, but will of course make their choice in the best interests of the residents, not the company.

Phase three: the final choice

This takes the form of a free vote on which site should be chosen; it is called a free vote because representatives disregard any previous allegiance to company or local community (which is *not* easy to do!) and simply cast their votes according to their *own personal* viewpoint. They cannot do this, of course, without being aware of the discussion which has taken place in the other meeting. This difficulty can be overcome by:

1 holding the two meetings at different times, so that one group can listen in to the comments made by the other group of representatives. They may be told to take notes of what they find most useful, and perhaps make individual summaries of these later on.

2 holding the two meetings at the same time, in which case one or more people will have to do the note-taking and summarising for each group.

8.2 Coastal barrage planning exercise

The purpose of this enquiry is to assess the implications – the likely benefits and disadvantages – of building a barrage across the Severn Estuary. The enquiry ends with a vote on whether planning permission for the scheme should be granted. This decision will be based on all the evidence presented by its members. The basic information required to do this is contained in the map of the area (Figure 8.5) and the 'data sets' on the next page. All members of the enquiry are, however, advised to re-read Unit 7.1 before attempting the first phase of the enquiry. Individual members should also revise any previous work on topics linked to their roles (e.g. Unit 6.1 on sewage disposal). The role play exercise has three phases.

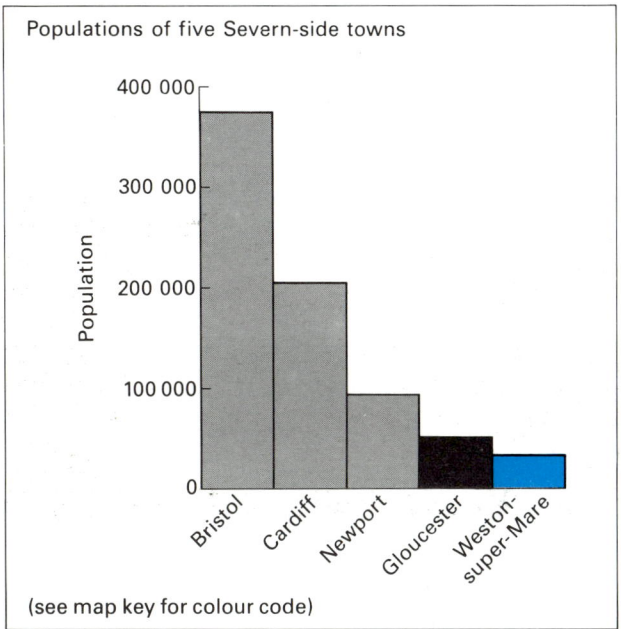

Populations of five Severn-side towns

(see map key for colour code)

▼ **Figure 8.5** Severn-side and the proposed barrage location

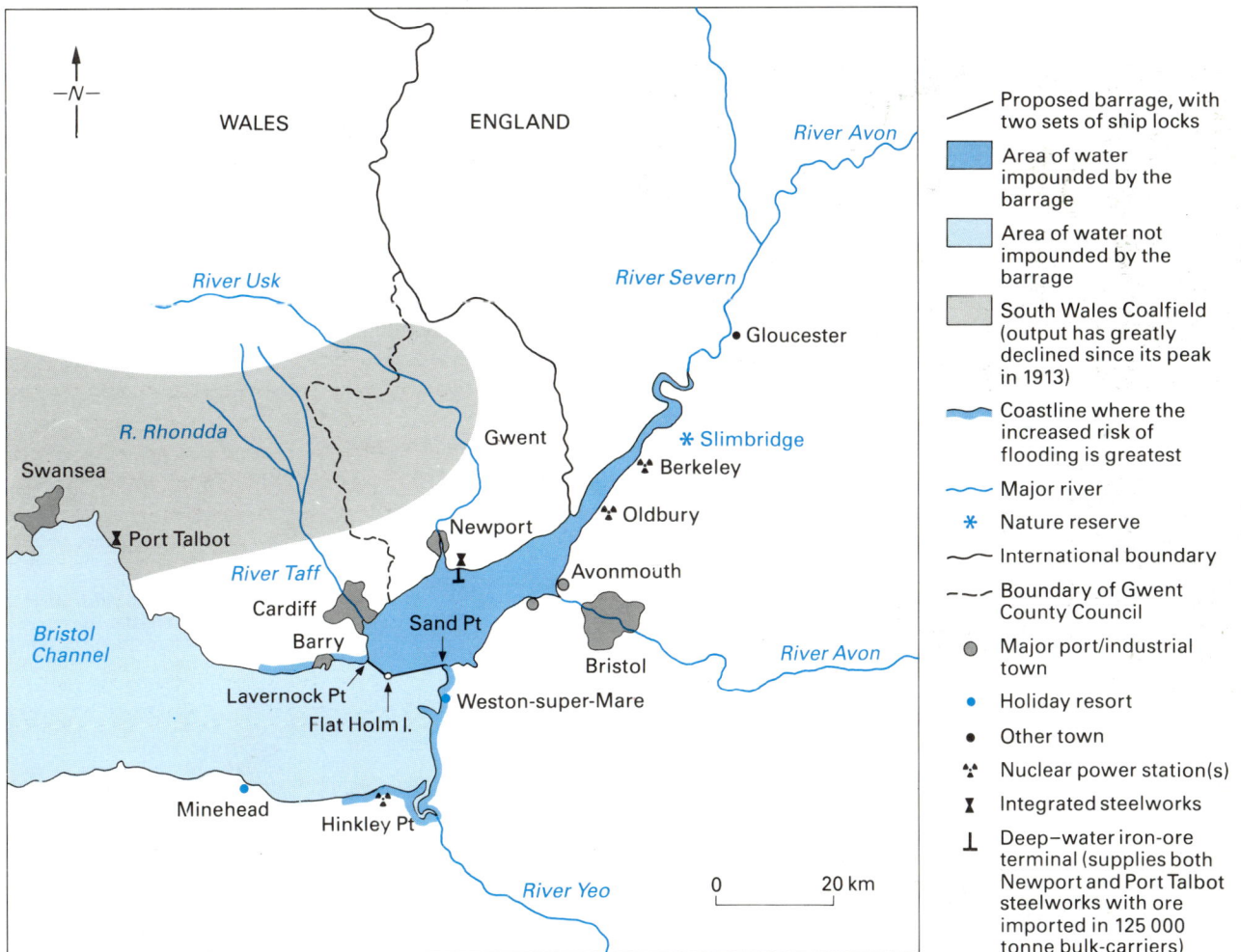

Data Set 1: Population

Bristol	387 977
Cardiff	273 856
Newport	105 374
Gloucester	92 133
Weston-super-Mare	57 980
Clevedon	17 915
Portishead	11 331
Chepstow	9 309

▼ Slimbridge Wildfowl Twist

The Severn Barrage would:
- Cost £6 000 million.
- Take nine years to build.
- Create 20 000 jobs during the construction phase, then 500 when operational.
- Provide 6 per cent of Britain's energy needs, but generate power for only a few hours each day.
- Have sluice gates which would open on a rising tide, trap the water behind it, then re-open at low tide.
- Make the Severn Estuary safer for recreational use; its natural currents are strong and dangerous.
- Limit the size of ships able to use the ports of Cardiff, Bristol and Newport because of the smaller tidal range created there.
- Make the disposal of sewage and industrial waste more difficult and more costly.
- Affect fishing (e.g. of salmon) in the rivers entering the Severn Estuary further upstream.
- Protect the coastline east of the barrage against flooding *but* increase the risk of this happening nearer the open sea. Sea defences would have to be built there.
- Reduce the area of coastal mudflats.
- Take advantage of the world's second largest tidal range of 30 m (the difference in depth of water between high and low tides).

▲ **Figure 8.6** The Severn Estuary

Birds at risk from Severn Barrage

THE BUILDINGS of the propsed Severn Barrage to provide tidal energy would have far-reaching consequences for birds, the British Association was told yesterday. The total area available to support the present numbers would be severely reduced.

Dr. Peter Ferns, senior lecturer in zoology at Cardiff University, said that preliminary calculations suggest that 60 per cent of the present intertidal area upstream of the barrage, Lavernock Point to Brean Down, would be permanently flooded, if the recommended stage one Severn Barrage Committee 1981 scheme were to be constructed, reducing feeding levels.

Last month, the Government announced that they will share the £4.2 million cost of fresh studies for a barrage, with the six companies involved in the project, which could provide five per cent of Britain's electricity needs. Proposed construction is on a line near to Cardiff and Weston-super-Mare.

The high tide period above the barrage would cut the time available for feeding, the salinity of the water upstream would decrease along with its food content, and the distribution of food supporting the birds could also be affected.

Tidal sluices

But Dr. Ferns conceded that the density of birds would have to increase to three times its present level if the same number were to be supported following the construction of the barrage.

A barrage would also affect birds of the coastal levels, as pumped water drainage systems replaced existing tidal sluices, reducing the water table.

He warned: 'The Gwent Levels the Welsh side of the estuary have already been drained and no longer support the regular winter flocks of Bewick's Swans, Wigeon, Pintail and Shoveler which they did in the 1960s.'

The Daily Telegraph,
4 September 1986

Phase one: role preparation

Members of the class will be given two types of role. The 'local people' must think carefully about how the barrage scheme is likely to affect their lives; their main task in Phase Two is to put questions to the expect witnesses – questions which should draw useful information about the matters of most concern to them.

It is vital that the experts do some 'homework' about their particular roles. Their task is to answer any questions which the local people wish to put to them, and that will not always be easy to do. Some will ask for facts, while others seek expert opinions. It is quite a good idea for all the expert witnesses to meet early on to ask themselves any likely questions, and so built up a stock of 'instant answers'.

Brief role descriptions for both groups of members are given below, but do not hesitate to ask you teacher for help if you find it difficult to think of extra ideas.

The local people:

1 Landscape painter

2 Unemployed labourer

3 Secretary of the local sailing club

4 Treasurer of the Severn and District Salmon Fisheries Co-operative

5 Owner of a small grocery store very near to Lavernock Point

6/7 A retired couple who live in a new bungalow less than ¼ km inland from Sand Point (2 people needed)

8 Resident of Flat Holm Island

9 Owner of Flat Holm Island

10 Coal miner who lives to the north of Cardiff

11 Chairman, Severn Bore Surf-riding Society

12 Farmer whose land is on the banks of the River Severn, very near to Slimbridge

13 Tourism and Publicity Officer for Weston-super-Mare

14 Community charge-payer living in Bristol

15 Harbour Master, Cardiff Docks

The expert witnesses:

1 Spokesperson for the Central Electricity Generating Board

2 Director of one of the large engineering companies which has helped to plan the Severn Barrage and belongs to the consortium (group of companies) hoping to be awarded to contract to build it

3 Chief Planning Officer, Gwent County Council

4 Chief Supplies Officer, British Steel Corporation

5 Sewage Consultant, Severn Water Authority

6 Representative, Department of Energy (which regards wind power as the most feasible of the new, alternative ways of producing energy)

7 Representative, HM Treasury (the Treasury has overall control of government spending)

8 Lecturer in Geography, Bristol University (who is a specialist in tidal features)

9 Recreation and Amenities Officer, Avon County Council

10 Representative, National Coal Board (South Wales Area)

Phase two: the enquiry

The purpose of the second phase is to give the local people an opportunity to put questions to the expert witnesses. They should choose questions which are likely to provide additional information about the likely effects of building a barrage across the Severn Estuary. After answering the questions put to them, the witnesses may wish to add questions of their own or state opinions which they believe to be important.

The chairperson (the teacher) will probably insist that all questions are directed though him/her. This can be done quite simply by saying 'Mr/Madam Chairperson, I would like to ask Mr/Mrs . . . why/ whether/if . . . .' This procedure is often used to make sure that lively discussion (which is to be encouraged) does not become too bitter or personal. The chairperson may also re-arrange the furniture so that everybody has a clear view of the proceedings, and issue each pupil with a card showing his/her role play name and character.

Phase three: the vote

When all the main implications of building the barrage have been debated thoroughly, the chairperson will summarise what has been said. He/she will then invite the local people to vote on the propsal 'That the Severn Barrage should be built as planned because it is likely to be more beneficial than harmful to the surrounding area.'

1 Make a copy of Figure 8.5.

2 Summarise the main points raised during Phase Two of the exercise.

3 State:
   a how your class voted in Phase Three.
   b whether you agree with this decision, in the light of the evidence produced during the second phase.

Additional Exercises

1 Pair up these key terms with their correct description:

Terms	Descriptions
A depression	can only take place where enough water has been stored to meet farmers' needs throughout the year.
Acid rain	completely cuts off a river or bay from the sea.
Barriers	describes an area where few people live.
Demersal fish	includes rain and snow.
Erosion	is a form of pollution caused when certain gases dissolve in rain water.
Perennial irrigation	is afforestation of an area where trees grew before.
Precipitation	is all those parts of the Earth where life can exist.
Reafforestation	is an area of low air pressure.
Sparsely-populated	is the opposite of deposition.
The biosphere	live near the bottom of the sea.

2 Pair up the following named places with their correct locations:

Names	Locations
Martin Mere	is a town in southern Japan.
Minamata	is a nature reserve in Lancashire.
Selby	is a town on one of Britain's newest coalfields.
The Mediterranean	is the densely forested region of northern Brazil.
The Selvas	is the sea between Africa and Europe.

3 State whether each of these statements is true or false:

a Acid rain has affected many lakes in West Germany.

b Jethro Tull's invention was most useful to arable farmers.

c Sugar beet grows very well on the island of Cuba.

d London's worst smog took place in the winter of 1963.

e Salmon can only breed successfully in rivers free from serious pollution.

f The Tennessee Valley Authroity was formed mainly to develop recreational facilities.

g The River Rhine acts as a natural national boundary between France and West Germany.

h The closure of the Suez Canal encouraged the building of much larger oil tankers.

i Antarctica is the wilderness area around the North Pole.

j Uranium is used to fuel nuclear power stations.

4 Choose the most appropriate ending to each of these statements:

a Wildfowl include . . .
   ducks.
   ostriches.
   tigers.

b The Dutch Delta Plan was built at the estuary of the River . . .
   Ganges.
   Nile.
   Rhine.

c The British government believes that the form of alternative energy best suited to our future needs is . . .
   solar power.
   wave power.
   wind power.

d Convection rainfall occurs mainly . . .
   in tropical regions.
   over mountainous areas.
   up-wind of large industrial areas.

e An example of biodegradable waste is . . .
   plastic bottles.
   rotten apples.
   tin cans.

f The Lancashire Conjunctive Scheme uses ...
only pipelines to move water.
only streams to obtain its supplies of water.
pipelines *and* rivers to move water.
g The Common Agricltural Policy has resulted in
...
a shortage of butter.
generally lower food prices.
large surpluses of certain types of food.
h One of the benefits of creating reservoirs is ...
the build-up of fertile silt behind the dams
the opportunity to generate HEP.
the spread of Bilharzia.
i Africa's savanna areas lie between ...
hot deserts and tropical rain forests.
Mediterranean climate areas and hot deserts.
Mediterranean climate areas and tropical rain
forests.
j The Greenhouse Effect is the result of ...
building more nuclear power stations.
more carbon dioxide in the atmosphere.
rising sea levels throughout the world.

5 Complete the following statements:
a Modern power stations need large quantities of
water because ...
b The Severn Estuary is Britain's finest location·for
a tidal barrage because ...
c The effects of the British drought of 1976 were
much worse than they need have been because ...
d It is often difficult to control the pollution of
major rivers because ...
e The recycling of waste materials is becoming
more common because ...
f Tall power station 'stacks' are a mixed blessing
because ...
g Only a fraction of the hydrosphere may be used
for large-scale commercial fishing because ...
h The pumped-storage method of generating HEP
is increasingly popular because ...
i Many of Britain's newest forests are sited in
remote, upland areas because ...
j Deforestation of the world's tropical jungles
seems certain to continue because ...

Study the map extract on page 144, then answer
questions 6–9 which are based on it.

6 What is the main land use at:
a GR 485330?   **d** GR 506278?
b GR 475276?   **e** GR 489350?
c GR 528350?

7 You live in the detached building at GR 475337 and
commute daily to the works on the northern edge
of Kegworth. Describe the route you take each
morning, assuming that it is the most direct one
using only A and B class roads, and minor roads at
least 4m wide (which are shaded yellow).

8 a How can you tell that the area south of grid line
30 is important for agriculture?
b Is irrigation likely to be necessary in this area?
c Give reasons to support your answer to **b**.

9 Assess the suitability of each location for its
proposed use:
a GR 506306 – for a picnic site
b GR 524287 – for further industrial development
c GR 470300 – as a landfill site for domestic refuse
d GR 513320 – for generating HEP
e Square 4830 – for a new housing estate.

10 a Which type of natural region is shown in the
map below?

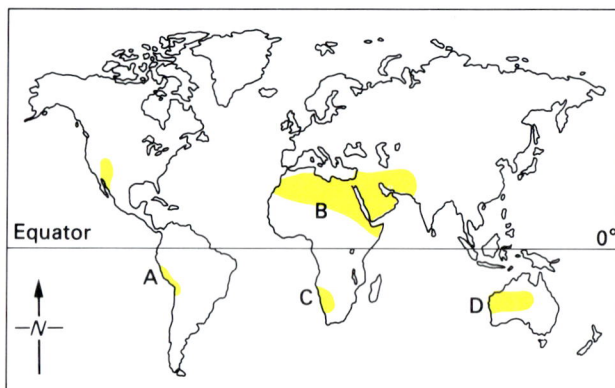

b Name the examples labelled A –D on the map.
c Describe the general distribution of all the areas
shown on the map.
d Suggest reasons for the distribution you have
just described.
e Describe any problems facing the inhabitants of
these regions *which are due to their climate*, then
explain how they may be tackled.

11 a Draw a line-sketch of the scene shown in the above photograph.
b Add labels to your sketch to identify any features which might endanger its environment.
c Describe the nature of the threat posed by each of the features you have labelled.

12 Draw flow-diagrams to illustrate the sequences within any two of the following:
a the Equatorial rain forest nutrient cycle
b a typical British dairy farm
c the urban water cycle
d a wildlife ecosystem within your local area.

13 a Describe the equipment and techniques which may be used to obtain data on any one of the following:
i daily rainfall
ii evaporation rates
iii stream volume.
b Identify possible weaknesses in the arrangements you have described in **a**, and suggest ways in which they might be overcome.

14 Draw *completely from memory* fully-labelled sketch maps to *locate* each of the following:
a sugar cane plantations in Cuba
b an oil tanker disaster which resulted in widespread coastal pollution
c a major British power station.

15 Write 1–3 page essays to *discuss* the following ideas. The last paragraph in each case should say whether you agree with the idea – having first considered all the evidence both for and against it.
a 'Whether self-sufficient groups of people such as the Aborigines should be encouraged to adopt highly-productive farming methods.'
b 'Whether the current British policy of flooding river valleys rather than building coastal barrages should continue.'
c 'Whether Britain should accept full responsibility for the acid rain problem in Western Europe.'
d 'Whether fish farming techniques *can and should* be used much more widely than at present.'
e 'Whether it is in the best interests of the world's poorer counties to build large water-storage HEP generating schemes.'
f 'Whether it might be possible to reverse the Greenhouse Effect.'
g 'Whether landfill sites near to built-up areas should continue to be used for waste disposal.'
h 'Whether the risk of oil pollution at sea can be virtually eliminated.'

Suggested Fieldwork Topics

Topics based on aims

To assess the potential of . . . (name of area) **for fish farming developments**. Locate and evaluate potential sites such as lakes and reservoirs.

To investigate changes in a wooded area within . . . (name of area) **over the last** . . . (number of) **years**. Use past and present maps and photographs plus information obtained from local land-owners and planning authorities.

To investigate climate patterns at . . . (name of weather recording station) **during the period** . . . – . . . (dates). Plot key temperature and rainfall data (e.g. monthly averages/maxima and minima) then suggest reasons for any trends identified. Synoptic charts from daily newspapers can be used to do this.

To investigate the water pollution problem in . . . (name of river or area). Link personal observations and map information of likely sources of pollution (e.g. factories, outfall pipes) to actual evidence of pollution (e.g. foam, litter, refuse, data from Water Authority).

To evaluate the water supply arrangements for . . . (name of town or area). Use Water Authority information to map the present water source and transportation arrangements. Suggest reasons for these arrangements (e.g. why a certain valley has been dammed to create a reservoir).

To investigate farming trends in . . . (name of rural area). Use the techniques described in Study 5 on pages 53–56 of *Fieldwork Studies in Geography*.

Topics based on hypotheses

That tourism has had a marked effect on . . . (name of 'honeypot' location). Use a variety of techniques (e.g. maps, photographs, questionnaires) to identify changes in land use, landscape, traffic patterns, inhabitants' quality of life, etc.

That the thickness of the humus layer in . . . (name or grid reference of area) **varies according to the** . . . (height and/or gradient) **of the land surface**. A practical investigation, based on soil horizon observations.

That the majority of . . . (e.g. shoppers, adults) **in** . . . (name of settlement or area) **believe that Britain's membership of the Common Market** . . . (has or has not) **benefited her people**. Questionnaire-based investigation.

That the present facilities for disposing of hazardous waste in . . . (name of area) **appear to be generally** . . . (adequate or unsatisfactory). Investigate existing facilities (i.e. local authority sites, the presence of companies specialising in hazardous waste disposal/ reprocessing).

That people's eating habits are having a marked effect on the food retail trade. Use questionnaires put to shoppers/retailer wholesalers.

That the changes in tidal height at . . . (name of location) **follow a set pattern**. Use the techniques described in Study 3 on pages 49–51 of *Fieldwork Studies in Geography*.

Glossary

Acid rain Rain which is contaminated with dissolved gas(es), so producing a weak acid solution.

Afforestation The planting of trees on a commercial scale.

Agribusiness The use of highly-efficient factory techniques in agriculture.

Anticyclone Area of high air pressure which is usually associated with calm, stable weather conditions.

Alternative energy Form of energy which avoids the use of naturally-occurring fuels.

Barrage Long dam across a bay or river estuary which creates a reservoir of fresh water.

Barrier Structure also built across a bay or river estuary, but whose main purpose is flood control.

Bilharzia Tropical disease spread by water-borne snails.

Biodegradable Describes a substance which can rot naturally.

Biosphere Collective term for all parts of the Earth where life can exist.

Biological oxygen demand (BOD) The amount of oxygen needed to break down sewage and industrial waste within a river or lake.

Common Agricultural Policy (CAP) Common Market agreement by which increased food production would raise its farmers' standards of living.

Conjunctive Describes a water supply scheme which combines different methods of collecting and transporting the water.

Deforestation Tree-felling on a large scale.

Delta Area of 'new' land built into a sea or lake where a river deposits large quantities of fine silt.

Demersal Describes fish which prefer to live near the sea bottom.

Densely inhabited district (DID) Japanese term for a heavily built-up densely populated area.

Densely populated Describes an area in which many people live.

Depression Area of low air pressure with warm and cold sectors separated by fronts.

Desertification The spread of desert areas due to human activity and long-term changes in climate.

Distributary Stream within a delta created when a river divides before entering the sea.

Drought Lengthy period of unusually dry weather causing serious problems.

Ecosystem The networks of links between different life forms.

Erosion The wearing away of surface material (e.g. soil by heavy rain).

Fish farming The breeding of fish commercially within a controlled environment.

Flow A movement of energy within an ecosystem.

Fossil fuel Fuel composed of decayed animal or plant matter (e.g. coal from wood).

Greenhouse effect The warming of the Earth's atmosphere due to changes in its carbon dioxide content.

Honeypot Extremely popular tourist attraction.

Humus Decomposed plant remains within a soil.

Hydrological cycle The sequence of events in which water constantly changes its form (e.g. ice) and location (e.g. in a lake).

Hydrosphere Collective term for the parts of the Earth in which water occurs in all its forms.

Impermeable Describes a rock which liquids cannot pass through.

Inaccessible Describes a place which is difficult to get both from and to.

Inexhaustible resource A natural resource which cannot run out (e.g. water).

Infiltration Seepage of water below the land surface.

Irrigation Putting water onto the land to help it to grow crops in areas without enough rainwater to meet farmers' needs.

Isotherm Line joining places on a map having the same temperature.

Landfill The disposal of unwanted material (e.g. household refuse) on land set aside for the purpose (often a disused quarry or gravel pit)

Leaching The movement of dissolved plant food deeper underground due to heavy rainfall passing through the soil.

Location factor Reason for siting a particular development (e.g. a power station) in a certain place (e.g. on the bank of a wide river).

Misconception Mistaken idea which people have about a place.

Natural environment The natural surroundings in which people (and other life forms) exist.

Natural region Large area having a certain set of natural characteristics (e.g. climate).

Over-populated Describes an area which cannot meet the basic needs of most of its people.

Pelagic Describes fish which prefer to live near the surface.

Perennial irrigation Irrigation in which reservoirs make water available throughout the year.

Plankton Microscopic plants and animals which are at the base of all marine food chains.

Plantation Large farm specialising in growing one crop, mainly for export – usually in a tropical region.

Pollution Harmful effect on the environment caused by human activity.

Porous Describes a rock which can hold a liquid or allow it to infiltrate.

Precipitation Collective term for rain, snow, sleet and hail.

Radiation The emission of rays from certain 'radio-active' materials. Those from uranium are especially powerful and dangerous to health.

Reafforestation Planting trees in an area where felling has already taken place.

Renewable resource Natural resource which may be replaced (e.g. wood).

Run-off The downhill movement of rainwater over the land surface.

Self-sufficient Describes people who are able to meet their own basic needs.

Selvas The Equatorial rain forest of Brazil's Amazon Basin.

Sink The use of the natural environment as a dumping ground for waste, without any regard to the likely consequences.

Smog A harmful mixture of *smoke* and *fog*.

Sparsely-populated Describes a place where few people live.

Spring tide Unusually high or low tide occuring when the Earth is in line with the sun and the moon.

Store Reserve of energy within an ecosystem (e.g. an animal's body).

Storm surge Very high wave(s) caused by freak wind conditions.

System Diagrammatic way of showing a human activity (e.g. farming, manufacturing) as a series of inputs, processes, etc.

Temperature inversion Occurs when the air temperature *rises* with increasing height.

Thermal power station Power station which burns fossil fuels.

Toxic Describes a substance which is highly dangerous to animal life.

Transpiration A plant's loss of moisture through its leaves.

Trophic level Life-stage within a food chain.

Wetlands Poorly drained, marshy area near to a river or coast. A rich natural habitat for wildfowl.

Wilderness area Large area of unspoiled countryside. Usually remote and virtually uninhabited.

Global Case Study Locations

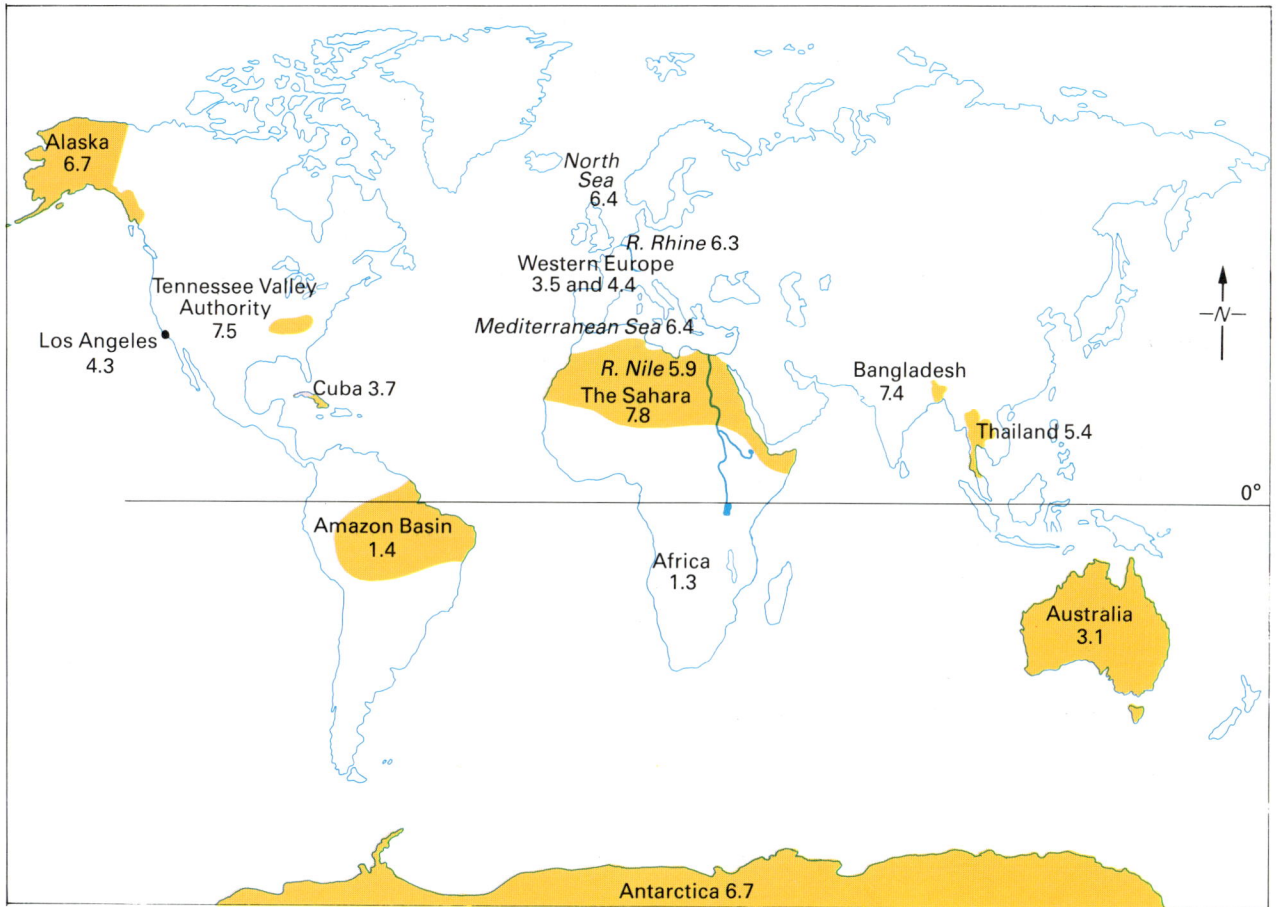

Alaska
6.7

*North
Sea*
6.4

R. Rhine 6.3

Western Europe
3.5 and 4.4

Mediterranean Sea 6.4

Tennessee Valley
Authority
7.5

Los Angeles
4.3

Cuba 3.7

R. Nile 5.9
The Sahara
7.8

Bangladesh
7.4

Thailand 5.4

—N—

0°

Amazon Basin
1.4

Africa
1.3

Australia
3.1

Antarctica 6.7

Index